Practical
Crime Scene Analysis
and Reconstruction

CRC SERIES IN
**PRACTICAL ASPECTS OF CRIMINAL
AND FORENSIC INVESTIGATIONS**

VERNON J. GEBERTH, BBA, MPS, FBINA *Series Editor*

Investigating Computer Crime
Franklin Clark and Ken Diliberto

Practical Homicide Investigation Checklist and Field Guide
Vernon J. Geberth

Practical Aspects of Munchausen by Proxy and Munchausen Syndrome Investigation
Kathryn Artingstall

Quantitative-Qualitative Friction Ridge Analysis: An Introduction to Basic and Advanced Ridgeology
David R. Ashbaugh

Practical Criminal Investigations in Correctional Facilities
William R. Bell

Officer-Involved Shootings and Use of Force: Practical Investigative Techniques, Second Edition
David E. Hatch

Sex-Related Homicide and Death Investigation: Practical and Clinical Perspectives
Vernon J. Geberth

Global Drug Enforcement: Practical Investigative Techniques
Gregory D. Lee

Practical Investigation of Sex Crimes: A Strategic and Operational Approach
Thomas P. Carney

Principles of Bloodstain Pattern Analysis: Theory and Practice
Stuart James, Paul Kish, and T. Paulette Sutton

Cold Case Homicides: Practical Investigative Techniques
Richard H. Walton

Practical Crime Scene Processing and Investigation
Ross M. Gardner

Practical Bomb Scene Investigation
James T. Thurman

Practical Analysis and Reconstruction of Shooting Incidents
Edward E. Hueske

Tire Tread and Tire Track Evidence: Recovery and Forensic Examination
William J. Bodziak

Bloodstain Pattern Analysis: With an Introduction to Crime Scene Reconstruction, Third Edition
Tom Bevel and Ross M. Gardner

Serial Violence: Analysis of Modus Operandi and Signature Characteristics of Killers
Robert D. Keppel and William J. Birnes

Practical Crime Scene Analysis and Reconstruction
Ross M. Gardner and Tom Bevel

Practical Crime Scene Analysis and Reconstruction

Ross M. Gardner and Tom Bevel

Contributions by

Matthew Noedel
Scott A. Wagner, MD
Iris Dalley

CRC Press
Taylor & Francis Group
Boca Raton   London   New York

CRC Press is an imprint of the
Taylor & Francis Group, an **informa** business

CRC Press
Taylor & Francis Group
6000 Broken Sound Parkway NW, Suite 300
Boca Raton, FL 33487-2742

© 2009 by Taylor & Francis Group, LLC
CRC Press is an imprint of Taylor & Francis Group, an Informa business

No claim to original U.S. Government works
Printed & bound in Singapore by Markono Print Media Pte Ltd
10 9 8 7 6 5 4 3 2 1

International Standard Book Number-13: 978-1-4200-6551-0 (Hardcover)

Library of Congress Cataloging-in-Publication Data

Gardner, Ross M.
   Practical crime scene analysis and reconstruction / Ross M. Gardner and Tom Bevel.
     p. cm. -- (CRC series in practical aspects of criminal and forensic investigations ; 49)
   Includes bibliographical references and index.
   ISBN 978-1-4200-6551-0 (acid-free paper) 1. Crime scene searches. 2. Criminal investigation. 3. Evidence, Criminal. 4. Forensic sciences. I. Bevel, Tom. II. Title. III. Series.

   HV8073.G317 2009
   363.25'2--dc22   2008048951

Visit the Taylor & Francis Web site at
http://www.taylorandfrancis.com

and the CRC Press Web site at
http://www.crcpress.com

Dedication

To our wives, Karen and Liz, and our children, Dawnielle, Jeremy, Christopher, and Cody, for their undying patience and love.

Table of Contents

7   Shooting Scene Processing and Reconstruction 131

Matthew Noedel

8   The Forensic Pathologist, the Body, and Crime Scene Reconstruction 175

Scott A. Wagner, MD

Series Editor

The series editor for Practical Aspects of Criminal and Forensic Investigations is Lieutenant Commander (retired) Vernon J. Geberth, New York City Police Department, who was the commanding officer of The Bronx Homicide Task Force, which handled over 400 homicides a year. Geberth has been president of P.H.I. Investigative Consultants, Inc., since 1987. He has more than 40 years of law enforcement experience and has conducted homicide investigation seminars for more than 60,000 attendees from more than 7,500 law enforcement agencies.

Commander Geberth is an author, educator, and consultant on homicide and forensic investigations. Geberth has published three best selling books in this series, *Practical Homicide Investigation, 4th edition*; *Sex-Related Homicide and Death Investigation: Practical and Clinical Perspectives*; and *Practical Homicide Investigation: Checklist and Field Guide*.

Commander Geberth created, edited and designed this series of more than 40 publications to provide contemporary, comprehensive, and pragmatic information to the practitioner involved in criminal and forensic investigations by authors who are nationally recognized experts in the respective fields.

Vernon Geberth welcomes the opportunity to review new proposals for books covering any area of criminal and forensic investigation, and may be reached at **vernongeberth@ practicalhomicide.com**

Foreword

Crime scene analysis and reconstruction has experienced a reawakening of sorts. The immense proliferation of television, print, and electronic media has generated significant public interest and helped shape public perception of our profession. Graduate level programs of investigative sciences have increased exponentially. Unfortunately, information about our profession is sometimes disseminated with little regard for accuracy and relevance. The net result of this condition is the creation of a morass of information with few guides available to navigate this wasteland. *Practical Crime Scene Analysis and Reconstruction* confronts this issue and bridges the gap between perception and reality.

For more than a century, noted criminal investigators have relied on the concept of reconstruction to aid them in their analysis of crime. There is nothing new about the practice of crime scene reconstruction, but the true practitioners are few and the methodology is varied. This book is the first serious attempt to resolve that issue and bring professionals to a common place of understanding. As the forensic community becomes more compartmentalized, there is a clear and distinct need to maintain a generalist perspective. Absent that perspective, we risk a discontinuity of facts comprising the criminal act. While the analytical scientist may be compared to the individual musician, the reconstructionist is the conductor. Each instrument may have a beautiful tune, but without the conductor to arrange the pieces there can be no melody.

The authors not only seek to enlighten the readers on the true nature of this discipline, but to guide them in their professional conduct. The readers of *Practical Crime Scene Analysis and Reconstruction* will understand the nature of scientific method and learn the proper application of its components. The text is generously augmented by realistic case scenarios, which highlight the relevancy of the concept being discussed. This is not simply the inclusion of crime scene photographs or case histories for the sake of imagery or theatrics. It is a careful selection of meaningful abstracts needed to convey each part of this complex methodology.

Those who read and study this text will gain a comprehensive understanding of the elements of crime scene analysis and reconstruction. Each author possesses a unique ability to distill complex issues into easily understood concepts. This book presents a clear and precise methodology that, when properly used, will give the practitioner the best opportunity to understand the events surrounding the commission of a crime. I have never been one to subscribe to the idea that any one book can be considered the "bible" of that profession. However, serious practitioners cannot afford to abstain from studying the information provided here. *Practical Crime Scene Analysis and Reconstruction* will be a welcome and well-used addition to a reference library.

Thomas W. Adair, President
Association for Crime Scene Reconstruction

Preface

Crime is a truly interesting phenomenon—not only in its root causes and long term effects on a society, but also in how society attempts to deal with it. When confronted with crime, communities ultimately find themselves asking a lay jury to decide the innocence or guilt of the parties involved. The expectation for these juries is immense: to objectively consider all information and judge who is, or is not, responsible. In the best of circumstances, this is no easy task, for even the best criminal investigation should not be expected to answer every single question relating to a criminal incident. This is not the nature of crime or the criminal investigation, for no one has an investigative crystal ball. Investigators arrive after the fact; they have only those pieces of the investigative puzzle found at the scene to work with, and are left to piece together the story using the oft times subjective testimonial evidence.

How is a jury to judge the truthfulness of those involved in alleged crimes? How are they to understand the true story of what really happened? Lacking this knowledge, the jury is left trying to decide who is truthful and who is not. Forensics and the criminal investigation exist for one reason—to answer such questions. They offer insight to the community on what really did occur. Unfortunately, forensic science, when offered as disparate disciplines (e.g., fingerprints, ballistics, DNA), doesn't always answer these questions for the jury. The jurors are still left pondering what took place. When presented with scientific evidence, that evidence is often offered in competing contexts, which does nothing more than confuse jurors.

In many instances, lawyers step forward to fill the gap of the jury's knowledge. In both opening and closing statements, counsel offer their own theories (valid or not) of what the "real" story is. They paint the scientific evidence in a context that works for them, many operating on what we now refer to as the Smorgasbord Theory of Science. They start with a conclusion, then choose that data that supports their theory, ignoring or dismissing any competing data. Like picking their favorite food at a buffet table, they choose only that information they like and then ask the jury to go along for the ride. This concept is not science; it is the antithesis of science.

Crime scene analysis (also known as *reconstruction*) is a discipline that fills this gap appropriately and effectively. The role of the crime scene analyst is to define as effectively as possible what occurred and in what order it occurred, as well as identifying what did not happen. This definition of events is never complete, playing out like a Hollywood movie; the limitations of the criminal investigation are ever present. There is only so much data to work with. But, crime scene analysis pulls the various forensic disciplines together and, using the refined conclusions from all of the experts involved, builds the most cohesive, most objective picture possible. This analysis guides the criminal investigation, assists both prosecution and defense in their tasks, and hopefully answers many of the questions being considered by the jury.

The role of the crime scene analyst is to answer as completely as possible what occurred and in what order it occurred. This idea of crime scene analysis is as old as the idea of the professional criminal investigation. The themes driving crime scene analysis have been written and discussed for over 100 years and are nothing more than the application of scientific method. As forensic technology progressed, the only real change in crime scene analysis has been the nature of evidence available for consideration. "How" one proceeds in crime scene analysis is the same today as it was 100 years ago, but the data available to the analyst has changed dramatically. That change demands caution on the part of the crime scene analyst. The analyst has to pull information from the various disciplines associated with the investigation and place it all into a functional and objective context. This is no easy task.

What we offer in this text is an approach to that task, a means of developing context. A way of taking all of the data from the disparate forensic disciplines and building an objective picture from it. The theory offered for crime scene analysis is as old as the concept itself. The principles we describe have always been in play, but perhaps in the form offered here, they will be more evident and understood by the analyst. Our methodology, Event Analysis, is a proven path that incorporates all of the basic historical themes of crime scene analysis. It is not the only methodology, but it works when used as described. Appropriate and objective crime scene analysis is the only effective way for achieving justice. We hope this book aids those who choose to pursue the task of crime scene analysis, guides those involved in criminal investigations, and eventually serves the best interests of our communities and juries by answering the questions that may lead us to true justice.

Acknowledgments

As with all writing projects, no one author or group of authors can take credit for every single aspect of the effort. We would like to offer our thanks to the following individuals for their input, assistance, or support:

Vernon Geberth, our series editor, for his continued support and encouragement over the years.

Tom Adair, Westminster Police Department. Tom has been an excellent source of archived material over the years as well as a good sounding board for ideas related to crime scene analysis.

Andrea McDonald, Arapahoe County Sheriff's Office. While attending a Crime Scene Reconstruction course several years ago, Andrea challenged our prior worksheets and suggested that instead of having two, we should combine the two to create a single, more effective worksheet. Her simple but effective suggestion has indeed helped and the new worksheet in Chapter 4 is a direct byproduct of her comment.

Becky McEldowney Masterman, our representative at Taylor & Francis. Becky has continued to be our greatest cheerleader over the years. When we asked Taylor & Francis to break out the crime scene analysis aspects for this book from the third edition of *Bloodstain Pattern Analysis with an Introduction to Crime Scene Reconstruction*, Becky never hesitated.

Cal Jenkins and Todd Zdorkowski for their guidance and direction as we addressed the underlying principles associated with crime scene analysis.

Iris Dalley, Laura Delong, Kim Duddy, as well as Chuck Merritt and the San Diego County Sheriff's Office Crime Laboratory, for their effort and support in pursuing the case examples utilized in the book.

Carolyn Gannet, San Diego County Sheriff's Office Crime Laboratory, for allowing us to use her research data on ethics.

Rebecca Shaw, Tom Adair, Matthew Noedel, and Kim Duddy for their input and perspective on the ethics of forensic science.

Christian Bachhiesl with the Hans-Gross Museum and the Bancroft Library, University of California, Berkeley, for their assistance and support in providing figures for Chapter 1.

The instructors at the Scenes of Crimes Officers Course (SOCO) in England, who set cogs in motion for the authors of this book; those cogs would later mesh and, when joined, ultimately became the Event Analysis methodology.

Richard Wintory, one of the first district attorneys with whom Tom had occasion to use these methods. Richard understood their value and supported the development of these ideas.

Lt. Travis Witcher, retired Oklahoma City Police Department. Travis secured Tom's early training and encouraged him to go beyond Bloodstain Pattern Analysis.

The entire staff at Taylor & Francis for the support and assistance in bringing this book to reality.

About the Authors

Ross M. Gardner worked for the United States Army Criminal Investigation Command (USACIDC) as a felony criminal investigator for nearly 20 years. He retired as a Command Sergeant Major and Special Agent in 1999 after serving a total of 24 years in U.S. Army law enforcement. Gardner subsequently served four years as the chief of police of Lake City, Georgia, a small suburban Atlanta police department. He now serves as vice president of Bevel, Gardner and Associates, Inc.

Gardner holds a master's degree in Computer and Information Systems Management from Webster University, a bachelor's degree in Criminal Justice from Wayland Baptist University, and an associate's degree in Police Science from Central Texas College. He graduated first in his class at the Scenes of Crime Officers Course, New Scotland Yard, Hendon, United Kingdom, in 1985 and between 1988 and 1996 served as an adjunct professor for Central Texas College in the Police Science Program. He is a former president of the Rocky Mountain Association of Bloodstain Pattern Analysts (RMABPA), as well as the Association for Crime Scene Reconstruction (ACSR), and has served as the chairman of the education committee for both the RMABPA and the International Association of Bloodstain Pattern Analysts (IABPA). Gardner was recognized as a Distinguished Member of ACSR in 2006. He is a charter member of the FBI Scientific Workgroup on Bloodstain Pattern Analysis (SWGSTAIN) and is the current chairman of the taxonomy and terminology subcommittee.

Gardner is certified by the International Association for Identification as Senior Crime Scene Analyst, a rating he has held for 18 years. He is an active instructor and consultant throughout the United States in crime scene analysis, bloodstain pattern analysis, and crime scene investigation; teaching to a variety of groups ranging from police and investigative organizations to trial counsel professional development groups. He is the author of the text *Practical Crime Scene Processing and Investigation* and co-authored with Tom Bevel *Bloodstain Pattern Analysis: With an Introduction to Crime Scene Reconstruction,* 3rd edition.

Capt. Tom Bevel (Ret.) is president of Bevel, Gardner and Associates, Inc., a forensic education and consulting company. He is also an associate professor in the Masters of Forensic Science program at the University of Central Oklahoma, Edmond. He retired after 27 years with the Oklahoma City Police Department. His last assignment was commander of the Homicide, Robbery, Missing Persons and the Unsolved Homicide Units.

Bevel holds a master of arts degree from the University of Central Oklahoma in the Administration of Criminal Justice. He also is a graduate of the Scenes of Crime Course, Hendon, United Kingdom; the Technical Investigations Course, Central U.S. Police Institute, Oklahoma State University at Oklahoma City; the FBI National Academy; and the Postgraduate Medical–Legal Course at London Medical College, United Kingdom.

Bevel is a charter member of the FBI Scientific Workgroup on Bloodstain Pattern Analysis (SWGSTAIN) and is on the Board of Directors. He also is a Fellow of the

Association for Crime Scene Reconstruction (ACSR), a Distinguished Member of the International Association of Bloodstain Pattern Analysts (IABPA), on the editorial board for the *Journal of Forensic Identification*, and a member of the Southwestern Association of Forensic Scientists (SWAFS), and the American Academy of Forensic Sciences (AAFS). He serves on the Board of Advisers for the Master of Forensic Science program for the University of Central Oklahoma as well.

Bevel has served as a crime scene consultant in 46 of the United States and 9 foreign countries. He has been qualified as an expert in crime scene reconstruction and bloodstain pattern analysis in both state and federal courts. He is co-author of the text *Bloodstain Pattern Analysis with an Introduction to Crime Scene Reconstruction,* 3rd edition.

An Introduction and History of Crime Scene Analysis

1

Introduction

Crime scene analysis is a relatively distinct concept in forensic science. In a nutshell, it involves evaluating the context of a scene and the physical evidence found there in an effort to identify what occurred and in what order it occurred. Note that we said "scene" and not "crime scene." The scenes in question are generally evaluated to determine if they are areas where crimes occurred, but that decision is not always apparent until after analysis. Throughout the book, *scene* and *crime scene* are used interchangeably; both are inclusive for all of the situations that crime scene investigators face. For purposes of this text, one may also consider crime scene analysis and crime scene reconstruction as synonymous terms. The Association of Crime Scene Reconstruction (ACSR) defines reconstruction as "the use of scientific methods, physical evidence, deductive and inductive reasoning, and their interrelationships to gain explicit knowledge of the series of events that surround the commission of a crime.[1] In Chapter 3, we will introduce the process of Event Analysis. All three relate to the same idea—defining the actions and order of actions at a given incident using the objective data found in physical evidence.

Crime scene analysis has a distinct history, which is described later in this chapter. Thus, the concepts of crime scene analysis are as old as the idea of professional criminal investigations themselves. In other words, this is not a new discipline. As we consider the history of crime scene analysis, numerous themes become evident, including:

- As with all scientific effort, data define the conclusion.
- Objective data are found in the scene, both in the general context of the scene and in the specific objects found there.
- Human testimony is always considered in a cautious fashion.
- Effective forensic evaluation of objects (evidence) leads to refined data, which leads to more objective and refined conclusions.
- "What happened" is not the only question considered by the crime scene analyst; the order in which it occurred is just as important.
- Crime scene analysis uses reductionism. The analysis is reverse engineered from the physical evidence.

From a practical consideration of these themes comes a working theory for crime scene analysis. This theory stated simply is: Nothing just happens. Every action has a preexisting set of circumstances, every action leads to a subsequent set of circumstances. By evaluating the scene and objects in it, we are able to define some of these. Chapter 2 will discuss this theory and its associated principles in detail. Although the definitions and themes of crime scene analysis are generally accepted, two distinctions are necessary when discussing the topic of crime scene analysis.

Distinguishing Crime Scene Analysis from Crime Scene Processing

On this point we want to be very clear—all crime scene processing involves some level of crime scene analysis. Any claim that it does not is a statement of ignorance. Chapter 2 will describe this informal analysis in depth; however, crime scene processing is distinct in its purpose and activities from formal crime scene analysis. Crime scene processing involves six steps. These include assessing, observing, documenting, searching, collecting, and analyzing scenes. The express purpose of these six steps is to document the context of the scene and collect any physical evidence present in a usable form. Crime scene processing is a definite procedure. Granted, to be competent, the crime scene technician must understand the underlying forensics. One cannot collect evidence in a fashion usable to the forensic scientist unless he first recognizes that the evidence exists and then realizes how it must be collected. But one does not specifically follow scientific method when taking overall evidence-establishing or evidence close-up photographs or when mapping a scene (e.g., triangulating a piece of evidence). Of course, the situation changes when the crime scene investigator is evaluating the scene—deciding what is or is not evidence or where to look for evidence. The crime scene investigator employs scientific method in these activities and certainly employs it when tasked with responsibility for specific on-scene analysis efforts (e.g., trajectory analysis). The concepts of processing the scene and analyzing the scene are significantly intertwined, but the difference between the two is important in certain discussions.

Distinguishing Crime Scene Analysis from Behavioral Profiling

To consider crime scene analysis in its entirety we must also contrast crime scene analysis from the work started by the Federal Bureau of Investigation's (FBI's) Behavioral Sciences Unit (BSU). This distinction is important as many people associate criminal profiling with the term *crime scene analysis*. In some discussions, the terms are often used interchangeably.

Criminal profiling is a service found in serial and violent crimes. It often assists the investigator in narrowing the search for a suspect. This evaluation considers the crime scene, the victim's background and actions, the apparent actions of the suspect, and, from this data, provides information that may define the suspect as an individual. This information can be valuable, but it also is quite subjective. Quality profilers usually explain that these methods are not without fault and are anything but completely accurate. The methods are based on statistical data developed over years of evaluating homicides, rapes, and arsons. Unfortunately, statistical data can be misleading when applied to a single instance. For example, in one case a profile identified 12 characteristics of the probable perpetrator. When the suspect was caught, none of the 12 matched. The reason for the disparity was that the case involved a female serial killer who decapitated her victims—a circumstance that fails to fit the statistical data used to assist in developing such profiles.

Crime scene analysis concentrates on the objective evaluation of the scene and physical evidence and then establishes any information that may safely be defined from it. This is in stark contrast to the idea of criminal profiling as a whole. Criminal profilers consider what happened in an effort to explain the "who" and "why" regarding the perpetrator. In crime scene analysis, the "why" of crime is the analyst's event horizon; physical evidence simply does not allow us to objectively explain the why of human behavior. However, using crime scene analysis to define objective statements of "what" happened, criminal profilers, investigators, and even lawyers can always expand their consideration beyond the crime scene analysis to develop hypotheses of "why" things occurred.

Criminal profiling is nevertheless inseparably linked to crime scene analysis, as it relies on the results of a *functional* crime scene analysis. The evolution of criminal profiling techniques has been significant over a relatively short period of time, but as Vernon Geberth noted, psychological profiles are nothing new to criminal investigations.[2]

In early criminal investigations, most profiles were completed after the suspect was in custody. More often than not, these methods applied standard psychiatric evaluations to establish the sanity of the individual involved. As Jerry Chisum reported, Edward Heinrich (the Wizard of Berkeley) was the first criminalist to go beyond scientific analysis of evidence and develop an early form of profiling, which included a victimology.[3]

Another notable profiler was Dr. James A. Brussel. Active during the 1940s and 1950s, Dr. Brussel used his psychiatric training in an attempt to identify personality characteristics of the individual known as the "Mad Bomber" who set off more than 30 bombs over a 16-year period. As Geberth reported, Brussel, after reviewing the investigative efforts spanning those 16 years, said simply:

> "Look for a heavy man. Middle age. Foreign born. Roman Catholic. Single. Lives with a brother or sister." He [Brussel] also added, "When you find him, he'll be wearing a double breasted suit. Buttoned." [The suspect] was exactly as described by Dr. Brussel. When taken into custody, he was even wearing a double-breasted suit.[4]

The most significant evolution in profiling came from the efforts of Howard Teten. Influenced by previous efforts, but with a greater understanding and appreciation of the role of all forensic disciplines, Teten developed the initial FBI profiling techniques. Over time those techniques have become the basis of modern profiling.

Modern criminal profiling generally consists of three stages:

1. Collecting profiling inputs: these include the crime scene, victimology, forensic information, police reports, background information, and photos.
2. Creating decision process models: defining the homicide style, primary intent, victim risk, offender risk, location and escalation.
3. Conducting a crime assessment: reconstruction of the crime, crime classification, staging issues, motivation, and crime scene dynamics.[5]

In terms of the relationship between profiling and crime scene analysis, the assessment stage is important. Ressler described assessment in this fashion:

> The crime assessment stage in generating a criminal profile involves the reconstruction of the *sequence of events* [italics added] and the behavior of both the offender and the victim. Based

on the various decisions of the previous stage [the decision process model], this reconstruction of how things happened, how people behaved, and how they planned and organized the encounter provides information about specific characteristics to be generated for the criminal profile.[6]

Chisum also commented on the necessity of integrating crime scene reconstruction techniques into the criminal profile process, stating:

> Criminal profilers have realized the need to reconstruct the crime. To explain the behavior of the criminal, they need to know what was done at the scene. The study of the crime scene holds many answers to the motives of the suspect, but only if the crime is understood.[7]

Criminal profiling relies heavily on a viable methodology for crime scene analysis. This reliance helps ensure the objectiveness of the profiler, in what can only be described as an otherwise subjective process. An integral and unmistakable part of the third step of criminal profiling, crime assessment, is reconstructing the crime in a manner that we will describe in this book.

Pioneers in Crime Scene Analysis: A History of the Discipline

The concepts behind crime scene analysis are not new. The history of crime scene analysis can be traced back to at least 1898 and Austrian jurist Hans Gross. To fully understand and apply crime scene analysis demands consideration of that history. Despite this history, however, many lawyers will claim that crime scene analysis is "new" and/or "unscientific." The fact is our stated theory that "nothing just happens" was first suggested by Edward Oscar Heinrich in the mid-1900s. Heinrich, in explaining the task, said, "One is confronted with scrambled effects, all parts of which separately are attributable to causes. The tracing of the relationship between isolated points of fact, the completion of the chain of circumstances between cause and effect, are the highest functions of reason... ."[8] As for the charge of unscientific, crime scene analysis shares significant similarities in purpose and action with a scientific discipline outside of forensics, as we'll discuss in Chapter 2. This discipline is archaeology and, due to the similarities, crime scene analysis adopts and applies several basic principles from this area of study.

Hans Gross was a pioneer in modern forensic science (Figure 1.1). It would not be an understatement to say that Gross is the father of modern criminal investigations. He set the stage for scientific investigations based on the analysis of physical evidence, and his contributions include discussions on crime scene analysis. Gross's 1898 text spoke of the necessity of reconstructing crime through the meticulous examination and collection of empirical facts. He warned investigating officers against heaping testimony upon testimony, stating that by doing so investigators will "almost always be led astray and found wandering from the goal [the truth]."[9] Gross' book discusses the basic aspects of all our current practices including making detailed observations, the collection of physical evidence, the scientific examination of evidence to obtain more refined data, and the application of this refined information to assess specific investigative questions. Gross' stated purpose was to "reconstruct the occurrence [and] build up by hard labor a theory fitted in and coordinated."[10]

Luke May was another pioneer in crime scene analysis. May published *Scientific Murder Investigation* in 1933 in which he stated that the investigator must "develop other facts, correlating and interlocking to make a whole from apparently disassociated separate

Figure 1.1 Hans Gross, (1847–1915) is considered by many to be the father of the modern criminal investigation. (Photo courtesy of Christian Bachhiesl and the Hans-Gross-Kriminalmuseum of the Karl-Franzens-University Graz.)

units."[11] His writings warn investigators against the practice of developing subjective personal theories and the penchant investigators often have of trying to force the pieces of an investigation into such theories. May advised that professional investigators seek out additional facts that may lead to novel and more accurate theories, rather than forcing evidence into a theory. May said the true mark of the scientific investigator was the ability to "work untiringly, obtaining facts upon which to predicate theories, changing his [initial] theories as the facts developed warrant."[12]

Henry T. F. Rhodes was the first author to make the case that crime scene analysis was a specific scientific process. His text, *Clues and Crime,* written in 1933, stated that the object of crime scene evaluation was to determine specifically how the crime was committed and in what order the events occurred. Rhodes explicitly defined scientific method as the underlying foundation for these decisions.

Another pioneer in the development of crime scene analysis was Edward Oscar Heinrich (Figure 1.2). Although generally unpublished, a biography detailing his career throughout the early 1900s offers insight into his beliefs and procedures for crime scene analysis. In it he described his work, saying:

This work of mine, it is not mysterious. It is a matter of understanding the scientific aspects of ordinary phenomena. Rarely are other than ordinary phenomena involved in the commission of a crime. One is confronted with scrambled effects, all parts of which separately are attributable to causes. The tracing of the relationship between isolated points of fact, the completion of the chain of circumstances between cause and effect, are the highest functions of reason... ."

Figure 1.2 Edward Oscar Heinrich (1881–1953), also known as the Wizard of Berkeley. A professor of physics at the University of Berkeley, Heinrich was also active as a consultant in criminal investigations and crime scene analysis. Heinrich was the first analyst to truly articulate a theory for crime scene analysis. (Photo courtesy of The Bancroft Library, University of California, Berkeley, CA.)

Heinrich saw cause and effect issues as the basis of crime scene analysis. This is anything but surprising because defining cause and effect relationships is in itself the basic definition of science. Heinrich added that one must first analyze the method (the progression of events) before one could properly understand the purpose of crime or hope to identify the criminal. This belief carries over into modern-day criminal profiling. Heinrich's stated methodology for crime scene analysis was quite simple. The analyst must define "what happened, where it happened and when [in what order] it happened."[13] Heinrich offered the analogy that analysis was like "a mosaic...[in which] every fact must be evaluated before it can be fit into the pattern. In that way, every fact as it is developed and equated becomes a clue." This is a widely familiar and accepted analogy used in crime scene analysis, where analysis is often described in terms of pieces being fit into a puzzle.

From 1930 to 1960, most of the reconstruction experts were individuals outside of police agencies (e.g., Heinrich, Rhodes) who supported law enforcement agencies when requested. With the onset of more professional policing and the development of general forensics, a greater emphasis on forensic analysis was evident in investigative texts. As technology fueled the development of forensic science, the new emphasis became detailed evaluation of physical evidence. This led to the refinement of many forensics disciplines and a trend away from the generalist. As a result of this emphasis, discussions of general methodologies for crime scene analysis were lost to some extent; however, methodology development was not completely idle.

Charles O'Hara was one of the more detailed authors on the subject of crime scene analysis methodology. His text, *Fundamentals of Criminal Investigation,* was first published in 1965. In it, O'Hara placed his emphasis on reconstruction and analysis on the objective value of physical evidence and its scientific evaluation. As every other author of the time, O'Hara drove home the belief that scientific analysis of evidence was extremely important, but was not the end-all of analysis. O'Hara also offered a specific methodology for reconstruction, which he described in terms of scientific method. It involved:

- Painstaking and comprehensive collection of data.
- Arrangement and correlation of that data.
- Defining issues and investigative questions.
- The development of hypotheses along the lines of the available data and subsequent resolution of any hypotheses.
- Testing of each hypothesis and elimination when possible of contradicting hypotheses.
- Testing of the final hypothesis before acceptance.[14]

O'Hara applied this approach to the entire investigation including subjective aspects, such as testimonial evidence; but, he is clear that physical evidence as well as the context of the crime scene shouldered a distinct responsibility in solving crime. He made the case for conducting a separate crime scene reconstruction (excluding testimonial evidence) using these techniques in an effort to determine the objective circumstances of the crime.[15]

In 1984, Jerry Findley and Craig Hopkins in discussing their beliefs on crime scene analysis stated, "In essence, reconstruction is the sum total of the investigation demonstrated in its tangible form."[16] They too recognized that after scientific analysis by the various forensics disciplines, someone (a crime scene analyst) had to bring all of this information together.

William Chisum and Joseph Rynearson described a specific methodology for crime scene analysis in their text, *Evidence and Crime Scene Reconstruction*. Their methodology, first published in 1984, emphasized the importance of contextual information: a belief that time and surroundings were a significant source of objective data. Their methodology included the use of logic pathways and a storyboard approach. In the latter, once identified, specific events were mapped out and then sequenced within the entire reconstruction.[17] Rynearson and Chisum spoke of three cause and effect relationships that are of specific concern to the analyst:

1. Predictable effects
2. Unpredictable effects
3. Transitory effects[18]

They identified things such as the progression of rigor or livor mortis as predictable effects. Predictable effects follow predictable timelines, which allow the analyst to better understand the scene. Unpredictable effects are things that cannot be controlled. An example of this is the opening of a door and disturbing the layering of items behind it. These effects alter or destroy the value of evidence at the scene and are often unintentionally produced by actions of the first responders or even the crime scene team. Unpredictable effects impact the way the crime scene analyst views the evidence, which can alter the way it is incorporated into the analysis. Transitory effects are fleeting. If unrecognized, they may well be lost forever. Examples include a cigarette burning or the fragrance of perfume wafting in the air. The same as fragile items of evidence, a failure to recognize and record the condition of transitory effects could be disastrous. When the crime scene analyst considers reports of transitory effects, where testimonial evidence may be the only record available, he must be confident of the witness's ability to have effectively observed and remembered such evidence. These three effects—predictable, unpredictable, and transitory—are significant tools for consideration.

In 1992, James W. Osterburg wrote *Criminal Investigation: A Method for Reconstructing the Past*. In it Osterburg made it clear that the investigative process must follow the scientific method. Osterburg offered no specific reconstruction methodology, but he discussed the importance of using physical evidence to reconstruct events.

Dr. Henry Lee has often commented on reconstructions, both in his text *Crime Scene Investigation* (1992) and his subsequent text, *Henry Lee's Crime Scene Handbook* (1999). Lee advocates the use of scientific method as the means of pursuing crime scene analysis.

Chisum went on to join another author, Brent Turvey, contributing a chapter entitled "An Introduction to Crime Scene Reconstruction" in Turvey's book *Criminal Profiling*. Chisum's primary point was that crime scene analysis is a necessary part of the profiling process. He, however, did not take the opportunity to outline in depth or expound on his previous beliefs regarding a methodology for analysis.

In 1997, we, the authors, introduced a methodology called Event Analysis. It relied on the themes and work of previous authors, but set forth a practical series of steps to follow. The initial ideas that would ultimately be put into Event Analysis were published as early as 1994, at a point prior to us becoming aware of Heinrich's work.[19] What is interesting about this point is that Event Analysis shares distinct similarities with Heinrich's beliefs. Heinrich felt that "crime presents a succession of methods—entrance, approach, attack, retreat, exit. Each of these must be learned [discovered] by the investigator as his work proceeds."[20] As Chapter 3 will outline, Heinrich's "succession of methods" in Event Analysis are called *Events*. Each event is a macro component of the crime and composed of "event segments." These event segments are defined actions supported by physical evidence.

We make this point, not as a statement of comparison between Heinrich and ourselves, but rather as a statement of the simplicity of logic behind the concept of crime scene analysis. The ideas behind "how to" reconstruct crime are almost self-evident. The true difficulty lies not in how to proceed, but rather in how to proceed objectively. This is an important point to understand; the dramatic changes in forensic science have not altered how the crime scene analyst pursues the analysis. The analyst uses the scientific method. All that the changes in forensic science have brought about is a change in the nature and quality of data available to incorporate into the crime scene analysis.

The Future

The ideas that drive the concept of crime scene analysis have not changed over the years, but that doesn't mean crime scene analysis as a discipline is unchanging. The expectations for the future of crime scene analysis are quite clear. Numerous professional associations exist that are actively seeking to guide and direct the discipline in an appropriate direction. For example, the International Association for Identification (IAI) initiated a certification program for crime scene analysis in the 1990s. Over the years, they have expanded that system to include a proficiency test for recertification and are now looking at developing a specific "crime scene reconstruction" certification. The Association for Crime Scene Reconstruction (ACSR) was formed in 1991, intended as a regional (Oklahoma and Texas) organization. Over its short history, ACSR quickly expanded to a national association and now boasts members from throughout the United States and around the world. ACSR is committed to offering professional education to those interested in the discipline as well as setting ethical guidelines for members. In one unfortunate ethical lapse, despite the fact that the involved individual was a member of many forensics associations, ACSR was the only association to censure and oust the involved analyst prior to a public outcry.

The IAI and ACSR believe the role of the crime scene analyst, now and in the future, is to understand and apply appropriate methods in as objective a fashion as possible. By doing this, the analyst can help bring clarity to the issues before the court, which may allow a jury to make a more informed decision. Thus, the continued development of curriculum, objective methods, and practices that assist the analyst in maintaining quality assurance are all important issues.

Summary

It is not enough that one can collect evidence and have that evidence examined for specific issues by a forensic scientist. At some point all of the information obtained from the crime scene examination and evaluation of the evidence must be brought together to forge a valid theory of what happened. This theory must be grounded in objective fact and should not be based on subjective information. The process of bringing this information together is known as crime scene analysis or reconstruction.

Crime scene analysis uses the context of the scene and the refined data developed through scientific analysis of evidence to establish specific actions that happened at the scene and whenever possible to define in what order these actions happened. Crime scene analysis relies heavily on the quality of the crime scene processing. The context and evidence recovered from the scene is the only data available to fuel the crime scene analysis. Thus, crime scene analysis and crime scene processing are distinct but inseparably intertwined ideas.

The themes that drive how crime scene analysis is pursued have been well defined by numerous authors over the past 110 years. Change in scientific technology has not altered the way we pursue crime scene analysis, nor will it. Changes in forensic science simply change the nature of the data used in the analysis. As forensic science advances, the crime scene analyst is provided with more and more objective data to turn to in order to build their reconstruction.

References

1. Association of Crime Scene Reconstruction By-Laws, 1995.
2. Geberth, V.J. 1996. *Practical Homicide Investigation*, 3rd ed., CRC Press, Boca Raton, FL, 706.
3. Chisum, J.W. April 1998. The History of Crime Scene Reconstruction, *ASCR The Scene*, 5 (2): 14–15.
4. Geberth, V.J. 1996. *Practical Homicide Investigation*, 707–708.
5. Ressler, R.K., A. Burgess, and J.E. Douglas, 1988. *Sexual Homicide: Patterns and Motives,* New York: Lexington Books, 137.
6. Ressler, *Sexual Homicide: Patterns and Motives*, 142.

7. Turvey, B.E. et. al. 1999. *Criminal Profiling: An Introduction to Behavioral Evidence Analysis*, San Diego: Academic Press, 76.
8. Block, E., 1958. *The Wizard of Berkeley*, New York: Coward-McCann Inc, 44.
9. Gross, H., 1924. *System der Kriminalistic* in the translated and edited version of J. Collyer Adam, *Criminal investigation: A Practical Textbook*, London: Sweet Maxwell Ltd., 37–38.
10. Ibid.
11. May, L.S. 1933. *Scientific Murder Investigation*, Seattle, WA: Institute of Scientific Criminology, 9.
12. Ibid.
13. Block, *The Wizard of Berkeley*, 42–43.
14. O'Hara, C.E. 1976. *Fundamentals of Criminal Investigation*, 4th ed., Springfield, IL: Charles C Thomas Publishing, 20–21.
15. O'Hara, *Fundamentals of Criminal Investigation*, 58.
16. Findley, J., and C. Hopkins. October 1984. Reconstruction: An Overview, *The Identification News*.
17. Rynearson, J.M., and W.J. Chisum. 1989. *Evidence and Crime Scene Reconstruction*, 100–108.
18. Rynearson, *Evidence and Crime Scene Reconstruction*, 93.
19. Gardner, R.M. 1994. Considerations in Crime Scene Analysis, *IABPA* News, 10(2): 10–18.
20. Block, *The Wizard of Berkeley*, 42.

Theoretical and Practical Considerations for Implementing Crime Scene Analysis

2

Introduction

Circumstances and situations that investigators and analysts alike are routinely presented with as crimes or suspected crimes naturally beg questions. What happened? In what order did it happen? Who was involved? Why did it happen? The function and expectation of any criminal investigation is to resolve these questions to the best of the investigator's ability. In order to meet that expectation, the investigator must wade through a wide array of different and disjointed facts trying to build from them a reasonable and valid theory that will answer these questions. Traditional forensic science has always played a role in helping to establish such a theory (Figure 2.1). Each of the forensic disciplines define specific facts and information from the artifacts and evidence left at the scene, all of which will ultimately help set a foundation for any theory of what occurred. However, forging a consolidated understanding of what those facts mean demands more than just possessing them. Context is everything in analysis and that means correlating all of the forensic facts and data together. Relational and chronological aspects between different data elements, even a smidgen of common sense have to be rolled together with all of the forensic data to define any reasonable hypothesis (Figure 2.2).

These considerations are beyond the role of the traditional forensic scientist to answer. In fact, the concept of forging a consolidated theory is counter-intuitive to the way most scientists are allowed to operate. Generally the forensic scientist or law enforcement specialist in today's specialty-driven environment is compelled to operate in an extremely compartmental fashion. Serologists work on serology issues, ballistic experts worry about the ballistics, fingerprint examiners worry about fingerprint issues. Rarely are they allowed to widen their conclusions beyond their own individual discipline. This is not intended as a statement of condemnation of the scientist or specialist; rather it is an acknowledgment of the current state of affairs. But it is only by considering all data that any functional theory can ever be developed. Crime scene analysis is an overarching discipline that integrates all of the disjointed data found in the scene and establishes a reasonable and hopefully

11

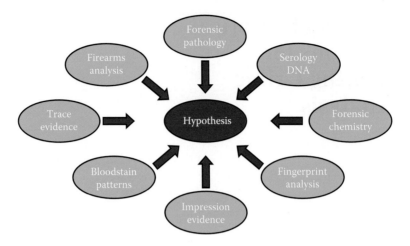

Figure 2.1 The information derived from forensic science evaluations has always been an integral part of the foundation for any hypothesis of "what happened" in a crime scene.

defensible theory. In this chapter we will present some foundational ideas that will guide the crime scene analyst.

Who Qualifies as a Crime Scene Analyst?

The question of who should conduct crime scene analysis often breaks down into a divisive and antagonistic discussion. Some authors rail against law enforcement, criminal investigators, and even forensic scientists, claiming that only a "true" scientist has the ability to be a crime scene analyst. One often hears a forensic scientist state that criminal investigators should not conduct crime scene analysis, claiming they are incapable of being objective. Criminal investigators, on the other hand, challenge forensic scientists claiming that their lack of scene experience limits their ability to be a true crime scene analyst. It is the

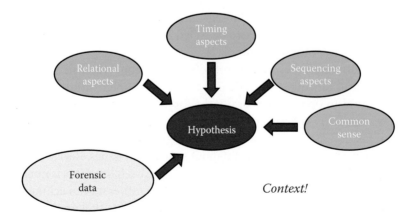

Figure 2.2 Above and beyond the standard forensic data, relational, timing, and sequencing aspects, as well as a little common sense, all contribute to our beliefs about what happened in the scene. Together they provide a context in which to view the forensic data.

authors' opinion that all of these arguments are based on personal agendas and, when considered objectively, haven't any absolute basis. Each is skewed in some aspect.

What is the reality? In our opinion, crime scene analysis demands three things of the analyst. The first is an understanding of general forensics; however one doesn't need to be an expert in every forensic field to be a crime scene analyst. The authors are not aware of anyone who could claim such a distinction. Being an expert in every field is unnecessary. The crime scene analyst takes all of the refined information from the individual forensic disciplines and then uses that knowledge. The crime scene analyst doesn't redefine what the sciences say; he takes these individual pieces of the investigative puzzle and puts them into a context.

Secondly, crime scene analysis certainly demands an understanding and level of experience in dealing with crime scenes—direct and specific experience, not that gained by simply visiting a scene or reviewing the work of others who have processed scenes. However, it should be stated that having experience with crime scenes is not always the same as pure "investigative experience." Thus, mere police experience in and of itself is not enough to answer this issue. The nature of this crime scene experience must be such that the analyst recognizes the problems associated with crime scene work, how these problems will become manifest in the scene or evidence, and how that can produce effects that may misdirect the analysis. One often hears the "scientist only" clique counter this latter concern with statements that, if scientists were at the scene, such issues would not present themselves. In other words, if scientists were in charge, the crime scene would be handled without problem or issue each and every time. This is pure arrogance and proves why real scene experience is a factor. As we will discuss in Chapter 5, crime scene processing is a task inundated with problems. No one, no matter how good they think they are, no matter how educated in science they may be, has *ever* processed a crime scene perfectly; nor can they. Understanding the realities and ambiguities of crime scene processing is a must for any crime scene analyst.

A final capability that is significant to the crime scene analyst is the ability and willingness to be objective. Understanding and applying scientific method is important to any analysis. Criminal investigators are not always trained in formal scientific method or adept at the task. Once again, this is not a condemnation of criminal investigators, for scientific method is an integral part of any proper investigative procedure. If one doubts that scientific method is not a part of investigative procedure, author Gardner would refer such skeptics to Crime Scene Processing I and II, a U.S. Army video training series created in 1990. In this training tape, two investigators go through a scene processing scenario in Part I of the series and then after submitting the evidence to the lab and receiving forensic data back, define and work through multiple hypotheses regarding their scene in Part II.[1] Anyone viewing the tape or who has actually experienced real world investigators operating in an appropriate fashion would immediately recognize this behavior as scientific method. Investigators may not refer to what they do as scientific method, but that is exactly what it is. If, however, investigations are not guided by these principles or investigators choose not to practice them, the resulting investigation is bound to slip into subjective traps. The most critical trap any analyst can fall into is to first define a conclusion, then set out to locate data to support that conclusion. Thus, it is important to build on the criminal investigator's understanding of scientific method. Scientists operate in an environment where they are constantly reminded that data define any conclusion and that experience gives them an edge in countering these issues. Unfortunately, in terms of remaining objective no matter what our background or level of training, subjectivity is a vice held by each and every human. Scientist, investigator, and laymen alike are all equally capable of ignoring data and forcing subjective conclusions. It is only arrogance speaking when any one of us presume we are operating in a totally objective fashion, as it is simply not in our nature as human beings to do so.

In our humble opinion, above and beyond any knowledge or skills that come with their primary position, those who intend to conduct crime scene analysis need an understanding of general forensics, actual experience in dealing with crime scenes, and a willingness to proceed objectively. Investigator or scientist, it doesn't really matter. Objectivity and adherence to the scientific method are best accomplished through a firm grasp and application of the underlying theory, principles, and proven methods of crime scene analysis. These tools will guide the analyst (scientist or investigator) through the morass of subjective traps found in crime scene analysis. In the end, each analysis should be judged on its merits and objectivity, not solely on who did it.

Fundamental Beliefs for Crime Scene Analysis

In Chapter 1, we defined the common themes found in the various historical discussions of crime scene analysis. These included the belief that data define the conclusion, and the more refined the data available, the more refined the conclusion. For the crime scene analyst, objective data exist in scene context and physical evidence. This data may lead to the recognition of specific actions that occurred during an incident, as well as the order of these actions. Crime scene analysis is reverse engineered, working from the evidence backward; it uses a form of reductionism. In order to implement objective and quality crime scene analysis, these themes must be incorporated into a practical methodology. These themes serve as a guide, defining a "how to" procedure. Lacking in these guidelines, however, is a succinct theory of crime scene analysis, not an absolute methodology. Is there an underlying theory applicable to crime scene analysis? If it exists, how can it be articulated? As authors go, Edward Heinrich was the first to suggest an overarching theory for crime scene analysis. He said that crime scene analysis was the "tracing of the relationship between isolated points of fact, the completion of the chain of circumstances between cause and effect."[2] In 1997, we restated this theory as "Nothing Just Happens."[3]

Theory and Applicable Principles for Crime Scene Analysis

Our theory of crime scene analysis is that "nothing just happens;" each action has something that precedes it, something that occurs during, and something that follows it. As simple as this may sound and as Heinrich pointed out, this theory is nothing more than a restatement of the founding principle of modern science itself, the principle of causality. From David Hume (Scottish philosopher) to the present, the concept of cause and effect as scientific explanation has driven the development of all science. Every action (a cause) has led to some subsequent condition (the effect). We can think of this in another way as well; it is "history." In the broadest sense, the crime scene analyst identifies and links actions through cause and effect relationships defining a history regarding the incident in question. This analogy to history is rather important because as we look for established principles to apply to our theory, a clear correlation to the study of archaeology will become evident.

A theory is always supported by principles that are applied through a specific methodology. Crime scene analysis is no different. There are four principles applicable to crime scene reconstruction (CSR). Three of these principles are found in the discipline of archaeology, the study of human behavior and culture through the examination of artifacts. Although this association is not often described and some may question the correlation, crime scene investigation as a whole (both processing and analysis) shares distinct similarities with the field of archaeology.

Correlating Crime Scene Analysis with Archaeology

The correlations between archaeology and crime scene analysis are clear and distinct. To recognize them, we need only examine each discipline. Archaeologists examine and excavate ancient scenes in an effort to understand the historical events and cultures associated to them. In part, they try to answer what happened and in what order it happened. This examination includes documentation of the overall scene context (e.g., mapping the location of artifacts in relation to the dig), as well as the careful collection of any artifacts and their subsequent scientific analysis in order to define more effectively what each artifact tells the archaeologist. Ultimately the archaeologist conducts an in-depth correlation of all of the available data developed from the scene using scientific method, in an effort to understand what can objectively be stated about that scene. The archaeologist takes the scene and artifacts found there and puts this information into a context. Thus, archaeology is often concerned with the recognition of events as well as the sequencing of those events. The archaeologist's dilemma is that he has no reference or standard with which to compare his analysis. As an archaeologist once described, the task is much like having someone walk up with a jigsaw puzzle, throw several handfuls of pieces in front of the archaeologist, and then throw the remaining pieces and the box away, yet still ask: "What does this picture look like?" The archaeologist is left to infer as little as possible, while still defining objectively as much as possible from those few pieces; this is no simple task.

The function and purpose of the crime scene investigator and crime scene analyst is the same, with the same basic end in mind. Crime scenes are examined in detail. The context of the scene is documented (e.g., mapping the location of evidence and artifacts in relation to the scene). Evidence in the form of artifacts found at the scene are collected and often sent for additional analysis by a forensic expert. That forensic analysis defines more effectively what each item of evidence tells the investigator. The refined information resulting from that analysis is used along with all of the scene data to identify specific events (e.g., what occurred) and the order of those events. All of this is accomplished using scientific method, but like the archaeologist, the crime scene analyst has no objective standard to compare his conclusions to. There is no investigative picture on a puzzle box top to refer to.

One real difference between the two groups is that the archaeologist is concerned with a more distant history and usually deals with large swathes of time (e.g., years, centuries, or eras). In crime scene analysis, the analyst deals with a not so distant past. An additional consideration is that typically the number of artifacts in the crime scene is greater than those found in the archaeological site, which allows the crime scene analyst a more effective analysis of microevents. This comparison is not intended to suggest that the archaeologist is a crime scene analyst, or that the crime scene analyst is an archaeologist. The two simply approach their respective tasks using extremely similar methodologies and techniques. Given this interrelationship of purpose and procedure, it is appropriate that as crime scene analyst we look to archaeology and draw applicable principles from it to apply to our own given theory. These principles include Nicolas Steno's Principle of Superposition, Steno's Principle of Lateral Continuity, and a principle shared by both crime scene analysis and archaeology, the concept of chronology.

Principles of CSR

Nicolas Steno was a pioneer in the study of geology. He authored three principles for the study of geology; all three of these concepts are still bedrock beliefs in geology and the associated discipline of archaeology. Steno's Law of Superposition was first proposed in 1669 and states that layers of rock are distributed in a time sequence, with the oldest on the bottom and the youngest on the top, unless a subsequent action disturbs this arrangement. Steno's principle of superposition recognizes that subsequent alteration is always possible and must be considered. In modern archaeology, Steno's law of superposition is carried over to artifacts as well, in which layers of artifacts will be deposited in a time sequence. The obvious ramifications to crime scene analysis lie in the deposition of objects on top of one another. These depositions provide chronological data to the CSR. As with its application in geology, superposition requires consideration of subsequent alteration as a result of ongoing activity in the scene, as well as the creation of postincident artifacts by first responders and others (Figure 2.3).

CSR Superposition Example: In a hypothetical scene, the body of the victim is found on the floor on top of a series of bloody footprints, one of which is only partial. Using the concept of superposition, the blood deposit from the shoe by necessity must precede the final position of the victim.

Figure 2.3 A crime scene example of superposition. The layering evident for the bottle, hair, purse, and cell phone tell us much about the order of their deposition. Based on superposition, the bottle must have preceded the hair's final position, and the hair preceded the purse's final position as well as the cell phone's position.

Figure 2.4 A crime scene example of lateral continuity. A woman claimed an intruder was standing in this area trying to enter the window, but the continuity of the dirt is undisturbed. The concept of lateral continuity can be used to define both when continuity is disrupted by some action and when it was not. (Photo courtesy of Sherri Wallace, Oklahoma County Sheriff's Office, Oklahoma City.)

Steno's Law of Lateral Continuity in effect recognizes that strata are not deposited in a way that they abruptly end. Instead, as one approaches their ending boundary, they become less pronounced. The principle is carried over to artifacts found in the strata as well. Thus, when presented with a strata that abruptly ends and when similar but disassociated strata are present, they are by association assumed to belong to the same occupation or depositional period. This concept of continuity, applied in CSR, allows us to recognize when continuity is intact or when it is disrupted, as well as making associations between disassociated layers. Disassociated layering is often encountered in one form or another in the crime scene context. For instance, any void (e.g., in a bloodstain or some other deposit) is an example of the disruption of lateral continuity (Figure 2.4).

CSR Association Example: In our hypothetical scene, a partial bloody footprint is found on a sheet of loose paper that was displaced and pushed to the side of the room. The print on the paper ends abruptly, with a sharp demarcation that literally splits some individual lug marks. The partial footwear mark on the floor beneath the body is consistent with the missing portion of the mark on the paper. The two can be, in the context of the scene, considered to be from the same depositional period.

The third CSR principle developed within forensic science. It is Edmond Locard's Principle of Exchange. As it is applied today, Locard's principle, in effect, states that whenever two objects come in contact with one another, there will be an exchange of material between the two. Given the capability of current technology (e.g., locating and identifying DNA deposited by mere touching), Locard (1877–1966) probably had no idea just how right he was when he first proposed the idea. This principle remains a bedrock belief that through the evaluation of evidence, associations can be made between suspects, witnesses, and scenes (aka: the evidence linkage triangle).

> *CSR Exchange Example:* Footwear marks were deposited in blood on a floor in our hypothetical scene. Using the various forensic disciplines, examination may allow association of the blood on the shoe and in the mark to the victim.

The last principle of concern for CSR is the concept of chronology. Both crime scene analysis and archaeology use these ideas in the development of any theory. Chronology is so important to the study of archaeology that any discussion of archaeological events without consideration of time and sequence is considered almost meaningless. Chronology is important for crime scene analysis as well. The practical means for evaluating chronology aspects in archaeology are well defined and lend themselves to the crime scene analysis task. In archaeology, there are two forms of chronology: absolute and relative chronology. Absolute chronology relates to time, the ability to date an artifact or event through some mechanism or relationship. Relative chronology is the ability to order a series of artifacts or events (e.g., layering of artifacts evident through superposition). Evaluating chronology in this fashion is described in depth in Chapter 3. These concepts of chronology have always been evaluated in CSR, but are typically referred to as *timing* and *sequencing*.

> *CSR Chronology Example:* Based on the data presented in the hypothetical example, the following chronology can be concluded. A bloodshed event involving the victim occurred, the suspect's shoes were subsequently stained, the shoes then crossed the floor, leaving the marks on both the floor and paper, the paper was subsequently disturbed, and the body was ultimately deposited over the bloody marks. As there is no transfer of blood from the shoe marks onto the overlaying clothing of the victim, this suggests a passage of time between the two.

Armed with the theory that "nothing just happens" and applying these four principles, the crime scene analyst has a set of tools to guide them in their purpose. The only remaining obstacle is to apply these tools in a practical fashion using the scientific method.

The Role of Scientific Method

As we described in our text *Bloodstain Pattern Analysis: With an Introduction to Crime Scene Reconstruction*, 3rd ed. (CRC Press, 2008), it is not uncommon to encounter opposing experts and lawyers who imply that only a true "scientist" can functionally apply scientific method. Investigators and police are often portrayed as incapable of understanding the tenets of this mysterious thing called *scientific method*. But, this claim is dishonest. Scientific method is anything but some mysterious or magical practice. It is the manner by which human beings reason through complex problems. Scientific method is often described as a circular path that begins with a specific question, which leads to an answer and then that answer begs or forces another question. Any effort of discovery following the scientific method creates an ever-expanding and self-correcting body of knowledge related to some specific issue.

Scientific method is not some distant concept relegated only for the elite and unattainable to the nonscientist; although this claim is common in the courtroom and is frequently used to paint any individual employed as a "nonscientist" as inferior. Paul Leedy sought to dispel this myth in the opening chapter of his book *Practical Research: Planning and Design,* stating:

> Everywhere our knowledge is incomplete and problems are waiting to be solved. We address the void in our knowledge, and those unresolved problems, by asking relevant questions and

seeking answers to them. The role of research [scientific method] is to provide a method for obtaining those answers. By inquiringly studying the facts, with in the parameters of the scientific method.[4]

    To mislead further, the word "research" has a certain mystique about it. It suggests to many people an activity that is exclusive and remote from everyday life…. The purpose of this chapter is to dispel these myths and misconceptions. Although this concept of research may seem somewhat remote or academic, many of us rely on a truncated form of it each day to dispose of less formal matters than those solved by the more elaborate methodology of pure research.[5]

Henry Rhodes succinctly stated that it is a fallacy to suggest that the academically trained scientist is more likely, from start to finish, to handle a criminal investigation better than others. Rhodes certainly furthered the idea that scientific method must be the underlying basis of any analysis, but never excluded any particular group from employing it. In fact, Rhodes was quite clear that the traits of trained observation, discrimination, and a sense of the value of evidence (our concept of scene experience) are necessary skills that police experience provides the crime scene analyst.[6]

Scientific method, however, is not a mere collection or regrouping of information. Possessing data without the ability to functionally put it into a proper context is worthless and is a failure routinely seen in many individuals involved in the criminal justice system. Lawyers are particularly well known for this failure. Analysis demands far more than mere ownership; one must put the data into a valid context to understand it.

What is scientific method? Humans resolve complex or abstract issues by making empirical observations, which are then considered using basic reasoning. This mixture is itself the very nature of scientific method, a method that blends empirical knowledge (that gained through observation and deduction) with rationalism (that gained through application of reasoning and inductive thought). Scientific method sets a structure to the process and although described differently by different authors, includes some basic steps (see Figure 2.5).

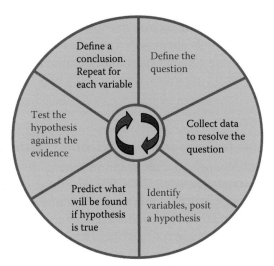

Figure 2.5 Scientific method is often described as a circular process. We ask a question, whose answer leads us to another question. It follows six basic steps: identify a question, collect data to resolve the question, posit a hypothesis, make predictions regarding the hypothesis, test the predictions, and then conclude.

These steps include:

- Identify the question to be resolved.
- Collect and gather data that may help answer the question.
- Posit a hypothesis regarding the question.
- Identify predictions relative to the hypothesis.
- Test the hypothesis by comparing the predictions against the observed data.
- Define a conclusion.

It is in the conclusion where the greatest misunderstanding of scientific method lies. The biggest myth promoted in the courtroom by lawyers is that "scientific certainty" defines something absolutely; that science always provides unwavering answers to the questions before the court. This simply is not the case. Science can often give definitive answers for specific issues and, in doing so, help us understand specific elements of the incident in question. But science will not always provide ultimate truths about the entire incident. Leedy commented on this issue when he cautioned research students to be wise enough to know that what they make from the data is truly only a glimpse of ultimate truth. Leedy stated:

> The English word for fact comes from the Latin. The Latin origin is in the word *facere*, meaning "to make"—what the situation makes or manifests to the observer. The etymology provides the first clue as to the nature of data; they are manifestations of the truth rather than the truth itself. No one has ever looked upon the truth itself—pure, undisguised, naked truth…. The mind yearns to understand the Ultimate. As a means to that goal, we have chosen the pathway of research [scientific method]. But it always ends at the farthest reaches of data, which are at the brink of a canyon in whose depths lies the inaccessible Ultimate Truth…. Truth is forever just beyond what is represented by the data and, hence, just beyond human grasp.[7]

Scientific method offers the analyst a pathway to seek answers to critical questions. In part, it forces the analyst to follow a repetitive process while maintaining a clear and distinct focus. The value of applying formal scientific method is that it defines discrete objective questions, seeks and finds answers to those questions, and ultimately applies the resulting answers to larger more complex questions. Because the core element of scientific method is posing and answering questions, that naturally begs the question: What is it the crime scene analyst asks?

Defining the Questions to Answer Using Scientific Method

Scientific method is simple enough to understand in general discussion, but it is a broad concept that overlays all human discovery. Thus, it is oftentimes difficult to put one's hands around it from a practical perspective for any given discipline. This concern is resolved by the use of discipline-specific methodologies. A methodology is simply a series of steps the analyst follows when pursuing his given discipline. These steps put scientific method into motion.

Chapter 3 presents a CSR methodology known as Event Analysis. There are other published CSR methodologies. No matter which model is used, there must be some basic questions crime scene analysts pose to achieve their end. In the development of Event Analysis, we defined four distinct questions the analyst must ask, but we feel these questions are appropriate no matter which model of reconstruction is employed. They are:

1. What is it?
2. What function did it serve?
3. What does it tell us about timing and sequencing?
4. What interrelationships does it hold to other items of evidence?

What Is It?   For each item we encounter in the scene, we ask simply: What is it? Presented with a door, a bullet casing, a baseball bat, or any other object that is familiar to us, on its face, this question might seem overly simple. But what about the myriad of objects we encounter for which we are not familiar? These unfamiliar objects can take almost any form. They might be specialty tools, parts of other objects; the list is literally endless. Just the same, we will encounter traces of material or broken pieces of other objects where the source is anything but obvious. In these latter instances, the crime laboratory becomes significant. They define if the white powder is talc or cocaine, whether the fluid on the carpet is water or diesel, or whether the glass fragment is safety glass or bottle glass. So, the first concern of the analyst is to know what is present in the scene.

Case Example: What Is It?

At a homicide scene located in a National Forest campsite, two victims were found shot with a .22 caliber weapon. Pieces of sisal-like fibers were found on the female victim. Also notable was a piece of burlap on the female victim's left shoulder (Figure 2.6). Although it was a camp setting, there was nothing made of a similar material in the campsite and the crime scene analyst was unfamiliar with the material. A U.S. Forest Service Law Enforcement Officer who was assisting at the scene observed the material and suggested it looked like part of a ghillie suit (a camouflage technique used by military snipers and hunters), something the crime scene analyst had never personally seen.

A week after the victims were found, a woman called the local sheriff's office with concerns about her missing boyfriend and his recent odd behavior. Part of the behavior she described included the construction of a ghillie suit and camouflaging his .22 rifle. When investigators served a search warrant, a ghillie suit was located in the subject's pickup (Figure 2.7). A .22 rifle camouflaged with strips of burlap was also located in the pickup. Subsequent fiber analysis of the ghillie suit, camouflaged rifle, and the questioned fibers from the female's body showed they all had the same characteristics. The composition of the ghillie suit helped explain the various fibers on the female's body. (Example courtesy of Iris Dalley, Oklahoma State Bureau of Investigation (OSBI).)

What Function Did It Serve?   Not every item found in the scene was utilized as it was designed. Thus, the next question the crime scene analyst must pose is: What function did this item serve? As in the case of "what is it," the role of some items will be obvious. Pantyhose or lamp cords may be used as ligatures or restraining devices. Lamps or other

Figure 2.6 Fibers found on the female victim at a double homicide. They were unfamiliar to the analyst, but by pursuing the question of "what are they?", the resulting answer suggested the source might be a ghillie suit. (Photo courtesy of Iris Dalley, Oklahoma State Bureau of Investigation, McAlester.)

Figure 2.7 A ghillie suit was recovered from the suspect of the double homicide. The fibers in this suit were found to be consistent with those recovered from the scene shown in Figure 2.6. (Photo courtesy of Iris Dalley, Oklahoma State Bureau of Investigation, McAlester.)

heavy objects may be used as blunt force weapons, with obvious trace evidence indicating this relationship. Functionality, however, can be a vexing question for the analyst. In some instances, an item may simply be in the scene; its presence and purpose unrelated to the incident being investigated. Or, an item may be present with no clear or obvious purpose, but, given context or layering aspects, the analyst will recognize that it was interjected into the situation in some fashion.

Case Example: What Function Did It Serve?

At a rape–homicide scene, the victim was found face down on the floor of the bedroom. The bed sheets were slightly bloodied and beneath her. Direct blood staining was also present on the mattress of the bed. Also present on the mattress was an open bottle of shampoo.

Given the superposition issues, it was clear that a struggle occurred on the bed, that the bedding was stripped from the bed as the struggle continued onto the floor. Some point after this, the shampoo bottle was introduced onto the bed.

In the scene was a condiment bottle, the cap of which was missing. On the stomach of the victim was writing in fingernail polish. The writing in polish on the stomach was not smeared and there was no transfer to the floor or to items beneath her. This suggested she was rolled after the polish dried to some extent. On the victim's back was additional writing in the condiment. At autopsy, the cap of the condiment bottle was located inside the victim's anal cavity along with additional evidence of a foreign body insertion into the victim; however, no traces of shampoo were found on the victim, the bottle, or anywhere else in the scene.

The condiment bottle served two different functions in this scene. Its primary use was for the sexual assault, but its contents were also used as a writing medium. The shampoo's use, however, was another question. Its introduction on the top of the mattress after the struggle was without question, but its purpose and function in the scene was anything but evident.

What Relationships Does This Item Hold with Other Items in the Scene? A constant concern of the crime scene analyst is recognizing interrelationships between items, objects, and individuals. The analyst constantly and repetitively asks: What relationship does this item hold to other items in the scene? These relationships can exist in so many forms that it would be impossible to outline them all. The crime lab often establishes significant relationships, either through class or individual characteristics, which allow us to recognize a relationship between two items. As in the case example involving the ghillie suit, ultimately the fibers and material from the scene were associated by class to the ghillie suit in the possession of the suspect. Casings and bullets may be associated to specific weapons. Fingerprints and DNA may associate individuals to the scene or objects from the scene. But interrelationships are not found solely in the efforts of the crime lab. We see contextual relationships in the scene everywhere. For example, combining the medical examiner's analysis of the terminal ballistic findings with the external ballistics defined by the crime scene investigator may allow us to functionally position the victim in the scene at the time of their wounding. Viewed independently, this would not be possible. Or, we may see a series of cast-off patterns rising out of impact spatter in a bludgeoning scene that helps us understand the orientation of the blows to the victim's position. This is not, as some lawyers suggest, the application of simple common sense. Recognizing the interrelationship of seemingly disassociated data elements is a significant aspect of CSR that demands proper effort, experience, and training. There simply are no limits to the nature and value of the relationships we are likely to encounter.

Case Example: What Relationship Does It Have to Other Items in the Scene?

A husband called to report his wife had killed herself at their home during an argument. At the scene, the victim was found on her back. The subsequent autopsy established that she had received a single contact gunshot injury to the left ear, with an exit at the base of the skull centered on the back of the neck.

A single bullet defect was located high in a wall behind the victim's final position, but, as the bullet was tumbling, no specific trajectory was possible. The ballistics examination associated the bullet to the weapon present in the scene. During an examination of the victim's clothing, a number of small directional impact spatter were found on the back of both heels of the victim's shoes (Figure 2.8). The directional information indicated the droplets were moving back to front and downward in relation to the shoe's normal position. No spatter was present on the front or top aspects of the shoes. Additional directional spatter of similar size were found on items on the floor to the right of the victim's final position. These indicated the droplets were moving toward the wall with the defect as expected, but low to the floor. The various spatter were analyzed against the victim's blood and determined to be consistent with her DNA.

The presence of directional spatter contradicted the husband's statement regarding the wife's position. He placed her standing in the scene at the time of the shot. However, the directional spatter on items low to the floor, as well as those spatter showing back-to-front movement on the shoes forced an issue with regards to position. The only functional method of explaining the spatter on the heels was if the woman were on her stomach on the floor, with her knees bent and the heels of the shoe facing the back of her head. Through relationships established at the lab (the DNA and ballistic exams), correlations could be recognized between the spatter and victim as well as the weapon and bullet. However, additional

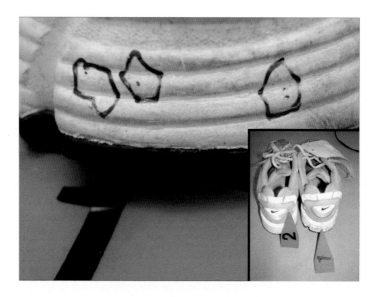

Figure 2.8 Spatter stains on the heels of a victim. These stains could not be reconciled with the claims of a "witness." Based on the various interrelationships of evidence, they forced a physical position for the victim that suggested a homicidal rather than suicidal act.

relationships established through the terminal ballistics from the autopsy and the location of the bloodstain patterns were just as telling, forcing issues in terms of the physical relationship of the victim's legs to her head at the time of the wounding.

Contextual relationships are not always immediately evident. A process that often assists the analyst in understanding these relationships during the reconstruction process is "role playing." The analyst undertakes to physically reconstruct a series of actions. In doing this, relationships may become evident that otherwise would never have been recognized. In some instances, role playing may be accomplished in the actual scene. In other situations, the analyst simply role plays the series of actions in a similar environment.

Case Example: Role Playing

Analysts investigating an in-custody prison death were presented with several possibilities as to how the prisoner received his fatal injuries. The prisoner was found in his cell with evidence of an attempted hanging, but with additional blunt force injuries to the head. One possible scenario involved the prisoner having fallen while attempting to hang himself, but striking his head on the concrete floor did not functionally explain the head wounds. As the analysts were role playing the activity, they positioned themselves on the floor in the cell. In that position, they could see the underside of various surfaces including a metal swing out stool (Figure 2.9). The role-play effort was conducted seven months after the death, but while in this position the analysts discovered not only blood, but also hair on the stool support

Figure 2.9 A prison cell where an in-custody death occurred. Note the swing-out stool at the end of the bed.

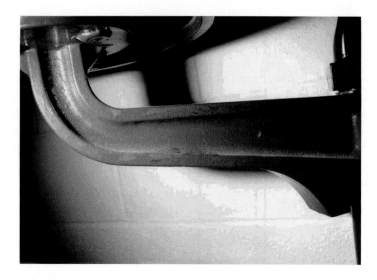

Figure 2.10 Seven months after the death while role playing in the scene, the crime scene analyst discovered not only blood, but also hair on the support arm of the fold-out stool. Consideration of the stool offered a context in which to understand blunt force injuries that otherwise had not been explained.

(Figure 2.10). The DNA from both items was subsequently identified as that of the prisoner in question. The support arm of the stool offered a valid explanation as to how one of the head injuries occurred. The presence of blood and hair indicated that this scenario was not only possible, but the best explanation possible.

What Does This Item Tell Us about Timing or Sequencing?   To ignore aspects of chronology (timing and sequencing aspects) in crime scene analysis is to ignore what is often half of the data available to us. Timing and sequencing relationships exist throughout the scene and are often critical to the overall analysis. Oftentimes it is sequencing information alone that will make or break the believability of a given hypothesis. The question before the court isn't simply "if" certain things happened, but rather the issue may hinge on "in what order" did they happen? The previous question—What relationships does this item have to other items?—sought to find relationships between objects; this question seeks to identify relationships between actions. These relationships can be quite intuitive (e.g., one must first have an injury before one can have a bloodstain) or they may be anything but obvious (e.g., the order in which several weapons were employed during an attack). If based on common sense, chronology relationships may require no significant effort or analysis; however, not all chronology is obvious and the situation may demand consideration of ideas like Steno's Principle of Superposition to make any sense of it. Once again sequential information is found throughout the scene; it is limited only by the analyst's recognition of details. Timing data are less evident. In the past, analysts looked to issues of livor or rigor mortis onset, interruptions of schedules, or devices that were broken (e.g., broken clocks) to give some indication of time. As digital surveillance, computer-aided dispatch, and other audio and video capture systems become more common in society, timing data are becoming more common place in the analysis.

Case Example: What Does It Tell Us about Timing and Sequence?

Following a domestic dispute where a drunken husband fired numerous shots, SWAT officers were called to the scene after the man retreated into his home and refused to exit. The SWAT team ultimately entered the house. After a dynamic entry through the front door, they found themselves in a living room with a hallway opposite their position. The two lead officers observed a man in the dimly lit hallway armed with a revolver. They were heard making repeated demands that he drop the weapon. The officers stated that when he failed to comply and pointed the weapon in their direction, they fired on him. Both officers fired simultaneously (verified by witnesses) and in one series (all shots fired one after the other with no pauses). The bullets struck the man multiple times, with several bullets striking and passing through an intervening living room wall. The man was immediately observed by other SWAT officers falling back from the door. Significantly wounded, his bloodstain patterns verified that he was not upright at the point of encounter for any period following the gunfire. Once the scene was secured, his weapon was located on a plastic container at the point where the officers first observed and fired on him (Figure 2.11).

In evaluating the condition of the weapon, it was obvious that there were layering issues present. The weapon was partially beneath several clothing items. These items had both blood stains and wall residue on top of them. Additionally, the portions of the revolver exposed in the final scene were covered with a white dust. This included the handle and trigger. When the revolver was moved, there was a distinct void of white particles where it had been laying (Figure 2.12).

These data elements indicated that the weapon had been placed on the plastic container and had not simply fallen to the surface. The particles on the weapon clearly demonstrated the handle and trigger were exposed when the bullets passed through the intervening wall and the void in the particles beneath the weapon validated its position when the wall was damaged. All of these elements supported a belief that the man was complying or had complied with the officer's requests to put the weapon down when he was shot.

Unfortunately, in his drunken state, he chose the worst scenario for trying to comply. In terms of the officers firing on the man, the crime scene analysis also supported their

Figure 2.11 The position of the revolver indicates it did not fall from above to the container. The presence of white dust and larger particles also tell us it was exposed to the event that produced these particles.

Figure 2.12 When the revolver was moved, a void of white dust was present beneath the position of the revolver. This indicates that it was in this position when the action (bullets passing through an intermediate wall) producing the white dust occurred.

perceptions and actions. In order to place the weapon on the container as it was found, the weapon would either have to be raised or lowered to the container. In its final position, the barrel of the revolver was clearly pointed directly back toward the officers' positions, thus they perceived him raising the weapon in their direction and acted in response to what they thought was a threat. Based on the crime scene analysis and specifically the sequencing information, the district attorney accepted a plea from the man for the associated charges, but did not pursue a charge of attempted murder against a police officer.

These four basic questions of CSR/CSA are asked and answered for each item encountered in the scene and they are continuously reevaluated throughout the analysis. The resulting answers serve as the foundation for the analyst's conclusions. These answers provide the means by which any claim about specific actions or order of actions is possible. Using these questions, each piece of the crime scene jigsaw puzzle is evaluated and placed into a context in relation to other pieces. Not every piece will have a relationship to every other piece, but through the relationships established, a framework or lattice will develop that should objectively guide the analyst's overall understanding of the incident.

Defining Additional Investigative Questions

As we ask and answer the four basic questions, a scene context begins to unfold, but with this context come additional questions. These additional questions will be pointed and specific to the scene, most often dealing with contradictions observed in the data. Of course, once the analysis is complete there may be contentious issues as well, areas where testimonial claims and/or defense and prosecution theories diverge in significant ways. These issues often require additional effort to properly bring them into focus and eliminate claims that are not valid or possible.

Whether encountered as an integral part of the crime scene analysis (e.g., a contradiction encountered in the analysis) or as a matter of testimonial claims about the incident (e.g., divergent claims by counsel), these specific investigative questions are answered using scientific method as well. The techniques of using the investigative worksheets, described in Chapter 4, are the most effective way of dealing with these questions. As in all scientific method, the analyst must seek and maintain a focus when dealing with these specific investigative questions. This often requires breaking down the primary question into smaller, more easily answered questions. Identifying these smaller questions is itself application of the scientific method and reductionism. Whether the analyst chooses to use the investigative worksheet we suggest or utilizes some other method, the analyst still follows the scientific method. They do this by defining a focus issue, pursuing data that may assist them in resolving the issue, positing hypotheses and predictions for each hypothesis, and then functionally testing each hypothesis in an attempt to prove it false. Not every question presented to the analyst will be solvable and not every issue resolvable to the benefit of the court or jury, but when a decision is made it will be based on a traceable and, hopefully, reproducible logic pathway whose foundation is found in the artifacts and context of the crime scene. Rather than presenting an opinion of "I don't think that is possible" or "In my experience that is unlikely," the analyst will be able to point to specific aspects of the scene and show how the scene facts either align or diverge from the claims being presented to the court.

When Is Crime Scene Analysis Employed?

Based on the discussion so far, it should be obvious that much of what has been described appears to be a last act in the investigative process. But is that really true? Crime scene analysis is accomplished in two very distinct venues. The first is on-scene and is less structured; the second is a formal analysis, using the specific techniques described throughout this book. Formal analysis is accomplished after the crime scene examination is complete, after analysis of artifacts and evidence is done, when all of the data are relatively complete and available for consideration. Formal crime scene analysis is a conscious and deliberate effort on the part of the analysts that follows a specific methodology. That methodology is discussed in detail in Chapter 3. It involves both time and significant effort. Formal analysis, however, is only one side of the crime scene analysis coin. The flip side of that coin is informal crime scene analysis.

Informal (Ad Hoc) Crime Scene Analysis

As the actual scene examination proceeds and throughout the investigation, issues and questions present themselves to the crime scene team. These questions are answered most often using a form of informal analysis, an ad hoc, on-the-spot effort. On-the-spot or not, this effort is still crime scene analysis. It is most evident during the crime scene examination. As the crime scene investigator arrives at a scene, he is not greeted by pretty yellow placards lying in the scene, saying: "Look here, I'm the evidence you want and need." The investigator walks into the scene, often with incorrect information (e.g., told it's a stabbing when in fact it's a shooting). He does not know the full extent of the scene. He does not know who was or was not a participant or what motives drove these individual's actions. What he does know is that something happened. In order for the crime scene investigator to do his job, he must evaluate

Figure 2.13 Crime scene investigators are not garbage collectors, picking up every piece of trash that has accumulated in a scene. Imagine arriving at a homicide. A witness reports the shooter stood in this area for several minutes smoking. When the victim arrived, he shot him and left. The cigarette butt at C is weathered and intertwined in debris. Superposition tells us this is not evidence. The three butts at F are significantly weathered. The butt at D is smashed and weathered as well. These do not correlate to an hour-old event. The butt at A is smashed in a fresh footwear mark, with ash and tobacco still present. The butt at B is fresh with the ash still intact. Both A and B are the same brand. In this context, these two cigarette butts are likely evidence and everything else can be ignored.

all of the items present, document the full extent of the scene, and decide what are pre- or postincident artifacts; in other words, he must decide what he feels is evidence and what he will seize. As processing proceeds, he must also consider and decide where to direct specific investigative techniques (e.g., fingerprinting effort, chemical enhancements for blood).

There are currently "experts" in crime scene analysis who decry all of this crime scene activity as rote compliance with a procedure or checklist, claiming that crime scene investigators are incapable of independent analysis. Such claims show an utter lack of experience and belie these individuals understanding of crime scene procedure. The individuals who make these claims have never done it, they have only read about it, and they don't understand how it is actually accomplished. Crime scene investigators are not garbage collectors. They do not enter a scene and collect every single item they find, "hoping" that it is evidence (Figure 2.13). They don't enter the scene in a "poke and hope" mindset throwing powder or chemical enhancements on every surface they find.

What they do, using critical thinking, is gain direction on where to look for evidence and make informed on-the-spot decisions about what is or isn't evidence in each scene. These decisions (informal analysis) guide them in every aspect of their on-scene effort. It tells them why they should print one area versus another, when they need to expand their perimeter and locate a secondary scene, or when they should be cautious because they believe they are looking at a staged scene. The crime scene investigator's informal analysis is the only reason anyone can perform a formal reconstruction. Without this effort, evidence would not be recovered and critical aspects of the scene context would not be captured. Crime scene documentation doesn't just happen and critical evidence doesn't just fall into the lap of the crime scene investigator. It is only through analysis and critical evaluation of the scene that the crime scene investigator locates and collects pertinent and critical items.

Case Example Informal Analysis: Recognizing a Staged Scene

Police were called to a home where a woman claimed to have been asleep on the ground floor of her apartment when she was awoken and assaulted by a male. The alleged point of entry was a second-floor window, which had numerous cuts to the screen, yet the screen was still in place and had not been ripped out. Beneath this window was an aluminum ladder, which lay on the ground behind various bushes and landscape plants.

There were numerous contradictions in the physical evidence, one of which was the condition and position of the ladder outside the alleged point of entry. Although the ladder was sufficient in height to reach the second-floor window, the ladder lay on the ground, wedged between the wall and bushes. Dried leaves were noted on the exposed top surface. No branches or leaves were evident in or around the ladder suggesting any recent movement (Figure 2.14). Additionally, the sill of the second-floor window (the alleged entry point) had

Figure 2.14 At an alleged assault scene, this ladder was reported as the means of entry into a second-floor window. First, if actually involved, the ladder was put back by the perpetrator, odd behavior in anyone's book. But, from a crime scene analysis perspective, leaves are present on the top surfaces of the ladder and there are no indications of broken twigs, leaves, or disruptions in the rocks to suggest it was removed or replaced in this position. (Photo courtesy of Laura Delong, Arapahoe County Sheriff's Office, Centennial, CO.)

Figure 2.15 The entry point. Note the cobwebs on the screen and the leaves on the opposite side. Nothing just happens. Given the manner in which the screen was damaged, if someone passed through this window, these areas would have been disturbed and their continuity disrupted. (Photo courtesy of Laura Delong, Arapahoe County Sheriff's Office, Centennial, CO.)

significant levels of dust cobwebs and leaves, which were for the most part undisturbed (Figure 2.15).

These aspects of the scene, along with numerous other inconsistent findings, suggested the woman was not being truthful in her claims. Presented with the inconsistencies, the woman quickly acknowledged that although she was sure she wasn't untruthful, she felt she might be "crazy." Based on the totality of the circumstances and the simple informal analysis conducted at the scene, the case was unfounded.

Staging and alteration of crime scenes by various parties is always a consideration for the crime scene investigator. It is one thing to recognize this alteration after-the-fact during formal analysis, but if this issue is not recognized on-scene it is possible that an adequate scene examination will not be completed (e.g., pursuing and understanding staging issues when the staging was produced by the perpetrator to misdirect the investigation). Or it will result in the waste of significant investigative resources (e.g., failing to recognize faked scenes staged by a person for attention). Recognition of staging and alteration is certainly important, but another critical aspect of informal analysis is the recognition of what is or isn't evidence.

Case Example Informal Analysis: What Isn't Evidence?

Investigators were called to the scene of an alleged accidental shooting. Present was a male victim seated in a chair with a single gunshot injury to his right ear (Figure 2.16). There was no exit wound. To the immediate left of the victim was a significant number of directional impact spatters on the wall and calendar (Figure 2.17). This spatter pattern was totally inconsistent with the position of the victim. Based on additional bloodstain patterns, there was no evidence of movement of the victim and no functional way to position the victim's entry wound toward this wall. Given this contradiction, the stains suggested some other event, unrelated to the wounding of this particular victim. As investigators tried to resolve the contradiction, they discovered several interesting aspects. In other rooms in the home

Figure 2.16 Arriving at a death scene, investigators found the victim seated with a single gun-shot injury to the right ear and no exit wound. On the wall to the immediate left of the victim is a significant impact spatter pattern.

Figure 2.17 A closer view of the spatter pattern on the wall and calendar. The presence of this pattern contradicted the position of the victim. It was quickly recognized that the pattern was from an unrelated event that occurred in the house days before, but was never cleaned up.

were spatter patterns similar to that observed on the wall calendar in the kitchen. An older resident of the home was identified as having a bleeding ulcer and responsible for many of these patterns (e.g., expectorate stains). Additionally, an assault had been reported and investigated in the same house several days before. Bloodstain patterns related to all three events were still present in the home, many in a 4-foot area around the body. The spatter pattern on the wall was verified as a preincident artifact to the shooting and had no relationship to what had occurred on this date. Lacking informal analysis by the crime scene team, which recognized the contradiction in the relationship of the bloodstain pattern and the victim's position, significant investigative and laboratory effort could have been wasted on this pattern.

Case Example Informal Analysis: What Is Evidence?

Five women were found stabbed in a small house in Oklahoma. The bedroom scene was exceptionally bloody, with patterns of every nature in and around the room. Crime scene technicians found several drip stains at the front door and porch (Figure 2.18). Given the volume of blood in this scene, these stains could have easily been considered drips of the victims' blood coming from the killer or his weapon. But, their presence and orientation also suggested the killer might be the source, particularly because self-wounding in stabbing attacks is a common occurrence. Given these considerations, the blood in the drip pattern was sampled. The drips were later found inconsistent with any of the victims' blood. The case occurred prior to the existence of any DNA database, but investigators sent the resulting DNA profile to other organizations and asked that they watch for any similar profile. Years after the murder, a DNA analyst in California made a cold hit on the unknown blood. This allowed the detectives to associate a name to the blood. When the palm prints of this individual were checked against a bloody palm print from the crime scene, they also matched. Informal analysis on scene suggested the possibility that these stains were not associated to

Figure 2.18 A drip pattern at the door of a scene involving five women who were stabbed to death. Given the bloody scene, these stains could have easily been dismissed as a victim's blood dripped here as the perpetrator left, but the crime scene team recognized the potential that it might also be the perpetrator's blood. It was and subsequent DNA work years later led to his identification.

the victims and, given this consideration, of the literally hundreds of drip stains present in the house, these were sampled. If they had not been sampled, it is unlikely the case would have been solved.

Another function that informal crime scene analysis provides to the crime scene investigator is the recognition of scene limits; in other words, what is the scene and how far does it extend? The first responding officers are responsible for establishing an initial crime scene perimeter. They do this using obvious evidence, their experience, and certainly a little common sense. Their decisions are usually driven by major focal points (e.g., the body, bloodstains), but very often this initial perimeter fails to encompass the full extent of the scene. On arrival, the crime scene team is charged with reevaluating the initial perimeter. Using simple informal analysis (e.g., considering how individuals came or departed the scene), the crime scene investigator evaluates if the scene perimeter has been fully identified. Based on this effort, he may extend or even limit the initial perimeter. This analysis can also suggest or demand the existence of additional scenes that have not, as yet, been discovered.

Case Example Informal Analysis: Recognizing Secondary Scenes

Investigators arrived at a scene to find an individual shot and seated inside a vehicle in an office complex parking lot. The scene was secured and held waiting the arrival of crime scene technicians. On arrival, the crime scene investigator noted significant flow patterns from the individual that abruptly terminated on the driver's side door rocker panel. There were no stains on the pavement outside the vehicle. Based on this simple continuity analysis, the crime scene investigator advised the agency officers that this was not the original location of the vehicle and that it had been moved from another location. Initially, the officers argued the issue and did not believe the crime scene investigator. The crime scene investigator initiated a search beyond the secured scene. Some 300 yards from the initial scene, a blood pool and series of bloodstains were found grouped on the pavement, which correlated to the patterns in the vehicle and indicated the initial scene where the shooting took place. (Case example provided by Kim Duddy, Washington State Crime Laboratory, Eastern Washington University, Cheney.)

Individuals who have even the slightest level of experience with crime scene processing understand that analysis, albeit on-the-spot and certainly anything but a formal process, is a routine and on-going activity the crime scene investigator engages in. This ad hoc/informal analysis is significant to the overall effort, for it leads to the recognition of what is or is not evidence and what is or is not the scene. The crime scene investigators may not follow a specific methodology in achieving this effort, but they certainly use critical thinking (aka: the scientific method). They see issues, ask themselves what it means in the context of the scene, and then make predictions based on these observations. Without this analysis effort, critical aspects of scene context would not be captured, critical elements of evidence would not be found, and red herrings in the form of pre- and postincident artifacts would not be recognized early on when they can still be validated and, thus, ignored in later stages of the investigation. These on-scene decisions by the crime scene team will significantly affect any subsequent formal analysis. This informal analysis is an integral and important aspect of the crime scene technician's job. It doesn't need to be, nor should it be structured, but it must follow scientific method. Therefore, the underlying concepts discussed here in terms of formal crime scene analysis are still applicable to any informal analysis efforts.

Summary

Crime scene analysis/reconstruction is a distinct discipline. It operates on the theory that "nothing just happens." Underlying this theory are four principles that guide the analyst. Two of these principles are bedrock concepts of archaeology. Because crime scene analysis mirrors the scientific discipline of archaeology in terms of process and purpose, it utilizes Nicolas Steno's Principle of Superposition and Principle of Lateral Continuity. The concept of superposition is simply that artifacts are deposited in layers at the scene in a time order. The concept of lateral continuity allows us to recognize disassociated strata or to recognize when the continuity of a layer has been disturbed. Additionally, crime scene analysis shares with archaeology the concept of chronology. In CSR, absolute chronology is the ability to date an action, while relative chronology is the ability to sequence a series of actions. The final principle of crime scene analysis is the application of Locard's Principle of Exchange. This concept states that scenes, items, and individuals can be associated by the transfer that occurs between each when they are in contact with one another.

These ideas guide the crime scene analyst and are always framed in a specific methodology based on the scientific method. Chapter 3 will present one practical methodology for formal crime scene analysis, known as Event Analysis. But crime scene analysis is accomplished in a less formal fashion as well; this is done by the crime scene investigator while at the crime scene. This ad hoc analysis guides the crime scene investigator in his effort to locate, document, and collect relevant physical evidence. Without this analysis, the crime scene investigator would not accomplish his goal and this failure would seriously hinder or prevent the subsequent efforts of the forensic scientist and crime scene analyst.

References

1. Department of the Army, Crime Scene Processing I and II, U.S. Army Visual Information Center, Joint Visual Information Activity, Tobyhanna Army Depot, PA, 1990.
2. Ibid.
3. Bevel, T. and R. Gardner. 1997. *Bloodstain Pattern Analysis With an Introduction to Crime Scene Reconstruction*, Boca Raton, FL: CRC Press, 36.
4. Leedy, P.D. 1988. *Practical Research: Design and Planning*, New York: Macmillan Publishing Co., 3.
5. Ibid.
6. Rhodes, H.T.F. 1933. *Some Persons Unknown*, London: John Murray Publishing, 5.
7. Leedy, *Practical Research: Design and Planning*, 3.

Event Analysis

A Practical Methodology for Crime Scene Reconstruction

3

Introduction

Given the history of crime scene analysis, it would be ridiculous to state that there is a single absolute methodology associated to the discipline. Over the years, various authors have presented different ideas on how to proceed and all of these ideas have merit. Whatever method is utilized, as the previous chapter discussed, there are basic themes that any methodology must incorporate and it must follow the scientific method. Event Analysis is one methodology that incorporates all of the basic tenets that have been described over the years. Event Analysis consists of seven steps that involve:

1. Collecting data from the scene and evidence.
2. Establishing specific *event segments* (time snapshots).
3. Establishing which *event segments* are related to one another.
4. Sequencing related segments, establishing a flow for that *Event*.
5. Considering all possible sequences, auditing the background evidence when necessary to resolve contradictions.
6. Based on the *Event Segment* sequence, final ordering of the *Events* themselves.
7. Flowcharting the entire incident and validating the sequence.[1]

To fully understand Event Analysis, we must first define its components. Any situation the analyst might be asked to evaluate can be considered as an *incident*. The incident encompasses all of the associated activity from the beginning of the incident to the end. Using an analogy of a book, the incident is the entire book, the story of what happened. Thus, if our incident is a burglary/murder, the incident comprises all of the actions, the story of the burglary/murder. Unfortunately, analysts are rarely presented with "short stories" in terms of the incidents they investigate, so most incidents are made up of macro components, known as *events*. Using the book analogy, each event is comparable to the chapters of the book. In the burglary/murder example, these chapters might be stated as: Entry, Encounter, Murder, Burglary, and Departure.

Each of these events, the chapters of the analyst's story, is made up of a series of individual actions. These actions are called *event segments*. Think of them as time snapshots, moments of activity captured by the data. For example, in the act of accomplishing the event of murder, the subject after encountering the victim in the hallway might strike the victim several times with a weapon, knocking the victim to the floor, where the subject then delivers the fatal blow. Each of these specific actions, the event segments, is defined by the resulting evidence it produces. Each is a part of the story. In the book analogy, they are like the paragraphs in a chapter. The primary focus of Event Analysis is to identify as many of these event segments as possible. The more paragraphs in the chapter, the more detailed the chapter and the better the reader understands the story. But, imagine a book where the paragraphs were randomly arranged and out of order. Without order, the paragraphs would be difficult at best to read or comprehend. It is the same with Event Analysis. Unordered event segments may assist us, but the more individual event segments identified and sequenced, the better the analyst understands what happened in each event, which ultimately allows better understanding of the incident. Thus, recognition and order are both important. How does the analyst recognize that any given event segment occurred?

Recall from Chapter 2 that a critical principle in crime scene analysis is the use of reductionism; crime scenes are reverse engineered from the available data. This data come in the form of physical objects (artifacts), the context in which those artifacts are found, and from in-depth analysis of the artifacts (forensic evaluation at the crime lab). It is data, in the form of objects and their context, that lead the analyst to know that a given event segment occurred. Using the book analogy, each paragraph is built on specific words (the data). Without the words, the paragraphs don't exist and we have no idea what the story really is. Therefore, data always define event segments; they are not based on guesses or supposition. To understand how they are defined, let's begin with something simple:

Hypothetical Example 1
Data Elements
- A pattern transfer (a right palm) is present on the west wall in blood. (Bloodstain pattern report)
- The blood is that of the victim. (DNA report)
- The ridge detail in the palm print is identifiable to the suspect. (Fingerprint report)

Event Segment
The suspect touched the west wall with his right hand subsequent to the victim's injuries.

Each event segment is in effect a miniconclusion. It is based on a series of premises, data elements that the analyst relied upon. If these premises are true (the blood is the victim's, the palm print is the suspect's), then the conclusion, that the suspect touched the wall, either must be true or it follows with a high degree of certainty. (A discussion of deductive and inductive arguments is presented in Chapter 10). Note that each data element is a fact, verifiable through observation (e.g., both its existence or its context in the scene) or from some detailed analysis (e.g., the fingerprint or DNA report). It should be obvious that over the course of any analysis, the number of such details used will become significant. In order that others can quickly validate the existence of the supporting data element, it is a good idea to list a reference for each element. In the example, they are listed in parentheses following their respective data element; this provides an immediate reference others may look at in order to validate the facts used by the analyst. Here is another example:

Hypothetical Example 2
   Data Elements
   - The victim has a single perforating injury through the abdomen. (Autopsy report)
   - Bullet A is recovered from the wall in Defect A. (Crime Scene report)
   - The victim's blood is located on Bullet A. (DNA report)
   - Defect A defines a trajectory path of…(however one might describe it). (Crime Scene report)

   Event Segment
   The victim was similarly positioned (in accordance with the trajectory defined by Defect A) when shot by Bullet A.

This is a slightly more detailed event segment, but still simple in concept and logic. If the bullet caused the wound, then the victim's injury path (the terminal ballistics) must align with the scene trajectory (the external ballistics).

Consider the following event segment definition from an actual case:

Case Situation: A man was found stabbed in his bed. In his final position, the sheets and blankets were pulled up to his chest, as if he were sleeping during the attack.

Example 1
   Data Elements
   - There are numerous spatter of the victim's blood present on the left hip of the victim's underwear, all of which are covered in the final position. (RMG physical exam, WA State Crime Lab Report, Olsen, 9/26/01, p. 2; BPA report, pp. 9–10)
   - Pattern transfers consistent with the knife were located on the fitted sheet, tip oriented to the south. These are covered in the final scene. (RMG 333, 334, 337, 349, BSPR pp. 8–9)
   - Additional pattern transfers were located on the fitted sheet at a level below the victim's chest, also covered, with no evident source of origin. (RMG 333, 334, 337, 338)

   Event Segment
   During the initial assault, the comforter and sheets were not positioned, as seen in their final position on the north side of the bed.

The relationships offered demand that the event segment as described, occurred. Arriving at it requires no in-depth consideration. The areas discussed had to be uncovered in order to become bloodstained. But not all event segments are as simple to define and, in many instances, it is the confluence of a number of many small observations that lead the analyst to know that an event segment occurred. Consider a second example from the same case:

Example 2
   Data Elements
   - Blood smears in the victim's blood were evident on the label of the electric blanket, which was tucked in and beneath the comforter. (KPD Curtis, p. 6, WA State Crime Lab Report, 9/26/01; Olsen, pp. 1–2)
   - The label side of the electric blanket was the surface facing up. (KPD Curtis)

- There were no sources of whole blood near this portion of the bed. (RMG physical examination, KPD photos)
- Patent and latent blood were present on the electric blanket, label side surface, to a position not greater than 12 inches up from the base of the blanket. (RMG physical examination, RMG 375, BPA report p. 9)
- Patent and latent blood were not present on the opposite surface of the electric blanket, other than along the base seam of the blanket. (RMG physical examination, BPA report p. 9)

Event Segment
   The attacker, after being bloodied, tucked in or adjusted the electric blanket in its final position in the scene.

In this instance, the victim is in the bed in his final position, blankets covering him. This includes the electric blanket. The blankets are all tucked in at the base, including the electric blanket. But when recovered, patent blood associated to the victim is present on the side of the blanket that is tucked in (the side exposed if one places a hand between the mattresses to tuck in the blanket). No incidental staining is near this area that would otherwise explain how the blood got there. The condition of the blood (still pigmented) and its context (tucked in) forces an action that the victim was incapable of doing. In the example, no single data element allows the analyst to arrive at the event segment. It is only through consideration of all of the data that any conclusion is possible. Consider another case example:

Case Situation: A husband returns home at midday to find his wife beaten and strangled. He claims he was alone, went to her aid, called 911, and never left her side until emergency medical services (EMS) and police arrived. He was taken from the scene by police.

Example 3
Data Elements
- Dr. X brought the Jaguar to the scene.
- Upon arrival on scene, Dr. X was alone in the house. (Sterling report, 2-14-01, p. 371)
- After arrival of EMS, Dr. X was accompanied in the scene and did not have access to the Jaguar. (Skalla report, 2-14-01, p. 005)
- Visible blood and a hair were evident on the driver door threshold of the Jaguar when processed. (Richardson report, 2-14-01, p. 214)
- The blood and hair found on the vehicle were consistent with the DNA of Mrs. X. (Labcorp report, 6-11-01, p. 2)
- Under both visible inspection and luminol enhancement, a substance consistent with blood was noted on the steering wheel of the Jaguar. (Richardson report, 2-14-01, p. 214)
- The substance on the steering wheel was consistent with the DNA of Mrs. X. (OCPD Forensic Services report, 2-28-01, p. 2)

Event Segment
   Subsequent to Mrs. X's wounding, Dr. X transferred Mrs. X's blood to the Jaguar.

The event segments in Examples 2 and 3 were both considered relatively critical to their respective reconstructions, as they each answered significant investigative questions.

However, that is not the case for every event segment. What the analyst defines through the various event segments may or may not assist directly in understanding all of the investigative issues developed for a given case. But with each new segment identified, the analyst gains more and more detail. Ultimately, all of the event segments will offer insight on what could have happened, what could not have happened, and in what order it happened. Using Event Analysis, the data define event segments, event segments define events, and the events define the incident. The entire concept of crime scene analysis and specifically Event Analysis is simple enough, but in practical application, the process can become quite convoluted.

One question that may arise from the previous discussion: How many data elements does it take to define an event segment? The answer is that any number (including a single data element) can define an event segment. Imagine finding a deformed bullet in a wall. Lacking any other information (e.g., specific ballistics), the presence of the bullet tells us a weapon was fired. The more data available, the more refined the event segment; however, in some instances, a single data element will offer the foundation for an event segment.

The Event Analysis Process

To better understand application of Event Analysis, we'll discuss each step and then offer an abbreviated case example. In the context of a chapter, we cannot discuss each and every question posed in the analysis or discuss each and every consideration that led to the final product. We can, however, offer a glimpse at how the event segments were defined and ordered. The example offered is courtesy of the San Diego County Sheriff's Office.

Case Example Details

The case involves a scene with two victims, a husband and wife. Following a welfare check request by family members, deputies found the victims present in their home on the kitchen floor. Both died of gunshot wounds. The male victim had a perforating gunshot wound to the head. The female had a penetrating injury to the head. There were two primary entry/exits to the home. The front door was blocked by furniture (apparently the standard layout for the owners); the rear door was blocked by the body of the female victim. No additional openings were evident. Deputies had to force entry through a window to gain access. Ultimately the weapon on scene was associated to both victims (based on ballistics). In terms of investigative issues, the critical question was who shot whom. Figure 3.1 to Figure 3.8 depict the scene. In any situation there are always apparent events. In this instance, the primary events that must be considered are: (1) the shooting of the male victim, (2) the shooting of the female victim, and (3) alteration of the scene (movement of a trash can and revolver).

Step 1: Collect Data. The first step of the methodology is based on scientific method and involves asking four questions of each item of interest in the crime scene. The answers to these questions will provide the data used in the analysis. These questions are:

1. What is it?
2. What function did it serve?
3. What interrelationships exist between this item and other items in the scene?
4. What does the item tell us about timing and sequencing?

Figure 3.1 A death scene involving two victims. The wife is positioned against the rear entry on the north side of the kitchen. The husband is located opposite her. (Photo courtesy of Chuck Merritt, San Diego County Sheriff's Office.)

The first question deals with the basic nature of the object of interest. What is it: a gun, a knife, an impact spatter pattern, or a fingerprint? In the instance of obvious objects, this is not a difficult question to answer, but in other situations identifying the basic nature of the object will demand significant effort. Examples include fragments of other objects (e.g., bullets, paint fragments), trace evidence (e.g., a white powder, accelerants), or simply items unfamiliar to the investigative team.

The second question deals with how the item was utilized in the scene. An object of a particular nature may be present in the scene that was not utilized as intended by its design. Examples include household items used as blunt force weapons or clothing used as bindings. Not all functional aspects may be obvious on first inspection, but the analyst must constantly be aware of such issues.

The third question looks at interrelationships between articles in the scene. The answers found here may assist in refining the answers to the first two questions. For instance, a

Figure 3.2 A revolver lies between the two parties, facing the male victim. (Photo courtesy of Chuck Merritt, San Diego County Sheriff's Office.)

small metal fragment may be found to be consistent with a deformed bullet recovered from the victim or an unknown liquid may be identified as diesel fuel consistent with fuel found in a gas can in the garage. Other relationships are also important. For example, recognizing a cast-off pattern rising from an impact spatter pattern will aid the analyst in understanding the position of the attacker, or consideration of the external ballistics along with the medical examiner's terminal ballistics may aid in placing the victim in a specific position at the moment of wounding. There is no limit to the nature of the interrelationships between objects that are of concern to the analyst.

The last question goes to the issue of chronology. What does this item tell the analyst about sequencing different actions or in placing an action at a specific point in time? Examples might include the presence of spatter overlaying a shoe mark or the deposition of ceiling debris in an arson scene on top of a victim with no underlying burns. Sequencing information is present throughout the scene and it is critical evidence.

Timing data is less evident in the scene, but on occasion it may present itself. Time of death estimations are a form of timing data, as are the interruption of regular activities by

Figure 3.3 The male victim is positioned on his back, feet oriented toward the north. There are two entries into the kitchen; the first is to his right at the southeast corner of the room. (Photo courtesy of Chuck Merritt, San Diego County Sheriff's Office.)

the involved parties. In this age of computer-aided dispatch (CAD), 911 calls recorded as a situation unfolds can offer timing data as well. Ongoing activity captured on CAD audio may aid the analyst in developing an absolute chronology (e.g., gunshot is heard at 4:04:20, followed by glass breaking at 4:04:28, followed by a series of two gunshots).

Together these four questions, when applied to every item of interest in the scene, will provide the data that will support the remaining steps. These four questions, however, are so integral to the CSR process that they remain in the analyst's mind and are continuously asked and answered throughout the analysis.

Case Example: Collect Data

It would be impossible to discuss all of the questions asked and posed to develop the data in the death scene analysis being discussed, but a few examples will illustrate the concept.

Figure 3.4 The second entry to the kitchen is behind the male victim, at the southwest corner of the room. A trash can is located on the floor there, between the entry and the male victim. (Photo courtesy of Chuck Merritt, San Diego County Sheriff's Office.)

In the sink (Figure 3.9) are several leaves. What are they? They are rose leaves. What function did they serve? No obvious answer is evident beyond the leaves having been deposited in the sink. What interrelationships exist? A bouquet of roses is in the trash can. Also present in and around the sink are white particles. What are they? They appear to be gypsum board particles. What function did they serve? This is answered by asking what interrelationships exist. The particles are artifacts of bullet defects found directly above the sink (Figure 3.10). What do they tell us about timing and sequence? The white particles are present on top of the rose leaves in the sink, but no similar particles are on the roses in the trash can. Thus, the roses were in or near the sink, the leaves deposited, the roses removed from the area, and the bullet holes produced.

Step 2: Establish Event Segments. As described, an event segment is a specific action that is identifiable based on one or several pieces of evidence. For example, the presence of a bloody handprint on a wall tells us something—someone touched the wall after being

Figure 3.5 A view of the male victim. Spatter extend from the victim's head toward the southwest beyond the trash can. The blood pool indicates he was not mobile after injury. A drip trail and associated blood into blood patterns to his left side indicate his wound moved from a position near his feet back to his observed final position. (Photo courtesy of Chuck Merritt, San Diego County Sheriff's Office.)

bloodied. If refined data are available (e.g., the crime lab tells us whose blood and whose palm print is involved), it tells us even more, for instance, that "Joe" touched the wall after coming in contact with "Mary's" blood.

This information creates a snapshot of a moment from the incident. How this snapshot interrelates to all of the other event segments is considered in Step 3. The concentration at this stage is on recognizing and defining as many of these snapshots as possible based on the physical evidence. These snapshots become the pieces of the analyst's puzzle, which ultimately must be fit together to form a picture of what happened.

Figure 3.6 The large spatter pattern that emanates from the male victim's head. Note that the trash can and tissue are not similarly spattered. (Photo courtesy of Chuck Merritt, San Diego County Sheriff's Office.)

Figure 3.7 A view of the female victim's position by the rear door, looking from the southeast entryway. (Photo courtesy of Chuck Merritt, San Diego County Sheriff's Office.)

Case Example: Identify Event Segments

Based on the scene, the following event segments were defined. Note that the event segment is shown in bold with the supporting data listed beneath it.

The flowers were in or near the sink.
> Numerous rose leaves are in the sink (Figure 3.9).
> The leaves are consistent with the bouquet of roses in the trash can (Figure 3.11).

The flowers in the trash were exposed to the male victim's (MV) spatter.
> Spatter are present on the sides of the trash can, including one facing opposite the MV (Figure 3.12 and Figure 3.5).
> Spatter is on the stems of the roses (Figure 3.13).
> The DNA in the spatter belongs to the MV (DNA report).

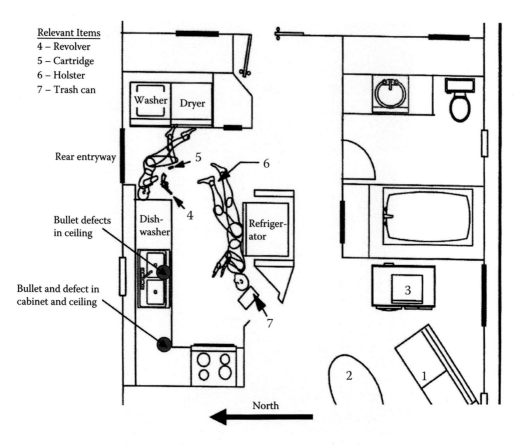

Figure 3.8 A crime scene sketch of the area showing critical evidence. (Photo courtesy of Chuck Merritt, San Diego County Sheriff's Office.)

Figure 3.9 In the sink located along the north wall are several leaves. They are rose leaves, consistent to those found in the trash can (see Figure 3.11). There is white powder material in the sink and on the rose leaves. No similar material is present on the roses in the trash can. (Photo courtesy of Chuck Merritt, San Diego County Sheriff's Office.)

Figure 3.10 Above the sink are two defects in the ceiling. The defects are consistent with bullet holes. (Photo courtesy of Chuck Merritt, San Diego County Sheriff's Office.)

Two shots were fired into the ceiling.

Two defects are present in the ceiling, consistent with bullet defects (Figure 3.10).
Four fired casings are present in the revolver in the scene (CS report).
A projectile and third defect are located in the cabinet and ceiling (Figure 3.14 and Figure 3.15).
A projectile is found in the female victim (FV) (ME report).

Figure 3.11 Spatter associated to the male victim is found on the leaves, the inner aspects of the trash can, as well as two surfaces of the outside of the can. Note that the white paper is both spattered and has had some form of contact staining. (Photo courtesy of Chuck Merritt, San Diego County Sheriff's Office.)

Figure 3.12 Small spatter associated to the male victim are found on the outer aspects of the trash can, one end and the associated facing. (Photo courtesy of Chuck Merritt, San Diego County Sheriff's Office.)

The trash can was repositioned after the large floor spatter event involving the MV.
A large spatter event radiates from the final position of the MV's head (Figure 3.5 and Figure 3.6).
The blood is that of the MV (DNA report).
The spatter radiate from a position on the far side of the trash can, consistent with the head of the MV (Figure 3.16).

Figure 3.13 Small spatter associated with the male victim is also present on the stems of the roses inside the trash can. (Photo courtesy of Chuck Merritt, San Diego County Sheriff's Office.)

Figure 3.14 An additional bullet defect and bullet are recovered from the cabinets in the north-west corner of the kitchen. (Photo courtesy of Chuck Merritt, San Diego County Sheriff's Office.)

Large spatter are found beneath and on the opposite side of the trash can on the floor (Figure 3.17).

The trash can has no similar large spatter present on its surfaces (Figure 3.5).

The trash can was repositioned after the MV's small spatter event.

Spatter are present on the sides of the trash can, including one facing opposite the MV (Figure 3.12 and Figure 3.5).

Spatter is on the stems of the roses (Figure 3.13).

The DNA in the spatter belong to the MV (DNA report).

No similar small spatter are present on surrounding surfaces near the trash can's final position.

Figure 3.15 The bullet recovered from the northwest upper cabinet. This bullet had trace bone tissue on it. Because the female victim had a single penetrating injury and a bullet was recovered at autopsy, this bullet and trajectory must be associated to the male victim's perforating gunshot wound. (Photo courtesy of Chuck Merritt, San Diego County Sheriff's Office.)

Figure 3.16 An overhead view of the spatter pattern that emanates from the male victim's head. The trash receptacle could not have been in position when this pattern was produced. (Photo courtesy of Chuck Merritt, San Diego County Sheriff's Office.)

One side where small spatter are present is facing away from the MV in the final position (Figure 3.12 and Figure 3.5).

The paper tissue was repositioned subsequent to the large floor MV spatter event.
A large spatter event radiates from the final position of the MV's head (Figure 3.5 and Figure 3.6).
The blood is that of the MV (DNA report).
The spatter radiate from a position on the far side of the trash can, consistent with the head of the MV (Figure 3.16).
These spatter are beneath the tissue lying on the floor (Figure 3.17).

Figure 3.17 Another view of the relationships between the male victim's head, the tissue paper, the trash can, and the spatter pattern. (Photo courtesy of Chuck Merritt, San Diego County Sheriff's Office.)

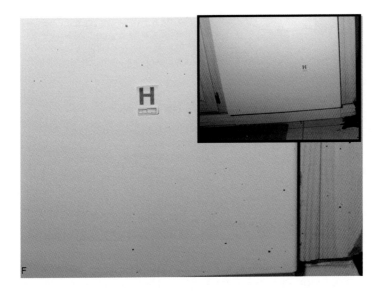

Figure 3.18 Small spatter (Pattern H) associated to the male victim were found to the north of his position on the vertical face of the dishwasher. The spatter struck relatively perpendicular to the surface. (Photo courtesy of Chuck Merritt, San Diego County Sheriff's Office.)

The tissue has small spatter on its surface, but no large spatter was observed in the floor pattern (physical examination).

The female victim's (FV) interior robe was exposed to male victim (MV) small spatter.
Seven to eight small spatter are present on the FV's robe, right interior side only (physical examination).
The blood is that of the MV (DNA report).

The MV received a single perforating gunshot wound to the head.
Entry wound to the right temple, with soot and no stippling (ME report).
Exit wound to the left frontal scalp (ME report).
A projectile and third defect are located in the cabinet and ceiling northwest of the victim (Figure 3.14 and Figure 3.15).
The projectile has blood and tissue present on it (physical examination).

The MV was facing somewhat north when shot.
The vertical face and floor in front of the dishwasher in the north wall is exposed to spatter (Figure 3.17).
The blood is that of the MV (DNA report).
Small spatter radiate out from the same area toward the southeast (Figure 3.18).
Spatter are present on the vertical face of the dryer (Figure 3.19).
A single entry wound to the right temple, with soot and no stippling (ME report).
A single exit wound to the left frontal scalp (ME report).
The wound track is right to left (R-L), slightly back to front (B-F) and slightly upward (ME report).
A projectile and third defect are located in the cabinet and ceiling northwest (NW) of the victim (Figure 3.14 and Figure 3.15).

Figure 3.19 Small spatter associated to the male victim were found to the southeast of his position on the floor at the southeast entry to the kitchen. These spatter struck at acute angles. (Photo courtesy of Chuck Merritt, San Diego County Sheriff's Office.)

The projectile has blood and tissue present on it (physical examination).
One additional projectile is present in the FV (ME report).

The revolver was exposed to MV's spatter event.
Spatter is located on the weapon (Figure 3.20).
The blood is that of both the MV and FV (DNA report).

The MV's head is low to the floor and positioned above his feet.
A drip trail and associated blood into blood patterns are present from the area of the victim's feet, on his legs, and leading to his final position (Figure 3.5 and Figure 3.21).

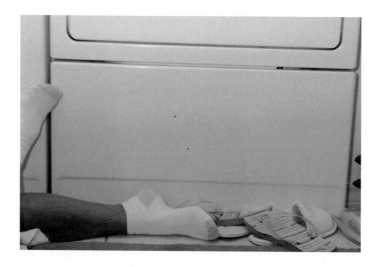

Figure 3.20 Small spatter associated to the male victim were found to the east on the vertical face of the clothes dryer. These spatter struck low and relatively perpendicular to the surface. (Photo courtesy of Chuck Merritt, San Diego County Sheriff's Office.)

Figure 3.21 The weapon that killed both victims. Note the cylinder is open and several casings are displaced. The weapon is facing the male victim in its final position. Contact staining in the male victim's blood is found on the opposite side of the revolver grip. (Photo courtesy of Chuck Merritt, San Diego County Sheriff's Office.)

The spatter in the MV's blood on the dishwasher strike low to the floor, but relatively perpendicular (Figure 3.22).

Spatter and drips are present on the inside left and inside right aspects of the victim's socks (Figure 3.23).

The spatter radiating to the southeast are striking the floor at acute angles, indicating their source was low to the floor (Figure 3.18).

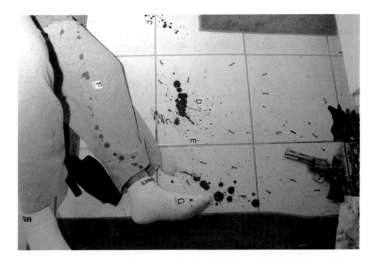

Figure 3.22 The bloodstains associated to the male victim include C, D, E, F, and G. They indicate that he was positioned wound over his feet at the time of his gunshot and after bleeding in that position a short time that he moved in a relatively continuous fashion backward to his final position. Note there are spatter on the floor, just below the black revolver holster. (Photo courtesy of Chuck Merritt, San Diego County Sheriff's Office.)

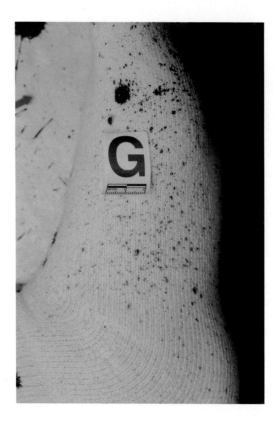

Figure 3.23 On the inside aspects of both the right and left socks are small impact spatter. These must be associated to the male victim's gunshot injury. Based on location, he cannot be standing at the moment of his gunshot. (Photo courtesy of Chuck Merritt, San Diego County Sheriff's Office.)

The spatter on the dryer strikes low to the floor, but relatively perpendicular (Figure 3.19).

The MV collapses to a supine position, consistent with final position.

A drip trail and associated blood into blood patterns are in the area of the victim's feet, on his legs, and leading to his final position (Figure 3.5 and Figure 3.21).

No additional drips and or pattern indicate movement in any other orientation.

The drip pattern on the legs is very linear and leads directly up the body, across the chest (Figure 3.5).

A large spatter event radiates from the final position of the MV's head (Figure 3.5, Figure 3.6, and Figure 3.16).

The blood is that of the MV (DNA report).

The FV received her gunshot wound near the rear door.

The FV has a single penetrating gunshot wound and no other bleeding injuries (ME report).

There are no drips associated to her wounds that extend from the general area where she is found (Figure 3.24).

Figure 3.24 The female victim was clearly bleeding and mobile in the area surrounding the door; however, no drips or patterns associated to the female victim are found beyond the revolver. (Photo courtesy of Chuck Merritt, San Diego County Sheriff's Office.)

Her injury bled significantly into the scene, producing a pool and saturations into her clothing (Figure 3.25).

The FV remained mobile subsequent to injury.

There are numerous swipes, smears, and transfer patterns on the facing of the cabinet adjacent the FV (Figure 3.25 and Figure 3.26).

Some of these transfer patterns appear to be hand/finger marks (Figure 3.26).

The blood in these areas is the FV (DNA report).

A large spatter event with a focused radiating pattern emanates out from the FV's position and occurred prior to the pooling (Figure 3.20).

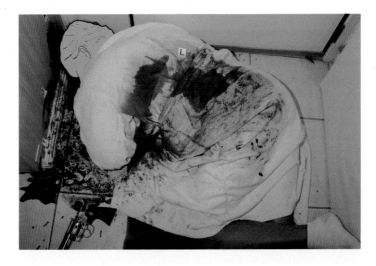

Figure 3.25 The area near the female victim. Note the patterns on the cabinet as well as the saturation stain on her back. (Photo courtesy of Chuck Merritt, San Diego County Sheriff's Office.)

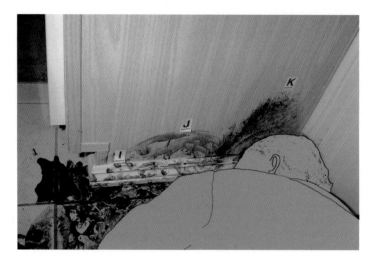

Figure 3.26 Patterns I, J, and K are associated to the female victim's blood. They make it clear that she remained mobile to some extent following her gunshot injury. (Photo courtesy of Chuck Merritt, San Diego County Sheriff's Office.)

The FV was positioned on her back subsequent to her injury.

Large saturation stains are present on the back aspects of the victim's robe (Figure 3.17 and Figure 3.25).

The DNA is associated to the FV (DNA report).

The blood flow cannot be attributed to her final position (BPA report).

The FV's cell phone was open in the scene.

The cell phone is open on the floor, with no evident contact staining consistent with the surrounding surfaces (Figure 3.27).

Figure 3.27 Beneath the female victim is her cell phone, which is open. (Photo courtesy of Chuck Merritt, San Diego County Sheriff's Office.)

Figure 3.28 The revolver and associated expended casings are shown. Two bullets appear to have been fired into the ceiling. One bullet entered and remained in the female victim. One bullet passed through the male victim and was recovered in the northwest cabinet. One additional cartridge was located on the green rug, adjacent to the revolver. (Photo courtesy of Chuck Merritt, San Diego County Sheriff's Office.)

A clear demarcation is present in a smear/saturation stain on the rug to the north of the cell phone, consistent with the shape and size of the phone (Figure 3.27).

The FV achieved final position (on her stomach) on her own.
The FV was mobile.
The FV was positioned on her back at one point subsequent to injury.
The final position is face and stomach down.

The revolver cylinder was opened/manipulated after the victim's were wounded.
The weapon is responsible for the killing rounds (ballistics report).
Four expended casings are present (Figure 3.28).
Two defects are present in the ceiling consistent with gunshot defects (Figure 3.10).
One bullet is found above the cabinets (Figure 3.14).
One bullet is found in the FV at autopsy (ME report).
The cylinder is open in the final scene (Figure 3.20).
An unexpended cartridge is present near the weapon, but not stained by any spatter events (Figure 3.29).

The MV's blood was transferred to the hammer and handle of the revolver.
Heavy smears are present on the hammer and right side of the handle (BPA report).
The bloodstains belong to the MV (DNA report).

Just as event segments are individual snapshots of the incident, an "event" is a macro view of some part of the incident. As the analyst fits a number of related snapshots together, they define a broader aspect of the incident: the event. So, recognizing related event

Figure 3.29 The revolver and the unfired cartridge are pictured. (Photo courtesy of Chuck Merritt, San Diego County Sheriff's Office.)

segments is an important step in understanding a particular *event*, leading the analyst to the third step.

Step 3: Establish which event segments are related to one another. In this step, the analyst looks for interrelationships between identified event segments. Instead of focusing on the individual snapshots (the event segments), the analyst shifts the focus to trying to understand different areas or activities that occurred during the incident. The initial consideration is very simply: which of the identified event segments are associated to one another. In some instances, immediate interrelationships are present. In the case example, the shootings of the two victims are obvious events. Both were shot, order as yet undefined. Thus, the actions associated to each wounding (bloodstains produced, trajectories, positions) all have some interrelationship. In other instances, however, event segments may appear quite disassociated and relationships may not be evident. In these instances, the analyst may only recognize something was happening (an event) without fully understanding what. The initial consideration of interrelationship may be based solely on the fact that the event segments occurred in or around one another.

Although it would be helpful to associate each segment to some specific event, that is both unnecessary and unlikely. Some segments simply will not easily fit into the investigative puzzle. The chronological associations defined during Step 4 often help fit these additional pieces into the analyst's puzzle.

Case Example: Identify Related Event Segments

MV gunshot event: associated event segments
>   The trash can was repositioned after MV's small spatter event.
>   The FV's interior robe was exposed to MV small spatter.
>   The MV was facing somewhat north when shot.
>   The MV received a single perforating gunshot wound to the head.
>   The revolver was exposed to MV's spatter event.

The MV's head is low above the floor and positioned above his feet.
The MV collapses to a supine position, consistent with final position.

FV gunshot event: associated event segments
The FV received her gunshot wound near the rear door.
The FV remained mobile subsequent to injury.
The FV was positioned on her back subsequent to her injury.
The FV achieved final position (on her stomach) on her own.
The FV's cell phone was out and open in the scene.

Activity involving the trash can movement
The trash can was repositioned after the large floor spatter event involving the MV.
The trash can was repositioned after MV's small spatter event.
The paper tissue was repositioned subsequent to the large floor MV spatter event.

Activity involving the manipulation of the revolver
The revolver cylinder was opened/manipulated.
The MV's blood was transferred to the hammer and handle of the revolver.

Activity involving the flower bouquet
The flowers are in or near the sink.
The flowers in the trash were exposed to the MV's spatter.
Two shots were fired into the ceiling.

Activity involving shots into the ceiling
Two shots were fired into the ceiling.

These basic associations give us somewhere to start when we begin sequencing the event segments. Sequencing begins in Step 4 and continues throughout the remaining steps. The analyst will find that, in practice, the activities in Step 4 through Step 7 are generally accomplished in a seamless fashion. Nevertheless, the analyst should recognize the individual aspects and importance of each step involved.

Step 4: Sequence these related segments, establishing a flow for that event. In this step, the analyst looks for sequencing information. The associations made in the previous step act as a focus point, a place to begin considering sequence. But these obvious associations in no way limit the analyst; any sequential aspect that is recognized between different event segments is considered and documented. By looking at interrelationships between event segments and using the consideration that every action is preceded by some other action and every action has some action that naturally follows it, the analyst begins to put order to the various related event segments. Relative chronology is the primary tool the crime scene analyst uses to put event segments in sequential order.

Applying a revised concept of archaeology's chronology (refer to Chapter 2), the crime scene analyst looks to identify three relative chronology relationships between various event segments. These relationships are known as: *terminus post quem, terminus ante quem,* and *terminus peri quem.*

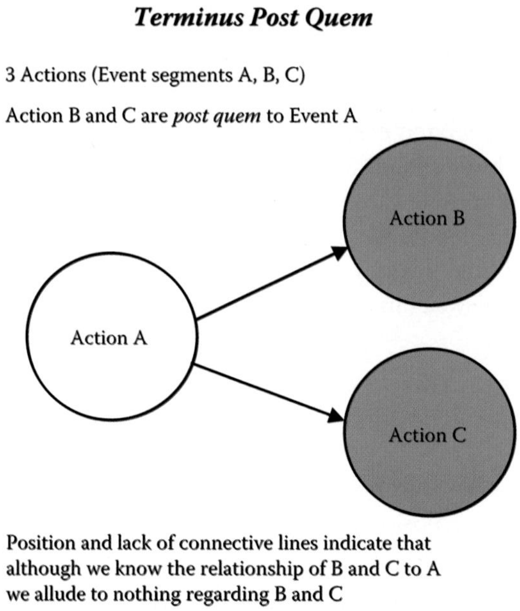

Terminus Post Quem

3 Actions (Event segments A, B, C)

Action B and C are *post quem* to Event A

Position and lack of connective lines indicate that
although we know the relationship of B and C to A
we allude to nothing regarding B and C

Figure 3.30 The concept of *terminus post quem* simply means that something happens after something else. Given three event segments (A, B, and C) as depicted, both B and C follow (are *terminus post quem*) to A. Note that no connecting line between B and C indicates there is no direct relationship known.

Terminus post quem: This defines a point in time (another event segment) after which an event segment must have occurred. Imagine a hypothetical burglary. A simple *post quem* example is that before a burglar can reach in to manipulate a dead bolt from the inside, he must first break the side window. In the hypothetical example, the segment "lock manipulated" must by necessity follow the segment "window glass broken," thus it is *terminus post quem* to that segment (Figure 3.30). In the case example, the final position of the trash receptacle must occur after (*post quem*) the large spatter created by the MV's head falling to the floor as well as the small spatter to the sides of the trash can (Figure 3.31).

Terminus ante quem: This defines a point in time before which an event segment must have occurred (Figure 3.32). A simple hypothetical *ante quem* example is an injury in relation to blood transfers in that person's blood. Some bleeding injury to the person involved (or other blood source introduction) must precede any deposition of blood in the scene. In the case example, the MV's position (low on the floor, head over his feet) must precede (*ante quem*) his collapse to a supine position (Figure 3.33).

Terminus peri quem: This defines a point at or near when the event segment must have occurred. In effect, it is a statement of near simultaneous actions. Archaeology uses only the *ante* and *post quem* relationships, but crime scene investigators deal with a much more recent past. When considering sequencing information, some event segments may be occurring nearly simultaneous to one another. A simple *peri quem* example is the deposition of gun powder particles on surrounding surfaces as a bullet is fired and strikes the body (Figure 3.34). In the case example, the gunshot wound to the MV and the spatter to the trash can and dishwasher are nearly simultaneous (*peri quem*) to one another (Figure 3.35).

Terminus Post Quem

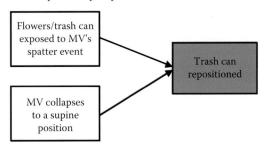

<u>3 Actions</u>
Flowers/trash can exposed to MV's spatter event
Trash can repositioned
MV collapses to supine position

It is impossible for the trash can to be present in its final position prior to the gunshot. There are no similar small spatter found at that location and the can is in the way of the subsequent large floor spatter event.

Figure 3.31 In the case example, the repositioning of the trash can occurs after (*terminus post quem*) both the male victim's collapse to the floor and the small spatter event. The collapse to the floor produced the large spatter event, which the trash can is literally on top of. The small spatter on the can are facing away from the male victim, thus they could not have been deposited after achieving this position.

Terminus Ante Quem

3 Actions (Event segments E, F, G)
Action E and F are *ante quem* to Event G.

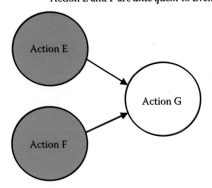

Once again the lack of connective lines indicate that although we know the relationship of E and F to G we allude to nothing regarding E and F

Figure 3.32 The concept of *terminus ante quem* simply means that something happens before something else. Given three event segments (E, F, and G), as depicted both E and F precede (are *terminus ante quem*) to G. Once again the lack of a connecting line between E and F indicates there is no direct relationship known.

Terminus Ante Quem

<u>2 Actions</u>
MV is low on the floor, head over feet
MV collapses to a supine position

| MV is low on the floor, head over feet | → | MV collapses to a supine position |

The drip trail indicates a position for the MV that must
have preceded the final position

Figure 3.33 In the case example, the position of the male victim with his head low and over his feet must precede the collapse to the supine position. The drip trail from the feet to the head shows only one passage of the wound.

Applying these three simple relationships (e.g., something precedes, is nearly simultaneous to, or follows something else) to as many event segments as possible provides critical input to the CSR attempt. This application of chronology rarely produces a complete and absolute flow (e.g., A followed by B, followed by C, *ad infinitum*) for each action in question. Simply put, not every event segment can be related to every other event segment. However, by combining the known chronological associations developed during this step (Figure 3.36), a structure and flow begin to take shape. As this flow is derived in a very objective fashion, it becomes a standard against which the analyst can evaluate any claims regarding the incident. Crossover event segments become critical at this point. A crossover event segment is one that allows the analyst to recognize a chronological relationship between two events (Figure 3.37). Without crossover segments, the analysis remains extremely fragmented and without form. In the case example, without crossover event segments, there would be no way to answer the question of who shot whom? Thus, in pursuing sequence, the analysts constantly challenge themselves to be sure they have recognized every

Terminus Peri Quem

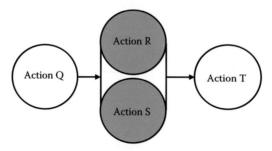

4 Actions (Event segments Q, R, S, T) Action R and S
are *peri quem* to each other

Figure 3.34 The concept of *terminus peri quem* simply means that several actions appear to be simultaneous to one another. Given the four event segments (Q, R, S, and T), as depicted both R and S are simultaneous (*terminus peri quem*) to one another.

Terminus Peri Quem

<u>3 Actions</u>
Flowers/trash can exposed to MV's spatter event
MV spatter event N face of dishwasher, low on floor
MV's GSW while facing North

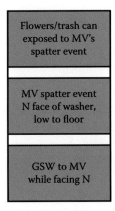

Figure 3.35 In the case example, the event segments trash can exposed to the spatter event, male victim facing north, and the male victim's gunshot wound are all nearly simultaneous to one another. The only evident bloodstain event similar to those found on the trash can is the male victim's gunshot wound. The trajectory information indicates a bullet path right to left and upward, which considered with the entry/exit aspects demands he is facing north.

possible chronological association. One missed association could prevent the analyst from recognizing if some testimonial claim is possible or impossible.

A practical and functional method for documenting sequence and producing the final flow chart is through the use of a whiteboard and post-it notes. As individual event segments are defined, they are transferred to a post-it note. The post-it notes are initially placed on the whiteboard in no particular order, but as associations and sequential relationships

Combining Sequence

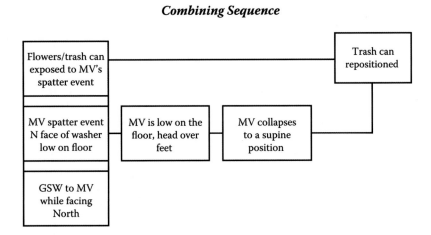

Figure 3.36 Not every event segment can be associated to every other event segment; however, when we combine the known chronological associations, the various relationships start to bring form and flow to the entire event.

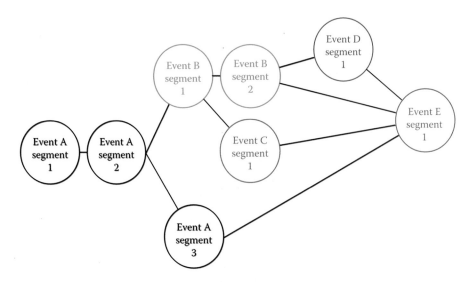

Figure 3.37 Crossover event segments are critical. They allow us to see relationships between events. In the figure, Event B Segment 1 has a sequential relationship to Event A Segment 2; this allows us to know that Event A preceded B. The same is true of B1 and C1 as well as B2 and D1. Without crossover event segments, the analysis will appear very fragmented.

are recognized, the notes are arranged accordingly. Over time, the analyst will go through multiple iterations of order. As these changes are made, event segments can easily be repositioned and lines of relationship redrawn. After multiple iterations, a relatively stable flow will ultimately develop and, at that point, the information can be transcribed onto paper or entered into some form of software on a computer.

Case Example: Sequence-Related Event Segments

Figure 3.38 shows the final flow chart developed from the sequencing effort. It is a graphic representation of each chronological association made during this step. This final form was not arrived at quickly or in a single iteration. In fact, no less than 10 iterations were developed as new associations were identified. A critical consideration was that the trash can was repositioned subsequent to the MV injury. The presence of the MV's spatter on the outside of the trash can and on the stem of the rose demands the can was in or around the position of the small spatter action (low to the floor and near the dishwasher and dryer). These could not occur in the can's final position. Just as obvious is that when the victim collapsed to his final position, he created a significant spatter action. The trash can and tissue could not have been present in their final position at the time, as they would have prevented the creation of the pattern. Thus, the alteration of the trash can occurred for whatever reason, after the shooting of the MV. This crossover segment suggests an order of events that forces an issue as to who moved the trash can.

The dotted line between the can repositioning and the FV's wounding in Figure 3.38 is significant. If the MV did not move the trash can, then the best explanation of sequence is the trash can was moved prior to the injury of the FV. But, this sequence remains dotted because the analyst cannot state with absolute certainty that the FV was the one who moved the trash can. Clearly the MV could not and the FV very likely did. But, is there anything present in this scene that excludes a third party from moving the trash can? No signs of a third party

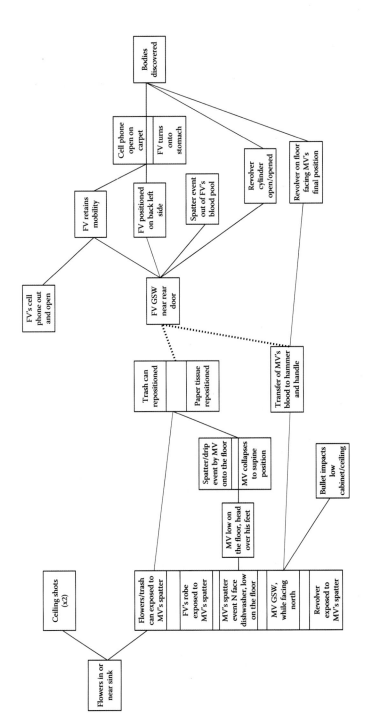

Figure 3.38 The final flow chart created from the analysis of the death scene is shown. Not every question is answered and, unfortunately, the crossover event segments are weak (note the dotted lines). Nevertheless, the analysis provides a best explanation of this incident and suggests that the female victim shot the male victim before turning the weapon on herself.

are present in the scene. Responding officers report that they did not move the can. However, testimonial evidence is still testimonial evidence, so is it possible someone altered the scene and forgot that action or was afraid to acknowledge it? Resolving the sequence of trash can repositioned and FV gunshot demands consideration of the fifth step: auditing.

Step 5: Consider all possible sequences, auditing the background evidence when necessary. As discussed, the sequence of various segments is not always evident, nor can we relate each and every segment to every other segment. For this reason, the flow that develops from Step 4 must be considered with alternative sequences or actions in mind. In some situations, the data may support several possible sequences. In these situations, the analyst audits the information available and tries to eliminate any of the possible sequences. This concept of auditing involves looking at background detail that may or may not be immediately relevant to the broader questions being considered. Answering an auditing issue, however, may ultimately answer a questionable issue.

Case Example: Auditing

Two areas of the analysis require additional effort, for as yet the data do not force an issue with the sequence of wounding. This lack of sequence in effect prevents us from understanding who shot whom. The two areas of interest that may assist our understanding are movement of the trash can and transfer of blood onto the weapon from the MV.

Some might ask: Why not look at the manipulation of the weapon? The logic being that this manipulation occurred after the two wounding shots, thus whoever is responsible for altering its condition was the last person in possession of the weapon. The MV lacked capacity to position the revolver as it was found and the scene forces a belief that the female victim must have repositioned it. However, she had mobility for some period, so answering this question in no way forces the sequence of who was shot first. It is possible the FV was shot first, the MV shot himself, dropped the gun, and with or without purpose, the FV manipulated the weapon before she died.

Movement of the trash, however, offers some hope for understanding the sequence. Because the trash can was exposed to the MV's small spatter action and then repositioned in the scene after he fell, if we can determine where in the scene the trash can was at the time of the MV's spatter action, that information may allow us to decide who repositioned it. The MV's small spatter radiate out nearly 130 degrees (from the dishwasher to the floor at the southeast entrance). Based on the radiating effect of the spatter, they must be associated to the gunshot in some fashion. Refer back to Figure 3.18 through Figure 3.20. Some minor blood into blood activity occurred on the floor, but it cannot explain the presence of these spatter. To receive small spatter on two surfaces and on the top of the stem, the trash had to have been positioned either within the cone of spatter produced by the gunshot or on the perimeter of the radiating effect. This presents the question: Where could the trash can have fit in a normal fashion? And where could it have been at the moment of the MV's wounding? The possible answers are limited.

If the can was present against the east side of the kitchen, the spatter on the can could be explained, but there is no obvious position for the can along the east side. Nor is there any area currently open with the exception of the actual entryway from the hall (see Figure 3.7 and Figure 3.19). In this latter position, the spatter on the floor struck at low acute angles, which is inconsistent with the location of the spatter on the trash can. This functionally eliminates this area as the position of the trash can.

There is no obvious "normal" location for the trash can against the north wall (in front of the cabinets and sink) (see Figure 3.1 and Figure 3.2). Granted, the presence of the green rug prevents us from knowing absolutely if the trash can could have been temporarily positioned here for whatever reason, but the lack of spatter on vertical surfaces to the west of the dishwasher suggest this is not the case. Close examination of these surfaces reveals that the dispersion cone of the gunshot spatter did not extend up onto them. The trash can was clearly exposed to the dispersion cone on two vertical surfaces, yet the cone of dispersion did not extend past the dishwasher face. This effectively eliminates this area as a prior position. There is no voided area present on the vertical face of the dishwasher, so the can was not present directly in front of the dishwasher.

The floor forward of the dishwasher and the MV offers plenty of open space for the trash can, but the floor is covered in various spatter and blood patterns. There were spatter actions oriented in multiple directions on the floor. There simply is no location where one could sit the trash can without it being spattered by all of these additional actions and, if present, then some form of void would also be present. Lacking these conditions, this eliminates this area from consideration.

There is one obvious position for the trash can, based on the can's size and the layout of the kitchen. The area in question is against the east side of the cabinet, immediately adjacent the door (to the west). The trash can could fit here and this is a more "typical" position for a trash can. In such a position, the two surfaces of the trash can facing into the room (toward the spatter event) would and could be exposed to the dispersion cone from the MV gunshot event. Spatter are found forward of this location at the same level as found on the trash can, but note that in Figure 3.26 no spatter are found on the east facing of the cabinet. If present here, the trash can would effectively shadow this area, preventing spatter from being deposited on the east facing.

If this is the true position of the trash can, this last position forces a sequential issue. It is clear that the FV was injured, bled, and moved in the very area we are discussing. Thus, if the trash can was exposed to the spatter at this location, its subsequent movement occurred prior to her gunshot injury. Because the MV did not have the capacity to move it, if this is the correct location, the FV must have moved it. This consideration is the strongest evidence that the FV moved the trash can.

Another auditing issue is how the MV's blood was transferred to the weapon. On the right side upper portion of the grip and on the hammer of the grip is blood associated to the MV. The nature of the blood on the grip is clearly contact; it did not drop down onto this area. But, the position of the contact prevents contact with the ground as a source. This portion of the handle is curved and was not and could not have been in contact with the ground. This eliminates accidental contact from the MV dropping the weapon. Can the stains be explained as a function of the FV's mobility? She clearly was responsible for the revolver's alteration, so can the contact stains be explained by her? The FV's position is limited to the corner and as far as she could functionally reach. The stains associated to her wounding that are forward of her (to the south) are undisturbed. No disturbed bloodstains associated with her husband are evident near her. The only true disturbance in his blood is the smear by the MV's pants, but his own movement explains this. His sock smeared that area. Thus, accidental movement after she was shot does not offer a reasonable way for the FV to come in contact with the MV's blood. If she can't make contact with a blood source, she can't transfer the blood. That, however, does not prevent her from touching his blood if she is uninjured and mobile.

What about the MV? Can we in any way attribute the contact staining on the grip and hammer to his action? Although we cannot eliminate his hands as being bloodied, as he lay in final position, his hands were a significant distance away from the revolver. The drip stains from his head wound indicate he made a single motion backwards, and once in final position did not move from that position. The blood into blood pattern on the floor appears along this path and is also dissociated from the revolver. His feet and pants were stained with his blood, but the stains on the revolver are oriented opposite the bloodied clothing and the grip is facing downward. This effectively eliminates the MV as a source of the stains.

The police arrived some days after the incident, after the blood had coagulated and dried. Thus, alteration by a police officer is effectively eliminated as a source of the revolver staining.

Unless an argument and reasonable explanation are offered as to how the MV could create the stains on the revolver, the only viable explanation is that the MV was injured; someone became wet with his blood and then touched the revolver. As the only two apparent parties present in the scene were the MV and FV, this appears to force a sequential issue.

Step 6: Based on the event segment sequence, final order of the events. As we develop an understanding of the event segment sequence for each event, the result often provides crossover data between events. An event segment related to one event will have a sequential relationship to an event segment associated to another event. This allows the analyst to better understand the general order of the events themselves. As described, this step is an integral part of achieving Steps 4 though 7, but in certain instances taking a moment to recognize event order is important.

In many situations, the order of the events naturally develops on-scene by logically considering what happened (e.g., they came, they killed, they left). Initial beliefs regarding event order are often made by the analyst during the initial assessment of the scene or by others in the investigative team. These initial beliefs die hard at times, whether in the analyst's or another investigator's mind. But, they are exactly that, initial beliefs. The relationships established between the event segments in Step 4 and 5 are more objective than any initial belief. If there is a contradiction between the initial assessment and the formal analysis, it will demand revising the initial beliefs. The reason the analyst takes Step 6 is to be sure he has not allowed such initial beliefs to color him in his overall analysis.

Case Example: Reorder the Events

The initial assessment of the scene suggested the female victim was the first shot. These beliefs were based on a number of factors including:

- Her wound was not hard contact; the MV's was.
- Her blood was not present in the barrel of the weapon; the MV's was.
- The weapons belonged to the MV. FV was not known for being particularly interested or trained in weapons.

In this case, the sequential aspects regarding the trash can movement and the staining to the revolver in the MV's blood do not absolutely establish an order of events. They do, however, suggest that contrary to the initial assessment, the MV was injured prior to the FV. But, in terms of being objective, the certainty of the order (MV then FV) is not there. Is this the most likely order? Yes it is, but lacking is a clear and absolute relationship. The only objective response is to use the dotted line between repositioning of the trash can and the FV's gunshot wound (see Figure 3.38).

Step 7: Flow chart the entire incident and validate the sequence. In order to recognize, understand, and demonstrate the overall sequence (the analyst's conclusions) requires some form of graphic tool. In most situations, these interrelationships are simply too convoluted for anyone, no matter how good they are to formulate and keep straight in their mind. Sequencing began in Step 4 and to be understood or meaningful it must be graphically demonstrated. Thus, creation of the flow chart begins in Step 4, and it is continuously altered and adjusted from that point forward. The final flow chart serves two basic purposes. First, it allows for more effective logic checking by the analyst. In a graphic form, the analyst can see logical errors that may occur when combining all of the interrelationships between the events and event segments. The second purpose of the final flow chart is as an effective demonstrative aid for the jury.

Before accepting the final flow chart, the analyst should validate it. This is a simple process of challenging each sequential aspect and determining if any logical errors are noted or if some alternate sequence is more appropriate (e.g., perhaps becoming more vague in some aspect). Validation of a flow chart rarely occurs overnight. The analyst should put away the case for a day or more, clear his head of the convoluted details he has challenged himself with and, once he has a clear head, return to the document. At that point, he starts fresh, reviewing each sequence described on the flow chart. By clearing his head and looking at the flow chart at a later time, logical errors are more likely to become evident.

In the end, the final flow chart is a graphic representation of the analyst's opinion. If developed appropriately and objectively, it is used to test any and all investigative theories as well as any and all claims about the incident in question. Any theory or claim must fit within the final form and sequence of the event analysis. Depending on the detail in the data, any theory or claim that fails to do so will at the very least be suspect, if not completely refuted.

Case Example: Flow Chart the Entire Incident

Figure 3.38 is the final flow chart for this analysis. Based on the effort, the best explanation of the incident is that the FV shot the MV and then turned the weapon on herself.

Summary

Event analysis is a functional methodology that conforms to the expectations of CSR. It asks the basic CSR questions and applies the themes developed over the history of CSR. The four basic questions asked are:

- What is it?
- What function did it serve?
- What interrelationships exist between this item and others?
- What does it tell us about timing and sequencing?

The themes that drive all crime scene analysis include:

- Data defines the conclusion.
- Objective data are found in scene context as well as artifacts.
- Human testimony is always considered cautiously.
- Effective forensic examination leads to more refined data.
- What happened is not the only question. In what order did it happen is important as well.
- Crime scene analysis uses reductionism. The analysis is reverse engineered from the physical evidence.

Event analysis incorporates all of these themes and questions and frames them within the scientific method. It considers the overall issue being evaluated as the Incident. It recognizes that each incident is made up of macro components known as events and then brings substance to these events by identifying and ordering as many specific actions, known as event segments, as the available data will allow. This is accomplished using seven steps. These include:

1. Collect data from the scene and evidence.
2. Establish specific event segments (time snapshots).
3. Establish which event segments are related to one another.
4. Sequence related segments, establishing a flow for that event.
5. Consider all possible sequences, auditing the background evidence when necessary to resolve contradictions.
6. Based on the event segment sequence, final order the events themselves.
7. Flowchart the entire incident and validate the sequence.

Reference

1. Bevel, T., and R.M. Gardner. 2002. *Bloodstain Pattern Analysis: With an Introduction to Crime Scene Reconstruction,* 2nd ed., Boca Raton, FL: CRC Press, p. 45.

Resolving Significant Investigative Questions in CSR

4

Introduction

Reconstruction and analysis use the scientific method to consider and evaluate various aspects of the scenes the analyst encounters. Event Analysis, described in Chapter 3, is an overarching methodology for evaluating the entire incident. It defines specific actions, orders those actions, and offers significant insight into understanding what did or did not happen in the course of the incident in question. As described in Chapter 3, the foundation of Event Analysis is scientific method, asking and answering four basic questions:

1. What is it?
2. What function did it serve?
3. What interrelationships exist between this item and other items in the scene?
4. What does the item tell us about timing and sequencing?

As this overall reconstruction is pursued, specific investigative questions may present themselves—distinct issues that the methodology of Event Analysis alone may not answer. In an effort to resolve them, these significant investigative questions must be considered independently. Once again, the method employed to resolve these questions must be the scientific method. Most discussions on how to resolve such specific questions in a crime scene context simply identify *scientific method* as the accepted methodology and fail to further explain the process or individual steps required to achieve that end. Functionally applying scientific method is not particularly complex, but it does require an understanding of what the steps consist of and how one goes about applying each step to the question being analyzed. Although it can be argued that scientific method can always be pursued as a mental exercise, when dealing with these critical issues their complexity demands a more formal effort. In this chapter, we will introduce the use of event analysis worksheets as a means of resolving these significant investigative questions. The worksheets utilize a memory aid, "*PhD etc*," to help identify each of the six basic steps of scientific method. Lucien Haag first suggested this memory aid and described it as "*PhD ic*," which stands for Problem, Hypothesis, Data, Interpretations, and Conclusion.[1] We have replaced the "*ic*" with "*etc*," which reminds the user that to employ scientific method, we must also consider Expectations/predictions as well as Testing those predictions and ultimately defining some Conclusion. This mnemonic aid represents a standard procedure for crime scene reconstruction (CSR Figure 4.1).

PhD etc

Problem	The Investigative Question (IQ) being considered
hypothesis	Identify all the viable ways an action could have been accomplished, based upon incident review and observations
Data	Collect all data that relates to the specific IQ under consideration
expectations	Identify any predictions of what one would expect to find: simple if "this" then "that" statements regarding the scene or evidence
test	Test each hypothesis against all data developed from the investigation (e.g., scene context, lab analysis) seeking to falsify each hypothesis
conclusion	State an opinion based upon the results of this analysis

Figure 4.1 Shown is a CSR Memory Aid. The *PhD etc* mnemonic reminds the analyst of the basic steps of scientific method.

No matter who is describing it or how it is described, scientific method always begins with a question, which in CSR is often called the *investigative question* (IQ). The answer to this question frequently leads to another question and as a result, the scientific method is often described as circular. By following this circular route of asking and answering questions, in effect the process produces an ever-expanding, self-correcting body of knowledge (Figure 4.2).

The first consideration is to define or refine the IQ that needs to be resolved. This ensures that a focus is established and that all efforts are directed toward the intended question. Significant investigative questions arise from two general areas in CSR. The first results when

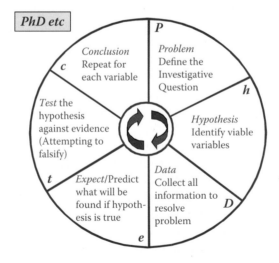

Figure 4.2 The Scientific Method Wheel with *PhD etc* added. The steps of the *PhD etc* mnemonic directly correlate with the steps in the scientific method.

Event Analysis or a similar methodology encounters a complexity or contradiction. The case example described in detail in Chapter 3 is an excellent example of such a contradiction. The initial analysis suggested that either of the parties might have been the shooter. The Event Analysis in and of itself did not force the issue absolutely. The complexities of that scene and the evident contradictions demand a more refined look at all of the various interrelationships in an effort to decide if any conclusion as to who the shooter was is possible.

Another source for investigative questions are counselors. Often a lawyer will ask the analyst if a specific issue can be resolved. In other instances as the trial looms, it may become evident that opposing counsels intend to argue some specific issue from mutually exclusive positions. In either instance, the responsibility of the analyst is to decide if the questions posed by the counsel can be resolved one way or another.

One of the most significant aspects of defining any IQ is taking the voluminous and often complex data, physical evidence, and lab analysis and breaking the complex issues into manageable smaller questions. Investigative questions have to be narrow in focus and very specific. The best and simplest question to consider is one with only two possibilities as an answer. For example, if the IQ revolves around claims by a counselor of a specific seated position for a victim, the investigative question could be posed in several ways, including:

Option 1: Was the victim seated at the moment of wounding? The answer to such a question is either Yes, No, or it could not be determined. Using the available data, the concentration is on whether the victim was seated. If it can be resolved that the victim was not seated, in this particular context it doesn't matter where else he was at the moment of wounding, as the counsel's hypothesis is effectively eliminated and is no longer in play.

Option 2: Where was the victim at the moment of wounding? In this version, the answers are limited only by the victim's potential positions. The manner in which the question is posed demands some answer, and, if not seated, it begs to define what position the victim was in. This may demand consideration of what could be an unmanageable number of possibilities, requiring significant effort, when, in this context and situation, all that is of concern is whether the seated position is the wounding position.

As the two options for the example demonstrate, how we pose specific investigative questions is important. Remember the purpose of the IQ is to focus the analyst's efforts. If we know what we want to answer (e.g., was the victim in a seated position), then all our effort is directed at answering that and only that aspect. Unfortunately not all questions can be posed in such a manner. Thus, a two part question is not always possible and questions with three or four possibilities will also have to be considered. Consider an IQ in relation to entry into the scene of a homicide. The question might be posed as: "How did the attacker gain entry into the scene?" This question is not as easily answered, as it has numerous potential answers.

If the analyst encounters an investigative question that has more than four possibilities, the investigative question should be reevaluated. In such instances, it is likely the question is too broad or complex and, with a little refinement of what is being asked, the question can be broken down into a more specific question or questions.

After identifying the issue we wish to resolve, the next step in the scientific method is to identify the viable ways the IQ may be answered. These possible answers (e.g., the victim was seated, he was not seated) become the stated hypothesis. Hypotheses are educated guesses based on the education, experience, case knowledge, physical evidence, analysis results, and the limited universe of the scene in question. The concept of a limited universe, first proposed by Lucien Haag, says simply that as analysts we don't have to consider every single possibility. All we are charged with is considering those possibilities that are valid within the context of that scene. If we consider the IQ example of how did the attacker gain entry into the scene, the answer might be found among four viable possibilities, which include: (1) forced entry, (2) used a key, (3) through an unsecured door or window, or (4) someone let him/her in.

The third step in the process is to collect any data that might assist in answering the question under consideration. Data in CSR are found in both objects and the context in which we find the objects in the scene. In the iconic view of scientific method, data collection is thought of as experimentation, but, for CSR, empirical data come from scene photographs, the physical evidence, and forensic reports. This is not to say that the crime scene analyst may not be presented with a situation demanding some form of experimentation, but our primary data are the very context of the scene itself.

The fourth step of scientific method is to identify predictions of what is expected if the stated hypothesis is true. These predictions are defined through a simple consideration of: "If this, then that." Remember our theory for CSR is that nothing just happens; we look for any testable cause and effect relationships. Predictions are based on that idea. If this (e.g., if entry was gained by force), then that(physical evidence of broken glass, a broken door or window lock, broken hinges, torn or missing window screens, and/or pry marks) will be present. As the number of predictions we can evaluate increases so too does our subsequent confidence level for any conclusion we draw from the data. These predictions are then tested in the next step.

In the fifth step, each hypothesis is tested by comparing our predictions and expectations against the known data and the scene context. If the hypothesis is true, then physical evidence or other data to support that the action occurred should be present. In our example of forced entry, if true, then physical evidence in some form must be present to support the hypothesis. We test the prediction by looking for evidence of broken glass, broken doors or window locks, broken hinges, torn or removed window screens, pry marks, etc. If any of the above are found, then the hypothesis of forced entry has to be considered as possible. If the evidence does not support the prediction, the hypothesis is considered refuted. In terms of refutation, each prediction must be considered in its own light and context. In some instances, a refuted prediction may be a deductive argument; thus it absolutely eliminates the hypothesis as possible. In other instances, refuting the prediction may involve an inductive argument and not fully eliminate a hypothesis as possible. This issue is best explained using several classic examples.

Example 1

Prediction: If the subject held the weapon, then his fingerprints should be present on the weapon.

Test: No fingerprints are present.

Discussion: In this instance although it does not support the hypothesis that the subject held the weapon, neither does it eliminate it. The argument is inductive in nature as there are many reasons why fingerprints are not left after contact with an object.

Example 2

Prediction: If the subject was present at a spatter producing event, such as a beating, then spatter will be present on his person.

Test: No spatter is present on his person.

Discussion: Once again this is an inductive argument. Although the facts do not support the belief that the subject was present, neither do they eliminate it. The production of spatter may have been focused and directed in quantity into the scene, but not back toward the subject.

Example 3

Prediction: If the subject is the source of the blood, then his specific alleles will be present.

Test: His alleles are not present.

Discussion: In this instance, the argument is deductive and demands elimination of the hypothesis that the subject is the source of the blood. There is no ambiguity.

The point is simple; each prediction must be considered independently as to how conclusive it is or is not. The more conclusive it is, the more important its refutation or corroboration becomes. Just as important as the nature of the predications themselves, the more predictions we can identify and test in any given situation, the more likely we can achieve a solid conclusion. In the end, if a hypothesis is functionally refuted in a conclusive enough fashion, then it is eliminated. This is where the application of the scientific method is most effective. It allows us to establish what could not happen. Each possibility we eliminate in effect adds clarity to the situation. We may not be able to define exactly what happened, but we should be able to define what did not happen. Scientific method is far less effective at proving that a single hypothesis is *the* answer. This process is often referred to as *premise negation*. If used correctly and all viable hypothesis are considered, then as the fictional sleuth Sherlock Holmes commented to his friend Watson, "…when you have eliminated the impossible, whatever remains, however improbable, must be the truth."[2]

In considering this idea of premise negation, a common mistake encountered in CSR occurs when the first hypothesis tested by the analyst is supported. If the analyst simply stops, accepting this "possible" answer, as "the" answer, and fails to consider the other possibilities, then the analysis is incomplete. Each of the possible answers must be tested under equal conditions. Granted, the remaining hypothesis may eventually be eliminated, but it is just as likely that one or more of the remaining hypothesis might survive the test and be supported as well. Once again, depending on the context and data the analyst is working with and the conclusiveness of the predictions made, any number of hypotheses can survive the premise negation process and remain as viable possibilities.

If the predictions we test are conclusive enough, then after testing a given hypothesis, the analyst is left with one of two possibilities. Either the hypothesis is supported by the data, meaning it is possible, or it is rejected and, thus, excluded as a possibility. Whatever the case, the analyst must live with the result no matter how it affects the theory of the hour. It is important to remember that the data ultimately define the conclusion and not the reverse.

The final step in the analysis process is to draw a conclusion from the information examined. In doing so, it is important to remember that nothing is ever 100% certain. The best the analyst can do in any CSR attempt is identify the "best explanation," given the data. This best explanation is based on the information known at the time of the analysis. As discussed in earlier chapters, in CSR we recognize that we never have all the pieces of the puzzle and we must be cognizant that additional information may be discovered in the future that could affect some part of the conclusions drawn. If additional data are subsequently discovered or brought forward, the analyst has a duty to consider if and how that data may affect earlier conclusions.

Using the Event Analysis Worksheet

Many aspects of a reconstruction are straightforward and obvious, so simply following the Event Analysis methodology as described is sufficient to maintain focus and clarity. Consider our example question of: "How did the attacker gain entry into the scene"? If the scene context is an occupied residence where the front door is precariously attached to the door frame by bent hinges, with screws stripped from the wooden frame, the analyst can in the context presented, safely conclude that forced entry was made into the structure. In another context, such as an unoccupied residence where the homeless have been sleeping, the conclusion derived from the door may not be as straight forward. Each incident is different and what is straightforward in one scene might require more in-depth analysis for a scene with a different contextual history. What issues or investigative questions require the use of the worksheet method is a decision best left to the individual analyst, given their specific context.

In some situations, particularly during informal analysis done at the crime scene, simply employing the mnemonic aid of *PhD etc* is more than adequate to keep the analyst within the parameters of scientific method. By considering *PhD etc* mentally, the analyst can move the analysis forward in his mind. The problem associated with this mental exercise of scientific method is that there is no documentation of the process and, thus, no way, other than verbal, to assess whether the method was effectively and adequately applied to the investigative question. Nevertheless, for simple straightforward investigative issues, this is not a significant problem, and a verbal explanation of the effort should be more than adequate to address any questions.

As the complexity of the issue increases, however, or in instances where the analyst is new to the application of scientific method, the situation changes and demands a more formal approach. The Event Analysis worksheet (Figure 4.3 and Figure 4.4) fills this niche. The worksheet forces the analyst through each step of the process and memorializes his effort, setting a foundation for how and why he arrived at any conclusion he made. Once documented, the worksheet is easily reviewed by both peers or an opposing expert and the analyst's efforts become observable, testable, and repeatable, the basic tenants expected of any scientific effort.

Investigative worksheets not only force the analyst along the path of scientific method, but they refine and focus that effort. While evaluating any issue, the analyst will often be confronted with a wealth of information—so much data that at times it will seem overwhelming on a cursory view. This information overload can cause the analyst to lose focus as he bounces from the question at hand to consideration of some newly discovered fact of the incident. As the analyst sifts through the available data, he must identify those facts that are germane and relevant to the IQ being considered. Using the worksheets as a guide, he culls these facts out and then with this refined context, takes on the investigative question at hand (see Figure 4.3 and Figure 4.4).

Event Analysis Worksheet Explained

The example worksheet (Figure 4.3 and Figure 4.4) has nine sections. Each section corresponds to the *PhD etc* formula following the scientific method. In Figure 4.5, the first section highlighted is the worksheet's administrative data. This section identifies the worksheet number, case number, date of analysis, and name of the analyst.

Event Analysis Worksheet (PhD etc.)

Worksheet # _____   **Analyst** _____

Case # _____   **Date** _____

$P =$ **Investigative Question:** _____

Event/Segment Issue
Identify the possible ways the above IQ could have occurred.

A-_____

$h =$ **B-**_____

Data on Specific Event/Segments
$D =$ Identify the various facts which will assist in solving this issue. Include a cross reference to where this information is found in the case
files. *Include only facts and __no inferences in this section__.*

<u>Cross Reference</u>

Expectations/Predictions

$e =$

Figure 4.3 This is the first page of the Event Analysis Worksheet that is used when evaluating complex investigative issues.

The second section, **P** (labeled Investigative Question), is for stating the problem or IQ under consideration (Figure 4.6). The specific question should be entered here. This serves as a ready reference that can be reviewed to ensure focus is maintained. Remember that the only data listed on this form is information relevant to answering this question.

Case #_____

Test

Test predictions for each stated hypothesis against all known information and explain for each hypothesis this tells you.
*Facts as well as inferences **may be included** in this section.*

$t =$ **A-**

$t =$ **B-**

Opinion

State your opinion based upon the analysis of the above data.

$c =$

Figure 4.4 The second page of the Event Analysis Worksheet. This is a two-part worksheet, meaning the answer to the question has only two possible outcomes. Worksheets can be used for three- and four-part questions.

The third section, h (labeled Event/Segment Issue), is where the hypotheses are listed (Figure 4.7). A hypothesis is simply one of the possible answers for the question being considered. In the example worksheet, there are two possibilities, labeled A and B. Worksheets are prepared for two, three, and four possible hypotheses. If there are three possibilities, the worksheet would list them as A, B, and C. If there were four, the worksheet would have A, B, C, and D. For example, if the IQ is: "Was there one attacker or more than one attacker?" then there are only two possibilities and each is written in no preference or order on the form:

A: There was one attacker.
B: There was more than one attacker.

Event Analysis Worksheet *(PhD etc.)*

Worksheet #_____   Analyst _____

Case #_____   Date _____

P = **Investigative Question:**_____

Event/Segment Issue

Identify the possible ways the above IQ could have occurred.

A-_____

h = B-_____

Data on Specific Event/Segments

D = Identify the various facts which will assist in solving this issue. Include a cross reference to where this information is found in the case files. ***Include only facts and no inferences in this section.***

Cross Reference

List what you would expect to find if the hypotheses are true.

e =

Figure 4.5 The top portion (boxed) of the worksheet is used for basic administrative data.

Each of these hypotheses must be analyzed independently. When considering possible hypotheses, only viable possibilities need to be addressed and these are based on the idea of the limited universe and on the context of the scene in question. For example, a spatter pattern in blood might be produced from various mechanisms, including but not limited to gunshot, blunt trauma, expectorate action, and even through some mechanical device, such as a spray bottle filled with blood. However, in the limited universe of the scene in question, if there is no blood-filled spray bottle, this possibility is not viable and requires no effort. A hypothesis is not based on flights of fancy, it must be reasonable and appropriate to the circumstance being considered.

Event Analysis Worksheet (PhD etc.)

Worksheet #_____   Analyst_____
Case #_____   Date_____

P = **Investigative Question:** _____

Event/Segment Issue
Identify the possible ways the above IQ could have occurred.

A-_____

h = B-_____

Data on Specific Event/Segments
D = entify the various facts which will assist in solving this issue. Include across reference to where this information is found in
the case files. *Include only facts and no inferences in this section.*

Cross Reference

Expectations/Predictions

e =

Figure 4.6 The P section (boxed) is used to define the problem or question being considered by the analyst. The question should be posed in as simple and focused a manner as possible. Convoluted questions must be broken down into simpler questions.

The fourth section, D (labeled Data), is where actual facts are listed. This is not intended to be a laundry list of facts from the entire investigation (Figure 4.8). Only facts and data that assist in answering the IQ being analyzed are listed here. This section should not contain inferences or circumstantial information. These facts are the foundation upon which the analysis is based. If the foundation is built on sand (e.g., based on inference) instead of bedrock (e.g., based on hard objective data), the entire analysis is weakened and the conclusions may be called into question.

The fifth section, e (labeled Expectations/Predictions), is where the analysts list what they would expect or predict in the scene if the hypothesis in question were true

Event Analysis Worksheet *(PhD etc.)*

Worksheet #_____   Analyst_____

Case #_____   Date_____

P = **Investigative Question:**_____

Event/Segment Issue

Identify the possible ways the above IQ could have occurred.

A-_____

h =   B-_____

Data on Specific Event/Segments

D =   entify the various facts which will assist in solving this issue.Include across reference to where this information is found in the case files. ***Include only facts and <u>no inferences in this section</u>.***

<u>Cross Reference</u>

Expectations/Predictions

e =

Figure 4.7 The h section (boxed) is used to identify the probable answers to the question, the analyst's hypothesis.

(Figure 4.9). For example, if the hypothesis under analysis was: "Forced entry was used," then this section might include predictions, such as: "I would expect to find broken glass, broken locks or hinges, torn or cut window screens, removed screens, etc."

On page 2 of the worksheet (Figure 4.4), there is an additional space for the case number, which aids in organizing the worksheets when multiple issues are in question.

The seventh section, t (labeled Test A), is where the predictions are compared against the data and which were listed in the prior sections (Figure 4.10). Here the analyst articulates how the various data elements, when considered against the predictions, support or refute the hypothesis in question.

Event Analysis Worksheet (PhD etc.)

Worksheet #_____   Analyst_____

Case #_____   Date_____

$P =$ **Investigative Question:**_____

Event/Segment Issue

Identify the possible ways the above IQ could have occurred.

A-_____

$h =$ **B-**_____

Data on Specific Event/Segments

$D =$ Identify the various facts which will assist in solving this issue. Include across reference to where this information is found in the case files. ***Include only facts and <u>no inferences in this section</u>.***

Cross Reference

Expectations/Predictions

$e =$

Figure 4.8 The D section (boxed) is used to list the specific facts available to the analyst that may assist in answering the investigative question. The analyst sorts through the myriad information present and culls those facts he believes may aid him in his quest.

The eighth section, t (labeled as Test B), is a continuation of comparing the second hypothesis against the facts and predictions (Figure 4.11). Once again the analyst articulates a foundation of why the hypothesis is supported or refuted.

The final ninth section, c (labeled Opinion), is where the analyst states his opinion and the results of this analysis (Figure 4.12). This section should simply state the analyst's opinion. Any justification or foundation for the opinion offered is already described in writing in the preceding sections of the worksheet. If the analyst finds that he is now describing

Event Analysis Worksheet *(PhD etc.)*

Worksheet #_____   **Analyst**_____

Case #_____   **Date**_____

P = **Investigative Question:**_____

Event/Segment Issue

Identify the possible ways the above IQ could have occurred.

A-_____

h = **B-**_____

Data on Specific Event/Segments

D = Identify the various facts which will assist in solving this issue. Include a cross reference to where this information is found in the case files. *Include only facts and* <u>*no inferences in this section.*</u>

<u>*Cross Reference*</u>

List what you would expect to find if the hypotheses are true.

e =

Figure 4.9 The e section (boxed) is used to list the analyst's expectations or predictions regarding the stated hypotheses. Expectation/predications are defined by thinking about the scene and data with a simple "if *this*, then *that*" mindset. Remember nothing just happens; every action has something that precedes it and something that follows it.

additional justification in order to make his point, then he should return to the earlier sections and incorporate that additional information. Figure 4.13 and Figure 4.14 show a case example of a completed event analysis worksheet.

Once completed, the worksheet is not normally used or presented as a report. A written reconstruction report should be prepared that outlines all of the analysis. This report may well refer to the worksheet effort, but the report should be a stand-alone document that summarizes any opinions offered.

Case # _____

<u>Test</u>

Test predictions for each stated hypothesis against all known information and explain for each hypothesis what this tells you.
Facts as well as inferences <u>may be included</u> in this section.

t = **A-**

t = **B-**

<u>Opinion as to The Best Explanation:</u>

State your opinion based upon the analysis of the above data.

c =

Figure 4.10 The first t section (boxed) is used to discuss the expectations and predications for the "A" hypothesis or possibility that was listed in the h section. Here the analyst considers all of the predictions listed in the e section associated with that hypothesis and decides if they are supported or refuted by the scene and data.

Statement Analysis Using the Worksheets

The primary focus up to this point for using investigative worksheets has been to resolve significant investigative questions that arise from the crime scene analysis. Testimonial evidence is considered after completing the analysis and is refuted or corroborated based on the conclusions drawn from the scene. The formal crime scene analysis is accomplished after all forensic work is complete, but can these techniques be used at earlier stages of the investigation or can we direct these techniques toward a specific statement presented to the

Case #_____

Test

Test predictions for each stated hypothesis against all known information and explain for each hypothesis what this tells you.
Facts as well as inferences __may be included__ in this section.

$t = $ **A-**

$t = $ **B-**

Opinion as to The Best Explanation:
State your opinion based upon the analysis of the above data.

$c = $

Figure 4.11 The second t section (boxed) is used to discuss the expectations and predications for the "B" hypothesis or possibility.

investigators? The answer is yes. One functional way that crime scene analysis can aid the investigation is through statement analysis. Statements from witnesses, suspects, or victims are, in effect, theories of what happened and as theories they can be evaluated in and of themselves on the worksheets. In considering any statement, like any theory, they may be correct in certain aspects (truthful) while diverging in other aspects (false). Avinoam Sapir calls the basis of this process of validating statements the Watermelon Theory.[3]

To understand the watermelon theory, consider that in any statement provided, particularly those presented by offending parties, rarely do individuals simply make up an entire story. What they tend to do is weave a story of fact intermixed with some fiction. They may leave out certain actions, make claims of actions that did not occur, or change the sequence

Case #_____

Test

Test predictions for each stated hypothesis against all known information and explain for each hypothesis this tells you.
*Facts as well as inferences **may be included** in this section.*

$t =$ **A-**

$t =$ **B-**

Opinion

State your opinion based upon the analysis of the above data.

$c =$

Figure 4.12 The *c* section (boxed) is where the analysts list their conclusions about the question based on all of the preceding effort.

of what happened, all in order to make their position more palatable to the interrogator and less culpable. As Sapir explains, the interrogator approaches the statement much as one does a watermelon. The vast majority of a watermelon is edible, but we are always on the lookout for the seeds—something we don't want to eat. We should approach any statement and confessions in a similar manner. Much of what we are told is likely true and accurate, but we are always on the lookout for the statement's seeds; those points where the statement giver has added, removed, or changed the sequence of what happened. The investigative worksheets can be used for statement analysis, comparing what a person said or claimed against the scene context and the physical evidence (Figure 4.15 and Figure 4.16).

Case:
Date:
Analyst:

P

State Investigative Question: Is Battle Damage Assessment Victim # 18 standing (e.g. fleeing) when initially shot?

h

Define Hypothesis 1
BDA 18 is standing when initially shot.

Define Hypothesis 2
BDA 18 is not standing when shot.

d

Define Data to Resolve the Investigative Question

Defect in right cheek, consistent with entry GSW	Defect left cheek, nose area, exit
Directional spatter into left rear shoulder (B- F, R-L)	Large exit left frontal lobe, with brain ejection
Brain matter restricted to large pool beneath V	Brain material, left collar inside
Spatter event W-E from pool toward feet	Right arm overlies, with no spatter
Large pool beneath the V	No disassociated spatter or brain material
Blood flow R-L from probable entry	Large volume flow right ear across forehead
2 Saturation stains, one a round right outer thigh	No blood flow beneath the Adam's apple
No blood onto left back of neck.	Blood flow R-L on left cheek, below ear
BDA 19 overlies V, with head wound close to saturations	Probable spatter on right side of victim
No disrupted dirt below boots	No blood or wounds evident on V's back
Lack of flows beneath obvious injuries	No brain material ejected onto left shoulder

Figure 4.13 A case example of the first page of a completed Event Analysis Worksheet.

Investigative Question: Is BDA 18 standing when shot?

e   State Predictions for Hypothesis 1

- Initial wound capable of incapacitation (drops V in place)
- Blood flows consistent with generally upright position
- Spatter/brain matter ejected into the scene, disassociated to final position
- Spatter ejected away from body and appendages consistent with upright position
- Drips onto lower clothing, shoes, hand or arms.
- Dirt marks on knees or buttocks consistent with falling
- Wound on posterior aspect (shooter to the rear of V)
- Dirt disturbances when shoes impact final position

t   Test Predictions by Identifying Information Relationships for Hypothesis 1

All brain matter is isolated to the pool, none spattered onto the left shoulder, indicating the frontal lobe wound occurs in the final position, excluding it as a first shot

There is no other incapacitating injury except the right cheek/nose. This wound creates directional spatter on the left shoulder, indicating the V's head was turned left somewhat, placing the shooter to the right of the V

This wound also produces a flow pattern, but the flow moves R–L and not downward, thus the victim was not upright when he received this wound

All flows on the victim show sideways motion

Injuries that were clearly free flowing did not bleed onto the neck, below the Adam's apple

There is no ejected spatter disassociated to V18, except the spatter on V19 (deposited while V19 was in his final position). This excludes any of these spatter as occurring while V18 was in a standing position

There are no drips onto the lower clothing suggesting a standing position

There are no disturbances in the dirt beneath the Vs shoes suggesting a standing position

There are no evident wounds that enter from the posterior aspect of the body

The right cheek, left nose wound has no clear reason for incapacitating the victim.

Hypothesis 1   Refuted

e   State Predictions for Hypothesis 2

- Blood flows consistent with other than standing position
- Lack of disassociated spatter and ejected material (all material in or around final position)
- All ejected spatter suggesting low position
- Hands in a neutral position
- Inter-related spatter on various aspects of V's clothing

t   Test Predictions by Identifying Information Relationships for Hypothesis 2

All evidence suggests frontal lobe wound is second, cheek injury is first, but no downward flow from the cheek injury. The immediate flow is R–L

V had mobility subsequent to his final wounding, the right arm was not in the final position when spatter was ejected L–R and backward toward his right side

A left side down position (based on flows) would result in the reposition of V18 towards V19's bloody head, accounting for contact stains on the right thigh

This would also expose and explain the spatter event deposited on V18's right side, associating it to the frontal lobe injury

All brain matter ejected backward from the head, consistent with the evident spatter event

Flow from the left cheek, flows R–L and never downwards, showing he was not in an upright position after receiving the injury

Heavy staining and flows move across the victim's face R–L and onto the upper neck, but not downward

There are no disruptions in the dirt suggesting V18 fell to his current position

Hypothesis 2   Supported

C   State Opinion as to the Best Explanation:

V18 is not standing when shot.

Figure 4.14   A case example of the second page of a completed Event Analysis Worksheet.

Event Analysis Worksheet *(PhD etc.)*

Worksheet# 1   **Analyst: T. Bevel**
Case# 96-32

$P =$ **Investigative Question:** ***Is the intruder's resting body position consistent with the husband's statement?***

Event/Segment Issue

Identify the possible ways the above IQ could have happened.

$h =$ **A** - *The intruder's resting body position <u>is</u> consistent with the husband's statement*
       B - *The intruder's resting body position is <u>not</u> consistent with the husband' statement*

Data on Specific Event/Segments

$D =$ Identify the various facts which will assist in solving this issue. Include a cross reference to where this information is found in the case files

Include only facts and no inferences in this section

	Cross Reference
01 *"There was a white male leaning and kneeling over her from behind striking her in the head with a hammer"*	*Rpt 3 p.3*
02 *When the husband was "3' to 4' from this white male, the white male was beating Mrs. Winger, the intruder raised his head up and looked at Mr. Winger...he fired his .45 semi-automatic at the subject"*	*Rpt 3 p.4*
03 *"He thought he struck him in the face or the head, but he was not sure he seen some blood fly and then the subject fell of of his wife and fell onto the floor on his back."*	*Rpt 3 p.4*
04 *Cast-off blood on wall beside female victim's body from floor to ceiling*	*Photo 6*
05 *Cast-off blood on ceiling traveling toward wall*	*Photo 8*
06 *Intruder has one bullet entry wound to left forehead*	*Photo 4, 22*
07 *Intruder has one bullet exit wound to top left side of head*	*Photo 5*
08 *Intruder has one bullet entry wound to top of head, no exit*	*Photo 5*
09 *One spent projectile through carpet by intruder's blood pool*	*Photo 39*
10 *Two separate blood pools by intruder, one under his head and one to the side of the intruder*	*Photo 9*

$e =$ *List what you would expect to find if the hypothesis is true. If this, then that*

Cross Reference

I would predict the blood cast-off will be down the wall as the intruder faces the hallway
There will be no stippling on or around the first wound
I would expect the intruder to be found on his back with his feet pointed toward the female victim
I would expect cast-off blood to travel along the wall and not from floor toward ceiling
I would expect cast-of blood on the ceiling to travel along the wall and not toward the wall
I would expect one bullet wound with no stippling to still be in intruder and one entry with an exit to be found in the carpet near intruder's body
I would predict there will be one blood pool under the intruder's head.

Figure 4.15 A completed two-part Event Analysis Worksheet. The question considered is whether an intruder's body position is consistent with a witness's statement. The second page of the worksheet is shown in Figure 4.14.

Worksheet# 1
Case# 96-32

Test
Test predictions for each stated hypothesis against all known information and explain for each hypothesis what this tells you.
Facts as well as inferences may be included in this section.

$t =$ A-

> *If the intruder after looking at the husband ducked his head, looking toward the floor at the time the husband shot, and if this is the first wound, it is consistent with the husband's statement as to position of intruder behind his wife for the first shot*

$t =$ B-

> *If the forehead is the first shot, the bullet upon exit would not be found in the carpet in the area where the intruder's head ended up on the floor. If the intruder is behind the victim and striking the right side of the victim's head, the cast-of blood on the ceiling would be highly improbable. If the intruder fell off the victim his body momentum should carry him beside and close to the victim. If falling backward his feet should be close to the victim and toward the victim. Instead his feet are away from the victim. I would not expect to find two separate blood pools by the intruder, but there are two separate blood pools consistent with the intruder being rolled over after the first blood pool formed in the carpet*

Opinion as to The Best Explanation:
State your opinion based upon the analysis of the above data.

$C =$ The intruder's resting body position is not consistent with the husband's statement

Figure 4.16 The second page of the completed Event Analysis Worksheet shown in Figure 4.15.

References

1. Haag, L.C. 2006. *Shooting Incident Reconstruction*, Burlington, MA: Elsevier Press, p. 8.
2. Doyle, Sir Arthur Conan, 1890. *The Sign of the Four*,
3. Sapir, A., Statement Analysis.

Understanding Crime Scene Protocols and Their Effect on Reconstruction

5

Introduction

As discussed in Chapter 2, there is no question that crime scene investigators conduct informal crime scene analysis on scene. This informal analysis guides the early investigative effort and leads to the collection of the available evidence. However, crime scene processing and formal crime scene analysis are two distinct actions and should not be confused. Crime scene processing is a methodical evaluation and documentation of the scene. It involves six basic activities, which will ultimately define if any level of crime scene analysis is possible. These activities include:

1. Assessing the scene
2. Observing the scene
3. Documenting the scene
4. Searching the scene
5. Collecting evidence
6. Analyzing specific scene aspects (e.g., bloodstain or trajectory analysis)

These six activities are conducted in the general order as listed, which involves doing the least intrusive actions first, followed by the more intrusive ones. The express purpose of taking these actions and following the sequence is to recover as much physical evidence from the scene as possible, in as functional and as usable a condition as possible, and to document fully through notes, sketches, and photographs, the conditions found on scene. From this effort, data in the form of scene context and physical evidence are produced. These data serve as the basis of any formal crime scene analysis.

The Importance of the Crime Scene Investigator

For many years the role of crime scene investigation was often taken for granted in some organizations. In these organizations, investigators were thrown into the position with little or no training. They learned by their failures or were simply taught a "this is the way we've always done it and this is the way we'll always do it" mindset. If one could point to a moment in time when this attitude changed, it would perhaps be the murder trial of O. J. Simpson in 1995. In some instances appropriately and in other instances not so appropriately, Simpson's defense counsel attacked every aspect of the crime scene investigation. The notoriety and circus-like ambiance of this trial gave it a life of its own, and every aspect of testimony was plastered on television screens throughout the United States and the world. Police supervisors and crime scene investigators took notice. They watched as the Los Angeles Police Department (LAPD) crime scene investigators were attacked, and they saw lawyers making claims about forensics skills. Many felt "better the LAPD than me," but in that recognition, organizations took a hard look at their own capabilities and started to change. It became routine to hear crime scene investigators talking about organizational change in procedures and claiming it was because of the Simpson trial. We should be clear, appropriate and defined crime scene methodologies existed long before the O.J. Simpson trial; these ideas were well published and many organizations of excellence existed. But, the Simpson trial got so much attention that it forced crime scene investigation across the board into the twenty-first century. No one wanted to be the next organization ridiculed in a televised circus act. That force for change continues to this day. Certainly the critics remain, claiming that police organizations do not understand or achieve their lofty goal. Nevertheless, crime scene investigation is receiving far more attention than it ever did before.

It should not be surprising that crime scene investigation gets this critical attention from both police supervisors and outside sources. Without proper and appropriate crime scene techniques, everyone's role in the criminal justice system is hampered. Without proper collection of evidence, forensic scientists cannot do their job. If the scene context is disturbed before proper documentation, that can affect the decisions of the medical examiner. Lawyers cannot argue functional theories of what happened or in what order things happened if they don't have valid data on which to test those theories. All of this can leave the jury in the lurch, scratching their heads when they are asked to decide the truth of a matter.

Proper crime scene investigation is the very foundation of a functional criminal justice system. Lawyers certainly love their testimonial evidence, but in the back of their minds they now understand that physical evidence speaks louder and more convincingly. One has to wonder why it took lawyers so long to wake up to this issue. This lesson was first made by Hans Gross as early as 1900. Gross made no bones about the fact that the crime scene offered the best evidence.[1] Putting your money on testimonial evidence is a bad bet every time. The application of formal crime scene analysis is recognition of this fact and without good crime scene processing technique, formal crime scene analysis cannot be accomplished.

What makes "good technique" in crime scene investigation? First and foremost it is knowledge and its proper application. The crime scene technicians must understand what they are doing and why they are doing it. The technician must know the underlying forensics, what a crime lab can do with various types of evidence, and in what condition the evidence must be recovered in order to do such an examination. Just as important, the technician must understand that the sequence of action he takes at the scene affects the overall result. Arbitrary or haphazard action at the scene can have disastrous results.

The crime scene technician must also have the proper tools and skills to put his knowledge into practical action. Knowing that good crime scene photographs are required is one thing; producing them is another. The technician not only needs an appropriate camera system, but he has to be able to use it. Knowing that trajectory analysis is possible is great, but if the technician doesn't have or use a trajectory kit, then what value is that knowledge?

Another critical skill is a methodical approach. There is a clear underlying order that drives the crime scene technician's action. The purpose of the crime scene investigation is to capture the scene context and condition *in situ,* or as found. Every action of the crime scene investigator has the potential to alter that condition, thus every action is taken in an appropriate order to preclude unnecessary alteration. Methodology ensures that all aspects of the scene are dealt with in a proper and functional order. Inherent in understanding methodology is the idea of flexibility. Every crime scene is unique; each comes with its own issues and complexities. If the crime scene investigator approaches each scene with a mindset of rote compliance to a checklist, he will ultimately fail. When scene unique situations are encountered, the crime scene investigator must be able to see through the issue and resolve it. Using his knowledge of both forensics and basic scene methodology, he finds a solution that allows him to achieve his ultimate purpose: the collection of the evidence in the best possible condition.

The final ingredient of "good" scene technique is coordinated effort. Crime scene teams, homicide detectives, and emergency responders, such as firefighters and emergency medical technicians, have to coordinate their effort. Everyone has a role, everyone has a purpose, and at times those purposes may be at odds with one another. Coordination of activity ensures that individuals are not making poor decisions independently that everyone else will ultimately have to live with.

How does one judge good scene technique? First and foremost there must be documentation. Five photographs of a murder scene or failing to take photographs of critical evidence won't cut it. The documentation produced must show the actual scene conditions, validating the crime scene integrity. If the documentation fails in this regard, then the processing was for naught. Whatever methods are employed by the crime scene team, those methods must consider and eliminate as effectively as possible three crime scene integrity issues. These issues include:

- Addition of postincident artifacts to the scene
- Movement of material or evidence in the scene
- Destruction of evidence in the scene

It is impossible to move or interact in a crime scene without causing some alteration. The addition of postincident artifacts occurs from various behaviors. Footprints or fingerprints created by police, cigarette butts deposited by visiting officials, or bloodstains created while moving a victim all have the potential to become "evidence." If these postincident artifacts are not eliminated or at least recognized, that "evidence" can alter our understanding of the scene. Postincident artifacts become red herrings, which can unintentionally mislead everyone involved or become something that lawyers may use later to intentionally mislead a jury.

Good scene technique demands eliminating the unnecessary movement of material before scene documentation is complete. Movement of items in the scene alters the scene context. Simple actions, such as taking a weapon from an individual's hand and placing it in a safer location, changes the way others view that scene. Lifesaving, officer safety, or the simple inability to access the scene can all impact this consideration. Whenever possible, things are not moved in the scene until after their original position is fully documented.

Eliminating the destruction of physical evidence is critical. Movement of evidence alters its context, but if our actions destroy the evidence, we lose everything. The placement of the body into a body bag before the bloodstained clothing is documented will effectively destroy evidence. Crime scene investigators that tromp through dust prints or dew prints in avenues of entry or exit, effectively destroy evidence. Almost any action taken while on scene has the potential to destroy what is there. The technician must consider what *may be in* the scene, carefully observe *what is there,* and ultimately take steps to prevent its loss.

In terms of preserving the scene, initial responding officers are a critical link in maintaining scene integrity. If the initial responding officers are not trained or concerned with scene integrity, nothing can undo the resulting damage, no matter how skilled the crime scene team or technician may be. It is important to understand that preserving evidence is not the initial responding officer's sole purpose on scene; the responsibilities of the responding officer are multifaceted. In the utter chaos so often encountered in the initial moments after arriving on scene, doing one's job is no simple matter. If the initial responding officers are not taught how to juggle contradicting concerns, crime scene integrity will suffer. Developing crime scene procedures then is not limited to training and coordinating the efforts of the crime scene investigator; all of the critical players including the initial responding officers must be involved.

Role of the Initial Responding Officer

The role of the initial responding officer is clearly multifaceted and a difficult role to accomplish effectively. It involves:

- Documenting the source and content of initial information provided.
- Preventing the officers from becoming causalities themselves.
- Providing for the care and safety of individuals found on scene.
- Securing and controlling the scene, including anyone present there.
- Transferring responsibility to the appropriate authority (e.g., the crime scene team).

Information that comes to the attention of initial responding officers, as well as investigative team members, must be appropriately documented. In the initial chaos of the scene, bits of information will be forthcoming from various sources, such as witnesses, other first-responders, and even those directly involved in the incident. These involved individuals may offer information in one version on scene and then later alter what they claim they knew or said. All of this information can be critical in the long-term investigation. Tidbits of information that are reported may have been misperceived by the witnesses themselves or misunderstood by the investigative team, leading to the creation of red herrings. These red herrings become clues that can use up investigative resources and mislead the investigation. Knowing what was said and who said it will help resolve these situations at later stages of the investigations.

The initial responding officers, as well as the crime scene team, must always evaluate the scene from an officer safety perspective. Are there natural or manmade hazards on scene that may affect operations? If so, how can they be mitigated to reduce the risk involved? Officers don't just rush into a scene. They have to look, consider the situation, and then act accordingly.

A significant issue for arriving officers is caring for injured parties. This is typically a greater consideration for the initial responding officers, but depending on the circumstances, even the crime scene team can be drawn into this issue. Lifesaving always takes precedence over evidence integrity. One of the most difficult juggling feats expected of the initial responding officer is curbing emergency medical and firefighter enthusiasm in order to preserve physical evidence. This simply isn't possible in every circumstance, but the officers have a responsibility to try. To do this, officers not directly involved in lifesaving can be directed to document initial scene conditions or preserve evidence that is subject to alteration by lifesaving actions.

Securing the crime scene and controlling those found in it has always been an expectation of the initial responding officer. The officers seek out primary focal points, look for secondary scenes, and any natural entry and exit points to the scene. These areas are brought under control by creating a perimeter, which is controlled within the limits of the situation. The express purpose of this action is to prevent damage to any evidence found in these locations. Another consideration of control is dealing with those who are in the scene. Victims, witnesses, or suspects may be present along with a throng of onlookers. While trying to ensure crime scene integrity, the officer has to deal with this group, preventing those who have no business from interfering, all the while keeping track of those who may be important. In the initial moments at the scene, the chaos encountered may prevent the officer from effectively controlling anything. As more assistance arrives, control becomes a significant concern; crime scene barriers are erected and involved individuals are segregated and identified. Once the crime scene team arrives, responsibility for the scene passes to them and crime scene processing begins in earnest. The bottom line in all of this is that the efforts of the initial responding officer set the stage for successful crime scene processing. They are a critical link for scene integrity.

Incorporating the Basic Crime Scene Activities into a Crime Scene Protocol

It is imperative to state that there is no one right way of processing a crime scene. Crime scene protocols may differ from organization to organization, but each will involve, in an appropriate sequence, the six basic activities of the crime scene investigator. These six activities are (1) assessing the scene, (2) observing the scene, (3) documenting the scene, (4) searching the scene, (5) collecting the evidence, and (6) conducting on-scene analysis. Each activity and its sequential application serve the express purpose of capturing the entire crime scene context and recovering as much evidence as possible.

Assessing

Assessment actions by the crime scene team serve many purposes and set the stage for subsequent action by the team. Assessment is the first action taken by the team, but it is a continuous action. The crime scene team constantly assesses the scene as processing proceeds, adjusting their approach when necessary. Assessment involves:

- Determining the full scope of the crime scene
- Ensuring crime scene integrity and control

- Ensuring any search warrants are correct and signed
- Developing an appropriate team approach
- Determining an appropriate search technique
- Ensuring the safety of the crime scene team

Although the initial responding officers will have established some form of perimeter based on their own assessment, once the crime scene team arrives they reconsider the circumstances. Using their knowledge and experience, they evaluate the scene to determine if all appropriate areas have been brought under control. This includes searching for secondary scenes or additional avenues of entry or exit that were overlooked.

In addition to considering if all the scene or scenes have been identified, the crime scene team also considers the level of control that is in place and adjusts as necessary. Initial officers usually establish a single perimeter that isolates the primary scene from onlookers. The crime scene team will likely create a second perimeter within the first in an effort to further isolate the actual crime scene. This prevents police and other emergency responders who have a purpose on scene but are not directly involved in crime scene processing, from arbitrarily entering or damaging the scene further. When defining access points for the various perimeters, the team considers the avenues of entry and exit used by perpetrators, the level of media exposure an access point may provide, as well as a basic consideration of what avenues are available (e.g., there may be a single functional entry point to a scene).

During assessment, the crime scene team also consider how they will compose the team and what search methods they will use. Considerations include whether the scene consists of a single location or perhaps multiple scenes, the order of specific examinations that may be necessary, the availability of resources to accomplish those examinations, and the physical size of the scene. The size of the scene, the lighting, and the environmental conditions present can all drive the decision of which search technique is used by the crime scene investigators. Flexibility during the assessment stage is a key concern, as any one of these considerations may force the hand of a crime scene supervisor to adjust his standard crime scene methodology.

Improper assessment can create havoc for the crime scene analysis. Information and evidence may be lost as a result of poor decisions made at this juncture in the processing methodology.

Observing

A critical quality of a crime scene investigator is the ability to observe. Observation begins immediately on scene, and good observation skills are used throughout crime scene processing. But, before taking any significant intrusive action, such as trying to enter the scene to photograph, sketch, or collect items, the crime scene investigator stops and takes an in-depth look. The investigator carefully examines the scene, observing details and content that may be altered by subsequent scene processing (e.g., the order of bedding on top of the victim) or details that may be lost as a function of time (e.g., ice cubes in a glass, the coagulated condition of a blood pool).

We want to be perfectly clear that observing is a distinct function, not just something the investigator does while assessing or preparing to move forward. The best approach is to find a vantage point on the perimeter of the scene and simply stop and look. The investigator should describe and document through notes or audio recording everything he sees. This act of observation takes only a few minutes, but it will pay major dividends. By taking this action, small, important details are observed by the crime scene investigator, details that might otherwise be missed and never recognized or captured in the documentation stage.

Observation by the crime scene team is absolutely essential to the crime scene analysis. If an item is missed as a function of poor observing skills, its context is lost to the analysis. Granted, some aspect of the item may be captured inadvertently in a photograph of another item, allowing its consideration in some fashion. But, that is not the same as knowing the item existed in the first place and purposefully describing and documenting what it does or does not tell us about the scene.

Documenting

Documenting the scene involves the creation of photographs, video recordings, and sketches that show the full and complete context of the scene as found by the investigative team. It also includes the notes prepared during the initial scene observations, as well as subsequent reports created to synopsize the crime scene team's efforts. Thus, the various aspects of documentation have an order and sequence as well.

The crime scene investigator observes before he enters to take detailed photographs; that way he knows what he needs to capture in the photographs. Intrusive actions, such as sketching, are taken only after photographs of the scene are created. Order and purpose drive the investigator's behavior; nothing is done out of sequence without a reason.

To capture the scene detail in photographs, the crime scene investigator creates three basic types of photographs: overall photographs, evidence establishing photographs, and close-up photographs. Overall photos are taken immediately upon arrival at the scene. They serve to capture the condition of the scene before any additional alteration can occur. Whatever the technique used, overall photographs will have overlapping coverage showing the entire expanse of the scene. They are not created to capture details (e.g., small items of evidence are not likely to be evident), but rather the overall context of the scene (e.g., doors open or closed, placement of furniture, and larger items of evidence) (Figure 5.1 and Figure 5.2). Overall photographs help establish crime scene integrity. After assessing the scene and making their observations, more detailed photographs are taken to capture all of the scene context and evidence. This effort will produce close-up photographs of the evidence, but just as critical is the evidence-establishing photograph. The purpose of the evidence-establishing photograph is to show where the evidence is in the scene. This photograph is taken in a way that frames the evidence along with a known landmark in the scene (Figure 5.3). Without the evidence-establishing photograph, the viewer is often lost with no way of knowing where the item depicted in the close-up photograph is. This is particularly true of items that are small or very similar in appearance. Examples include small bloodstains or shell casings deposited on similar surfaces. The purpose of the close-up photograph is to show details of specific items of evidence (e.g., a shell casing on the floor) or scene context (e.g., the layering of the bed linen) (Figure 5.4). These photographs document the conditions found by the crime scene team. Producing both evidence-establishing and evidence close-up photographs requires the crime scene technician move throughout the scene, but if done carefully this action is not intrusive and will not alter the scene context.

Figure 5.1 An example of an overall photograph. Its express purpose is to capture the initial conditions observed by the crime scene investigator. (From Gardner, R.M. 2003. *Practical Crime Scene Processing and Investigation*, Boca Raton, FL: Taylor & Francis. With permission.)

Figure 5.2 Another overall photograph. Note that on the tile floor to the left of the chair is an object. It may or may not be evident that this is a bullet casing. Overall photographs rarely capture details about specific objects. Evidence close-up photographs are used for that purpose. (From Gardner, R.M. 2003. *Practical Crime Scene Processing and Investigation*, Boca Raton, FL: Taylor & Francis. With permission.)

Figure 5.3 An evidence-establishing photograph is used to transition the viewer from the overall photograph to any close-up photographs taken of specific items of evidence. In this establishing shot, we can now make out the bullet casing. The photo is framed with the chair, desk, rug, and tile in such a way that by looking back at Figure 5.2, there is no question as to where in the scene this item is. (From Gardner, R.M. 2003. *Practical Crime Scene Processing and Investigation*, Boca Raton, FL: Taylor & Francis. With permission.)

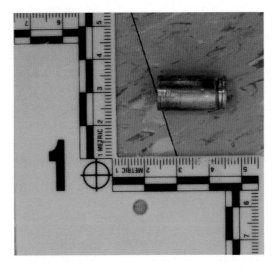

Figure 5.4 A close-up photograph of the bullet casing shown in Figure 5.3. The purpose of the close-up photograph is to show details about a specific item of evidence. Using the three basic photographs (overall, evidence establishing, and close-up), the context and condition of this item is fully documented. Once collected, additional close-up photographs of hidden sides of the evidence may be necessary as well. (From Gardner, R.M. 2003. *Practical Crime Scene Processing and Investigation*, Boca Raton, FL: Taylor & Francis. With permission.)

One concern in taking these photographs is to never replace an item of evidence that was moved and then present the replaced condition as the "original" condition. Once an item is moved for whatever reason, it is not replaced for documentation purposes. If an item, such as a weapon, is removed for safety or had to be collected to prevent alteration, an effective response is to place a photo placard back into its approximate position. Make the appropriate notes as to why it was removed and continue with normal processing efforts. Replacing and representing the "replaced" position as the original condition is not acceptable.

After photographing the scene, the next step it to sketch or map the scene. Sketching itself doesn't require any intrusive action on the part of the crime scene investigator. A sketch is a two-dimensional, diagrammatic representation of the scene (Figure 5.5). Sketching can be accomplished from the perimeter of the scene, much as observation was. It should include all pertinent scene details, depicted as accurately as possible in order to be of value (Figure 5.6). However, a sketch without supporting details, such as specific distances and size of objects, has limited value. In major cases, sketching is accompanied by crime scene mapping. Mapping the scene entails intrusive action by the crime scene team. Mapping serves to identify specifically where items depicted on the sketch are. Mapping involves the investigator moving in and around the evidence and measuring distances from the evidence to various objects. Items of evidence are "fixed" using a variety of mapping methods. These include the use of Total Stations, digital survey devices, or more traditional measuring techniques, such as triangulation, rectangular coordinates, or the baseline technique. In effect, the item of evidence is measured using one of these techniques and its physical position defined in the room or scene. In terms of mapping activity, the position of evidence is measured first and major scene details last. Scene details, such as lengths or heights of walls, doors, and windows, or the size of furniture and other objects, won't change. An item of evidence, however, can easily be displaced while trying to measure these unchangeable scene details. Document the placement of the evidence and other objects of interest first, then obtain the other details. This prevents inadvertently losing scene context and helps preserve scene integrity.

From the perspective of crime scene analysis, the information documented in photographs and by sketching and mapping the scene plays a significant role. What will or will not be in question at trial isn't always known at the time of the scene processing. When issues arise at later stages of the investigation or some claim is made regarding what did or did not happen on scene, small seemingly insignificant details captured in the scene documentation may suddenly play a major role in resolving the issue. Crime scene documentation must capture the entire scene context, not just what the investigator feels is important at that moment.

Searching

The act of searching a scene is very intrusive, taken only after the primary scene context is documented. The function of any search is to ensure that all evidence and details are noted. There are numerous search techniques (e.g., circle, strip, grid, and zone) and each has a place or circumstance for which it is best suited. Typically, the method of search is determined by the crime scene supervisor during the assessment phase, based on the particular circumstances of that scene. The manner in which the search is performed ultimately determines if all of the evidence at the scene is recovered. As discussed, critical observation plays a role throughout processing and is particularly important during any search.

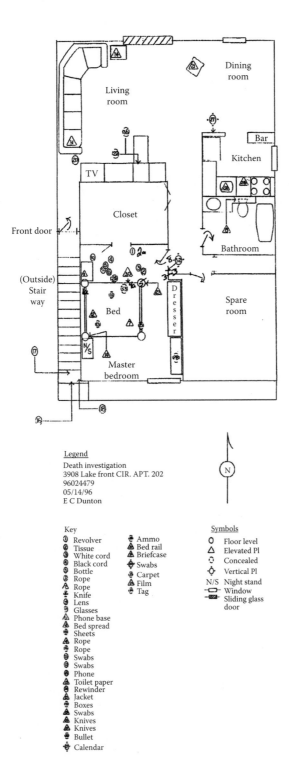

Figure 5.5 A typical crime scene sketch is designed to depict the scene from a bird's-eye view, showing the overall context of the scene as well as the location of all significant items of evidence. The sketch is often backed up with crime scene mapping details, data regarding the exact location of the various items.

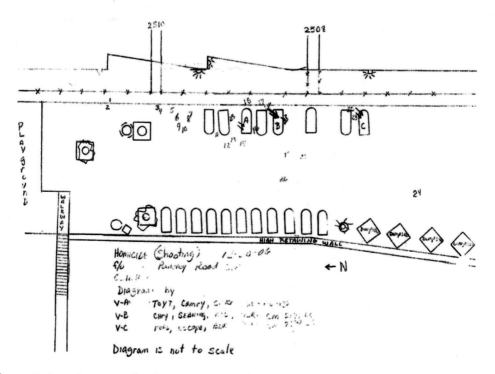

Figure 5.6 In this example of a crime scene sketch, all looks well initially. It is, however, a sketch associated to a shooting scene in which the victim's position was completely left off. The victim and his car were all positioned just to the right of the last dumpster depicted. A sketch that fails to capture pertinent data is of limited value and the position of a homicide victim is generally considered pertinent.

Poorly planned and performed searches have the potential to miss evidence and that will have a detrimental effect on the crime scene analysis. Not every item of evidence is immediately observable to the crime scene investigator. Items may be found beneath, behind, inside of other items or simply in positions where easy observation for whatever reason is not possible. The crime scene searches (and they are conducted in numerous iterations) ensure that all evidence is located and nothing is missed.

Collection

Knowing that evidence is on scene is one thing; collecting it in a usable fashion is another. Failing to properly collect an item in a usable form can prevent its subsequent use or limit its use in the crime scene analysis. Crime scene analysts rely on the scientific examination of evidence to provide more refined data. Knowing that a substance is blood is all well and good, but knowing whose blood it is is clearly of greater significance. Collection efforts must be accomplished with the forensic scientist in mind, securing the evidence in the most usable fashion possible. Collection, of course, is a very intrusive action. Once collected from the scene, the context of an item is altered forever. Thus, collection of items is taken only after scene documentation. The only exception is in the case of fragile items of evidence. Fragile evidence is anything that is prone to significant alteration on scene, as scene processing unfolds. Examples include a shoe mark in dirt as a storm is about to break, or the presence of a small fiber on the floor in the scene. If no action is taken to collect or preserve these items, they will be lost. In the case of fragile evidence, the crime scene team doesn't simply ignore the documentation efforts; they are simply taken out of sequence to whatever extent is possible, before collecting the fragile item.

In terms of crime scene analysis, the crime scene investigators knowledge of general forensics is critical. The investigator can't be an expert in every field, but he must know what kind of evidence is possible in any given scene, as well as knowing in what condition the crime lab wants that evidence collected. Authors, such as Chisum and Turvey, have suggested that crime scene investigators are just bagging and tagging things; this simply is not the case.[2] To be successful themselves and to make the forensic scientist successful in the endeavor, the crime scene technician must have and apply an underlying knowledge of forensics.

On-Scene Analysis

Not all analysis is best accomplished at the lab. On-scene analysis considerations include examining trajectories of bullets or defining an area of origin in bloodstain pattern analysis. It can also include activities like enhancing bloodstain patterns or large scale processing of surfaces with various chemicals for fingerprints. On-scene analysis is always intrusive and is accomplished only after normal items of evidence are documented and collected. When the on-scene analysis nets new information or evidence (e.g., shows a specific bullet trajectory or locates a chemically enhanced fingerprint), the context of that information must be documented with photographs and, if appropriate, the new evidence added to the sketch. At any point in the scene processing, the crime scene team should be prepared to stop when they encounter new evidence and return to an earlier stage of processing to play catch up. This process of "going back" ensures that the context of the new evidence or information is documented fully. In the case of on-scene analysis, no matter what its outcome (whether new evidence was discovered or not), the effort should be documented outlining what, where, and how it was done. This prevents lawyers from making fanciful claims later about police destroying "the real" evidence.

In terms of crime scene analysis, a failure to conduct on-scene analysis can certainly limit the context of the information available to the crime scene analyst. For example, a bullet trajectory in a car can always be examined after-the-fact at the police impound lot. The trajectory in the car will still provide information of value, but the physical position of the vehicle at the scene and its surrounding environment provide far more detail about what was or was not possible. Concerns of the vehicle's elevation and orientation, the relationship of additional surrounding objects, or the vehicle's backdrop all provide specific and important relationships when considered with the trajectory. Much of that detail can be lost once the car is moved off scene.

Summary

Proper crime scene processing is the key to crime scene analysis. Without proper scene examination, details of what was at the scene, where it was at, and in what condition it was found cannot be answered. Formal crime scene analysis relies on the quality and content of the crime scene documentation. It is only through the crime scene documentation that the analyst can establish the scene conditions and prove to the jury that the facts the analyst considered were the actual conditions. The forensic scientist cannot aid the crime scene analyst unless items are properly collected and secured for subsequent analysis. Items are found and collected only through proper crime scene investigation techniques.

No single individual's efforts have a greater impact on the end result of crime scene analysis than the crime scene technician's. Proper crime scene processing technique is anything but some random "bag it and tag it" approach. The crime scene technician has to have a clear understanding of evidence and forensics; he must approach the scene using a methodical process that is designed to capture as much scene context as possible. Just the same, he must be flexible enough in that approach to meet the unique conditions found at different scenes. All of this demands that the crime scene investigator fully understand the reasoning behind what he is doing and be competent in his mission. Nothing can harm an investigation more than poor crime scene technique and, unfortunately, nothing can undo poor crime scene technique. Crime scene processing is a one-stop shop; it must be done right the first time because there are no second chances.

References

1. Gross, H. 1924. *System der Kriminalistic*, as translated in *Criminal Investigation: A Practical Textbook*, Adam, J.C., ed., London: Sweet and Maxwell Ltd., p. 38.
2. Chisum, J., and B. Turvey. 2007. *Crime Reconstruction*, London: Elsevier Academic Press.

Applying Bloodstain Pattern Analysis to Crime Scene Reconstruction

6

Introduction

If we consider that crime scene reconstruction (CSR) is a function of defining what happened and in what order it happened, then it should be relatively obvious that two forensic disciplines provide significant input to that task. They are forensic pathology and bloodstain pattern analysis. The reason for their importance is simple: both define the "what" of crime. The vast majority of forensic disciplines help us understand the "who" of crime. Through trace evidence, DNA, and fingerprints, we make associations of individuals to objects and scenes. This information is certainly relevant and important, but this information becomes ancillary to understanding what happened. Contrast this with the information provided by the forensic pathologists. Much of their effort is directed at defining what types of injuries occurred, the orientation of those injuries to the body, and, in some instances, the sequence of those injuries. This information is critical in understanding the "what" of crime; it tells us what types of events occurred to the victim. Bloodstain pattern analysis mirrors forensic pathology in the respect that it allows us to peer back into the past and define the nature of blood-letting events that transpired on scene.

Defined, bloodstain pattern analysis is the in-depth evaluation of the physical bloodstains at the scene and on associated objects. The analyst considers a number of factors about the stain or pattern, such as shape, number, dispersion, and orientation. From this evaluation, a bloodstain pattern defines the underlying nature of the event that created it. The bloodstain, in effect, tells the analyst how it came to be. This information when considered in the context of the scene can be very enlightening. In addition to understanding how the stain came to be, the analysis may help in defining issues, such as direction of deposition, area of origin for a pattern, the nature of objects that were bloodied, or the relative positions of objects and individuals during the event. All of this helps us understand what kind, where, and how many bloodstain-producing events occurred.

A Background of Bloodstain Pattern Analysis

Although often referred to as a "new" discipline, bloodstain pattern analysis has a nearly 150-year consistent history. What bloodstain pattern analysts evaluate and how they evaluate it has not changed dramatically over the years, other than as science itself has progressed. As with all forensic science, our understanding of bloodstain pattern analysis has become more refined as more research and effort has been directed toward it. But, the recognition of basic pattern types or the issue of directionality and the manner in which it is evaluated has remained consistent since the discipline's inception.

The underlying theory of bloodstain pattern analysis is simple. Blood is a fluid, one in which particles are suspended, but a fluid nonetheless. As a fluid, blood is affected by both internal and external forces in a predictable manner. Internal forces of concern include surface tension and viscosity. External forces of concern are gravity and air resistance, as well as any external force that was directed at a blood mass (e.g., inertial movement of blood on an object or impacts to a blood source). These forces and their interplay during an event all affect the blood in their own manner, producing the patterns we observe. These forces are not significantly altered by temperature, humidity, or location; thus the pattern produced by impacting a blood source on a summer day in Bermuda would be similar to that produced at 14,000 feet at the top of Pikes Peak in the middle of winter. This predictability allows us to recognize basic classes of patterns. Bloodstain pattern analysis is, therefore, class characteristic evidence. Stains cannot be individualized to scene-specific events based on the pattern alone. It is only through consideration of scene context that the analyst can make such associations.

What are these patterns? By considering various physical properties, the analyst can recognize six basic mechanisms that produce patterns. Most of these groups have subset pattern types—more refined classifications that differentiate patterns within the group. The six major groups include:

1. Radiating patterns produced by an impact to a blood mass, such as impact spatter.
2. Linear patterns produced by blood flung from another object, such as a cast-off.
3. Patterns produced by streaming volumes, such as a spurt.
4. Patterns produced by blood falling as a function of gravity, such as drip trails.
5. Patterns produced by volume accumulations, such as pools and flows.
6. Patterns produced through contact with a bloody object, such as smears and pattern transfers.

The classification of bloodstain patterns is a confusing subject to those new to the discipline. The reason for this confusion is that numerous classification systems exist. Examples of classification systems in use today include:

- Low, medium, and high velocity
- Passive and dynamic
- Spatter and nonspatter
- Taxonomic

Within each of these systems, variations of terminology are found, all of which to the outsider appears confusing and or suggests that the discipline is without basis. This simply isn't true. Irrespective of the system in use, each system ultimately defines the same basic patterns. Their differences lie in the classification system's initial perspective. Some classification systems are concerned more with stain size, some with shape, some with mechanism, but despite these differences in initial perspective, each ultimately arrives back at the same pattern types and, with few exceptions, uses similar terminology to describe these patterns. A simple analogy to understand the issue would be if we sent four people to four different sides of the same hotel and then asked each to describe the path they took to go to the hotel lobby. Although each individual starts from a different vantage point, all would ultimately arrive at the lobby and recognize the lobby for what it was. Each might describe their journey in slightly different ways, but they would all agree about where they arrived. This is the case for the various classification systems in use in bloodstain pattern analysis; all ultimately arrive back at the basic patterns.

For the purpose of this text, stains will be described using the taxonomic classification system first outlined in the authors' book, *Bloodstain Pattern Analysis: With an Introduction to Crime Scene Reconstruction,* 3rd ed. (CRC Press, 2008). Although each classification system has merit, if we consider the concept of bloodstain pattern analysis— that by the evaluation of the physical characteristics of the stain or pattern, the analyst can identify the source event—then the taxonomic system has a value-added component. Although it finds its roots in other systems, a taxonomic classification system is physical characteristic driven. Like every other system, it certainly identifies mechanism, but it is concerned with comparing a questioned pattern against some standard physical criteria. The other systems of classification, although functional, are not as effective at articulating what criteria the unknown pattern should be compared against.

Impact Angle and Directionality

Before proceeding to a description of the various types of patterns, it is important to discuss two basic concepts of bloodstain pattern analysis: defining the impact angle and directionality of spatter stains.

Impact Angle

When a small mass of blood, a droplet, has been put into free flight by whatever means, that droplet will achieve a spherical shape. These drops are generally referred to as spatter. When this small sphere impacts a surface, it collapses in an orderly fashion that will consistently produce either a circular or elliptical shaped stain (Figure 6.1).

The impact angle of a spatter stain is a description of what angle it struck that surface (Figure 6.2). Droplets traveling perpendicular to a surface (striking at 90 degrees to the surface) produce circular stains. As the angle of impact becomes more acute (decreases), the momentum of the droplet causes it to skim laterally across the surface as it impacts. This results in an elliptical-shaped stain. The more acute the angle, the more elliptical the shape of the resulting stain.

There is a direct relationship between the length and width of the resulting stain and its impact angle. This empirical relationship was first established by Balthazard et al. and allows the analyst to identify the impact angle of nearly any well-formed spatter stain.[1] Using this relationship, MacDonell refined the method for calculating the impact angle, using the trigonometric relationship of the sin.[2] The practical application of this technique

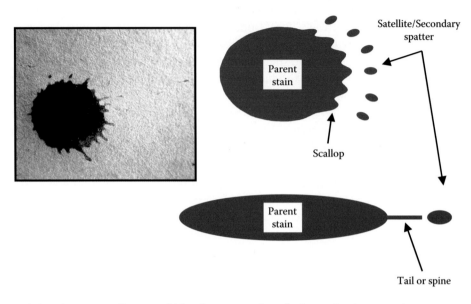

Figure 6.1 When a small mass of blood is put in free flight and subsequently impacts a surface, it produces a circular/elliptical shaped stain, most often referred to as spatter. (Bevel, T. and R.M. Gardner, 2008. *Bloodstain Pattern Analysis with an Introduction to Crime Scene Reconstruction*, 3rd ed. Boca Raton, FL: CRC Press. With permission.

in modern bloodstain pattern analysis is quite simple. The analyst measures the length and width of the spatter stain in question. He then divides the width by the length, which will always result in a number of 1 or less. This number is the sin and is converted to its corresponding angle by using a scientific calculator, with the inverse sin function.

Impact angle evaluation is always considered an estimate, with a known error rate. Recent studies indicate that when considering stains that fall at 60 degrees or less, the error rate is quite small (± 3 degrees). Above 60 degrees, as the stains approach 90-degree impacts, the error rate increases dramatically.[3] The same is true when considering directionality, which is described in the next section. The more elliptical the stain, the more effectively directionality can be established. Thus, when choosing stains for impact angle and directional analysis, the more elliptical stains are the best.

Directionality

Directionality relates to the path a droplet was following when it struck a surface. Directional angle (also called the gamma angle) describes the motion of the droplet as it impacts. Droplets falling straight down onto the target produce circular stains; there is no lateral movement and, thus, no directionality involved. Droplets that fall at more acute angles involve lateral movement along the target. This results in the droplet skimming the target as it collapses and produces one axis that is longer than the other. This long axis is oriented with the direction the droplet was moving at the time of the collapse. Of course, an axis viewed after the fact depicts two possible directions. When evaluating directionality, the analyst looks for the presence of scallops, tails, and satellite stains to decide which

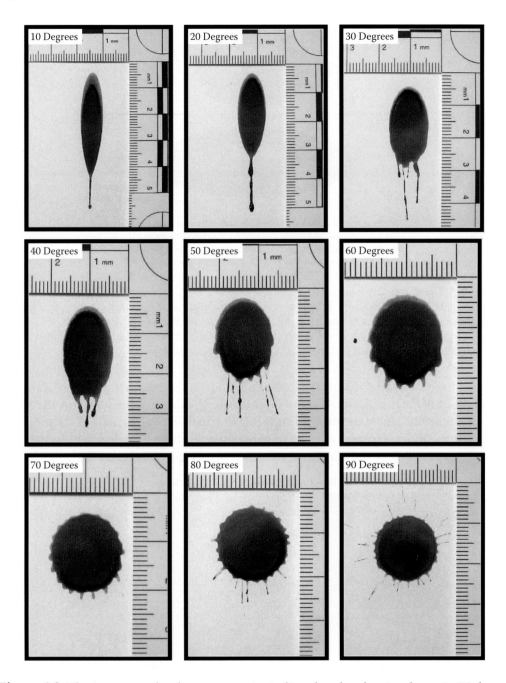

Figure 6.2 The impact angle of a spatter stain is directly related to its shape. In 90-degree impacts, the stain will appear circular. As the angle becomes more acute, the stain becomes more elliptical. (Bevel, T. and R.M. Gardner. 2008. *Bloodstain Pattern Analysis: With an Introduction to Crime Scene Reconstruction*, 3rd ed., Boca Raton, FL: CRC Press. With permission.)

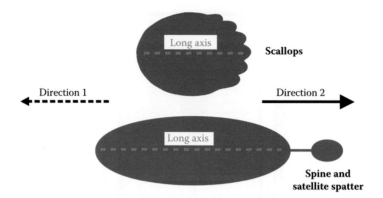

The long axis of a stain defines two possible directions of travel.
The analyst uses the presence of satellite spatter, scallops or
spines to distinguish the actual directionality of the droplet. In the
examples the directionality of both stains is in Direction 2.

Figure 6.3 Directionality is defined by looking for the long axis of the stain and then determining where the preponderant number of spines, scallops, and tails are located. In a parent stain, these characteristics are located on the side opposite the initial impact. (Bevel, T. and R.M. Gardner. 2008. *Bloodstain Pattern Analysis: With an Introduction to Crime Scene Reconstruction*, 3rd ed., Boca Raton, FL: CRC Press. With permission.)

direction the droplet was moving. These scallops, tails, and satellites form primarily on the side opposite of the initial contact point (Figure 6.3). The shape of the stain will affect how well directionality can be defined. It is difficult to visualize the long axis of the more circular stains, thus it is far more difficult to narrow the directional angle down. As the stain becomes more elliptical, the long axis becomes easily recognized (Figure 6.4).

Directionality Issues Based on Stain Shape

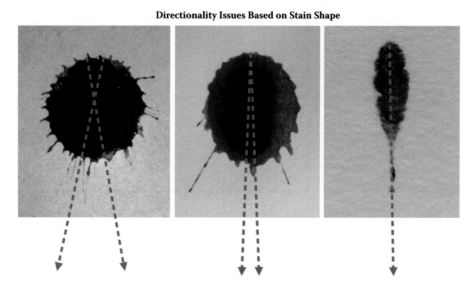

Figure 6.4 The more elliptical the stain, the easier it is to recognize where the long axis is, making directionality easy to recognize. As the stain becomes more circular, the long axis may be interpreted by different people in different ways (as shown by the blue lines). (Bevel, T. and R.M. Gardner. 2008. *Bloodstain Pattern Analysis: With an Introduction to Crime Scene Reconstruction*, 3rd ed., Boca Raton, FL: CRC Press. With permission.)

The concept of directional angle and impact angle are important to the analyst as they allow the analyst to recognize interrelationships of individual stains in patterns. Just as important, and as will be discussed later in the chapter, using these two ideas the analyst can identify an area of origin for certain types of patterns, known as impact spatter. Using the technique known as stringing and applying the information of impact and directional angle for a number of individual stains within an impact pattern will lead the analyst back to the probable area where the event originated.

Bloodstain Classification

Using the taxonomy concept, bloodstains can be grouped into two major classes: spatter and nonspatter. Spatter are drops that have been put into free flight through some mechanism. The analyst recognizes spatter stains based on shape. A small mass of blood in free flight will take on a spherical shape and produce a circular or elliptical stain when it collapses against a target (Figure 6.5). The spatter group is composed of patterns in which the primary stains are small circular- and elliptical-shaped stains. This group is further divided into linear and nonlinear spatter. These subgroups break down into the standard pattern types found in all classification systems. For linear spatter these include: spurts, cast-off, and drip trails. For nonlinear, these include: impact spatter, expectorate, and drips (Figure 6.6).

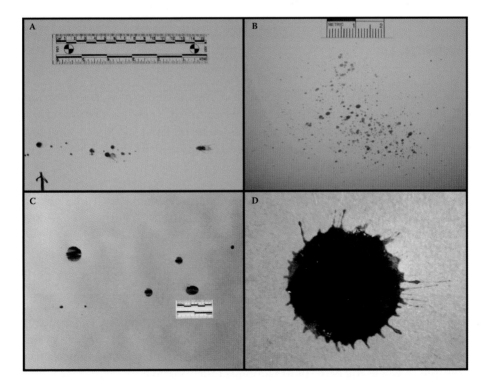

Figure 6.5 Spatter form in various ways when blood is put into free flight. The resulting patterns and stains are differentiated by their characteristics. Pattern A is a cast-off pattern, pattern B is an impact pattern, pattern C is a drip trail, and stain D is a drip. (Bevel, T. and R.M. Gardner. 2008. *Bloodstain Pattern Analysis: With an Introduction to Crime Scene Reconstruction*, 3rd ed., Boca Raton, FL: CRC Press. With permission.)

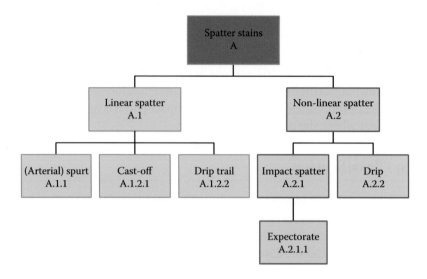

Figure 6.6 Using the taxonomic (physical characteristic driven, with established parent–child relationships) classification system, the spatter group is broken down into two primary categories: linear and nonlinear spatter. These two categories are broken down into six classic pattern types: spurts, cast-off, drip trails, impact spatter, drips, and expectorate. (Bevel, T. and R. M. Gardner. 2008. *Bloodstain Pattern Analysis: With an Introduction to Crime Scene Reconstruction*, 3rd ed., Boca Raton, FL: CRC Press. With permission.)

The Spatter Group

Spurt

Spurts are produced when blood is ejected in a stream under pressure. They are often referred to as arterial spurts because the primary source of a spurt is a breach to an artery or the heart; however, spurts can be produced by some odd and less typical circumstances (Figure 6.7). The physical criteria that help identify a spurt include:

- A series of related linear spatter stains.
- A large volume evident in the individual stains, demonstrated by flows from individual stains or a large volume in the pattern itself.
- Any of the following:
  – Large elliptical stains
  – Lines of overlapping stains deposited in Vs, arcs, or a serpentine pattern

Spurts are very informative as they are usually correlated back to a specific arterial injury. This allows us to recognize where the event occurred and any subsequent movement of the victim. Due to the volume and distance ejected, spurts are often found on assailants. By considering the directionality of the spurt, a general orientation of the victim in relationship to where the patterns are found is often possible.

Cast-Off

A cast-off pattern is produced when blood adheres to another object and that object is put into motion. Small drops of blood are ejected over time and space as the object is moved. The droplets produce spatter stains in linear or curvilinear orientations (Figure 6.8).

Figure 6.7 A classic spurt pattern extends from the floor up onto the surfaces of the washer and dryer, then back to the floor near the plastic item. The remaining spatter stains on the floor may be a combination of drips, drip trails, or additional spurt patterns. (Bevel, T. and R.M. Gardner. 2008. *Bloodstain Pattern Analysis: With an Introduction to Crime Scene Reconstruction*, 3rd ed., Boca Raton, FL: CRC Press. With permission.)

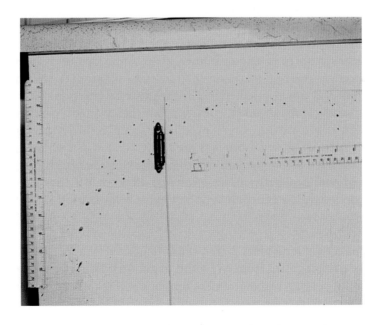

Figure 6.8 Two cast-off patterns on a cabinet facing. (Bevel, T. and R.M. Gardner. 2008. *Bloodstain Pattern Analysis: With an Introduction to Crime Scene Reconstruction*, 3rd ed., Boca Raton, FL: CRC Press. With permission.)

Cast-off are often produced by weapons, such as knives and bludgeons, but cast-off can also be produced by defensive actions, such as the swinging of a bloody hand. The physical criteria that help identify a cast-off include:

- A series of related spatter.
- Deposited in a linear or curvilinear orientation.
- With consistent parallel directional angles that change with the overall pattern.
- A consistent change in impact angle evident in the individual stains in the pattern.

Because the individual drops that produce the pattern are ejected at different times and positions in three-dimensional space, they will change in a consistent fashion. The idea of parallel directional angles simply means that the long axis of the stains will generally align with each other, but alter as the path of the object being swung changes. Thus, a swing of a club straight down will produce directional angles all aligned with the downward swing. However, if the swing starts down and then moves rightward, the directional angles will start in a downward orientation, but gradually show the movement to the right. The change in impact angle is also important. As they are released at different points in space, the angle of impact for each individual drop ejected will either increase or decrease in relation to the stains in front or behind it. This change may be very slight, but it will be present.

Cast-off patterns tell us about the orientation of objects as they are swung. If defensive actions are eliminated (e.g., the victim's hands, feet, and hair are free of blood), the cast-off are likely associated with the movement of weapons. By recognizing both the number of cast-off patterns present and their orientation (forward swings and backward swings) defines much about the attack. When considered with the information provided by the forensic pathologist (e.g., where and in what orientation are the wounds), this can allow the analyst to significantly limit the position of the victim and or subject at the time of the event. A particular form of spatter known as cessation cast-off is important as well. Although produced by a cast-off mechanism, unlike cast-off produced by the swing, cessation cast-off may or may not be oriented in a linear pattern. Cessation cast-off occurs when the object being swung stops abruptly. For example, when raising a club for an additional strike, the assailant may raise the weapon over his head and return it in a rapid movement. At the end of his backswing, small droplets are ejected and may be found on various surfaces, including the back of the assailant's clothing. Lacking specific characteristics (it may appear as linear or nonlinear pattern), cessation cast-off is not listed as a basic pattern type, but its recognition through scene context does provide helpful information to the analyst.

Drip Trail

A drip trail is a pattern of individual spatter stains deposited on a surface that demonstrate movement of the dripping item from one point to another. Drips form from any number of things, including people, weapons, and other objects (Figure 6.9). The physical criteria that identify a drip trail include:

- Inline distribution of spatter stains.
- Consistent size range in the pattern, relative to any change in surface characteristics.
- Stains lead from one point to another.
- Individual stains typically range in size from 3 up to 25 mm.

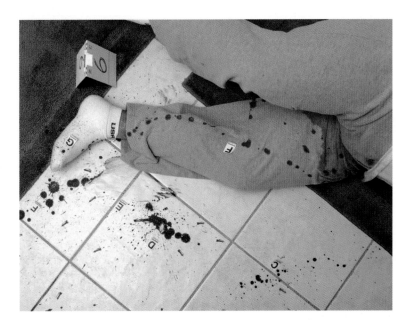

Figure 6.9 An example of a drip trail from the death scene considered in Chapter 3. The drip trail is marked as F and extends from the bottom of the left pant leg up to the left crotch area. Although not shown in this photo, the drip trail continues up across the chest of the victim's t-shirt. (Photo courtesy of Chuck Merritt, San Diego County Sheriff's Office.)

Drops falling from an object form on some surface of the object. The surface area available and the volume of blood flowing into that area all affect the size of the resulting drop, which affects the size of the resulting stain. There is a wide range of drip stain sizes, but in any given pattern the range will generally be consistent. If the drip trail leads across different surfaces, that may affect the size of the stains observed. For example, a drip trail that leads from a kitchen to a living room may look drastically different based on the different surfaces involved. Drops falling to linoleum in the kitchen may produce large 15- to 16-mm-size stains, but when the same volume drops fall to the carpet in the living room, the carpet fibers are absorbent and wick the blood down producing drip stains as small as 3 mm in size.

Drip trails may result from a replenishing source, such as a wounded individual, or from a nonreplenishing source, such as a bloody knife. In the former, the volume in the pattern will not change drastically and the trail may continue so long as the bleeding continues. In the latter, as the volume on the object drips off, the volume will ultimately decrease to a point that no further drips can occur. Given a large surface area (e.g., a butcher knife), a nonreplenishing drip trail may extend for as much as 100 feet. Drip trails are important. If we understand from whom or what the blood was dripping, this allows us to recognize movement of that person or item in the scene.

Impact Pattern

An impact pattern is a radiating pattern of small spatter stains produced when a blood mass is broken up at a point source. Typical impact patterns are produced from blows or gunshot wounds to a body. Impact patterns can also be produced when accumulations of blood outside the body are exposed to some force (e.g., a pool of blood forcefully stepped

Figure 6.10 An example of an impact pattern from the death scene considered in Chapter 3. The pattern is marked as A and radiates out from the victim's head toward the entryway. (Photo courtesy of Chuck Merritt, San Diego County Sheriff's Office.)

into). The radiating nature of the pattern is its most important attribute (Figure 6.10). The physical criteria that identify an impact pattern include:

- A series of related spatter stains.
- Deposited in a radiating distribution.
- With a progressive change in the shape of stains farther out in the pattern.
- Various sizes of stains, but a generally consistent size range throughout the pattern.

Impact patterns are extremely important. They occur when people are struck, shot, or simply impact surfaces. Based on both the direction and impact angle of the individual stains in the pattern, the bloodstain pattern analyst can often identify an area of origin, which effectively establishes where the source of the pattern was when it was produced. This often allows us to validate or refute claims about where individuals were or were not when wounded.

Expectorate Pattern

The expectorate pattern is similar to impact spatter, but with a slight difference. The blood source is broken up in the mouth or respiratory system by air pressure (Figure 6.11). The physical criteria that help identify an expectorate pattern include:

- A series of related spatter.
- Varying sizes of individual stains.
- Possible dilution of color from the presence of saliva.
- Possible presence of mucous strands.
- Possible presence of vacuoles (small bubbles that burst and leave behind a ring).

Impact and expectorate patterns can look very much alike, as both consist of small spatter that radiate outward. The presence of dilution, mucous strands, and vacuoles will

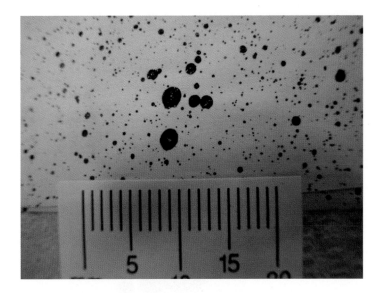

Figure 6.11 Shown is an expectorate pattern. Expectorate may be forced out of the nose, mouth, or from any injury in an airway. The presence of small, intermixed vacuoles (popped air bubbles) is an excellent indicator of expectorate. (Bevel, T. and R.M. Gardner. 2008. *Bloodstain Pattern Analysis: With an Introduction to Crime Scene Reconstruction*, 3rd ed., Boca Raton, FL: CRC Press. With permission.)

assist the analyst in making the distinction; however, in some instances, it may not be possible to differentiate between them. Some expectorate patterns will simply appear to be impact patterns. One critical consideration for the expectorate pattern is found in the scene context. If the pattern is expectorate, there must be a presence of blood in the respiratory system (e.g., nose, mouth, or lungs). Because the pattern is produced by air pressure, the size range of expectorate can vary greatly. If the victim is capable of forceful breathes, the spatter may be very small. If the victim is gasping or choking, the stains may be large. Because the victim's breathing can change during the event, a wide range of spatter size is possible in any given event. The expectorate pattern is important. If recognized as expectorate, it speaks to orientation of the victim in relation to where the pattern is found.

Drip

A drip is formed in the same fashion as a drip trail, by blood falling as a function of gravity from an individual or bloody object. Where the drip trail was a linear pattern of individual drips, a drip is simply a random deposit of drip stains (Figure 6.12). The physical criteria that help identify a drip include:

- One or more spatter stains.
- Parent stains (the primary stain and not the satellites) are generally large, 3 to 25 mm.
- Randomly oriented on a surface.

If an individual is injured and dripping blood in the scene, drips and drip trails are likely to be present as well as blood-into-blood patterns, which are discussed later in this chapter. Drips may be heavy, with multiple stains deposited randomly on surfaces, or they

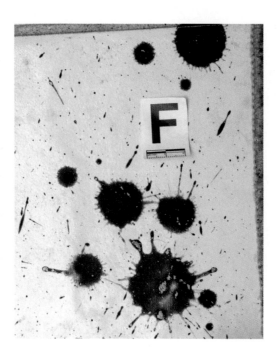

Figure 6.12 A drip is a random arrangement of large spatter and is often associated with drip trails (linear patterns). This example is from the death scene considered in Chapter 3. The drip is found at the base of a drip trail, also marked as F (see Figure 6.9).

may be isolated with one or two stains on a surface. Combining the location of the drips and drip trails allows the analyst to recognize movement and general positions of whatever or whoever was dripping the blood.

The Nonspatter Group

The nonspatter group is composed of patterns in which the primary stain is not a circular- or elliptical-shaped stain. This doesn't mean that a nonspatter pattern will not have *any* circular- or elliptical-shaped stains associated with them; they do. However, the primary stain in the pattern will not be spatter. The nonspatter group is divided into two subgroups: irregular and regular margin patterns. These subgroups are then divided into the major pattern types. The irregular margin group includes: blood-into-blood, gushes, smears, swipes, and wipes. The regular margin group includes: pattern transfers, flows, saturations, and pools (Figure 6.13).

Blood-into-Blood

Blood-into-blood patterns are created when drips fall into one another or into another liquid (Figure 6.14). The physical criteria that help identify a blood-into-blood pattern include:

- The primary stain is a pooling of blood or some combination of blood and another liquid. This pooling may consist of nothing more than several overlapping drip stains.

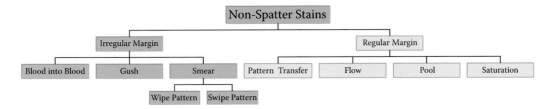

Figure 6.13 Using the taxonomic classification system, the nonspatter group is broken down into two major groups: regular and irregular margins. The subcategories to these two groups are the classic pattern types of: blood-into-blood, gush, smear, swipe, wipe, pattern transfer, flow, pool, and saturation. (Bevel, T. and R.M. Gardner. 2008. *Bloodstain Pattern Analysis: With an Introduction to Crime Scene Reconstruction*, 3rd ed., Boca Raton, FL: CRC Press. With permission.)

- The primary stain will be surrounded by a random distribution of small satellite spatter.
- The satellite spatter will show random variations in directional angles and shape.

As with drips and drip trails, the blood-into-blood pattern helps identify the general position of dripping individuals or objects, as well as identifying that there was a pause in any associated motion where the pattern is found. Depending on how long the pause is, the

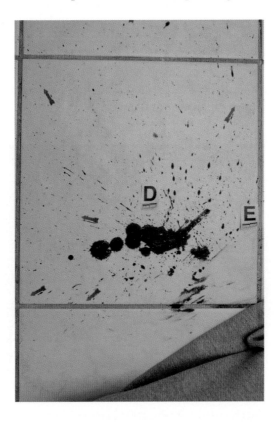

Figure 6.14 An example of a small blood-into-blood pattern (Pattern D) from the death scene considered in Chapter 3. Blood-into-blood occurs when a drip is stationary for any period and pooled liquid results. The primary stain is irregular, with a number of random satellite spatter surrounding it. (Photo courtesy of Chuck Merritt, San Diego County Sheriff's Office.)

blood-into-blood pattern may consist of only a few overlapping drips or it may be a significant pool that accumulated over time. The larger the pool and longer the pause, the greater the amount of associated satellite spatter surrounding the primary stain.

Gush

A gush is an irregular pattern created when a large volume of blood is ejected. A gush is created by similar circumstances as the spurt, typically when an artery or the heart is breached and a streaming ejection occurs. The primary difference between the two is in the volume ejected. In the spurt, the primary stains generally break up into individual spatter, whereas in a gush the primary stain is likely to be a large volume accumulation (Figure 6.15). The physical criteria that help identify a gush pattern include:

- An irregular stain exhibiting spines or associated spatter radiating out from it.
- A large volume accumulation evident in the overall pattern.
- Large elliptical stains may surround the pattern.

Where the spurt is a discrete linear or curvilinear pattern, the gush may appear as a pooling with associated spines and spatter around it. The volume ejected doesn't have time to break apart and either lands as a mass or is ejected into the same area, producing the large irregular stain. Gushes have significant numbers of spines and spatter radiating out from the primary stain, which will assist the analyst in recognizing directionality of the ejection. As with the spurt pattern, a gush helps us understand the victim's position and movement following breach of the arterial source. If a large volume of blood is ejected without pressure (e.g., a victim collapses after the cranium is blown off and blood has collected in the lower sections), the resulting pattern is often called a splash. The physical differences between a splash and gush are limited. Lacking the pressure ejection, the splash will usually have fewer spines radiating out from it.

Figure 6.15 In terms of mechanism, a gush pattern is produced from the same mechanism as a spurt, a volume ejection under pressure. Its physical appearance, however, is quite different, consisting of a large volume accumulation with many spines and satellite stains emanating from it. (Bevel, T. and R.M. Gardner. 2008. *Bloodstain Pattern Analysis: With an Introduction to Crime Scene Reconstruction*, 3rd ed., Boca Raton, FL: CRC Press. With permission.)

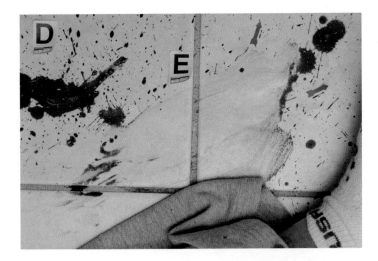

Figure 6.16 An example of a wipe pattern (Pattern E) from the death scene considered in Chapter 3. The male victim's foot moved through his blood after it was deposited on the floor. A corresponding saturation stain is present on the surface of the sock facing the floor. (Photo courtesy of Chuck Merritt, San Diego County Sheriff's Office.)

Smear

A smear is created when a bloody object makes contact with another surface often with some form of lateral motion. The smear is simply an irregular-shaped contact stain. There are two subcategories of smear: the wipe and the swipe. Smear as a classification is used when the analyst cannot differentiate between the wipe and the swipe.

Wipe   The wipe is a pattern produced when an object moves through a preexisting blood-stain on another surface (Figure 6.16). The physical criteria that help identify a wipe pattern include:

- An irregular-shaped contact stain
- A preexisting volume of blood
- Displaced blood from the original boundary
- Any of the following:
  –A feathered boundary
  –Striations (lines) across the body of the stain
  –Diminished volume of blood across the body of the stain
  –Accumulation of blood on the outer edges of the stain
  –Dried outer ring (skeletonization) of the original stain boundary

Wipes can be helpful in understanding sequence of events. As they involve some preexisting stain (e.g., impact spatter or a flow), they help the analyst recognize what event occurred first and, in some instances, how much time transpired between the two events.

Swipe   The swipe is any stain produced by the transfer of blood from one object to another with some form of lateral motion (Figure 6.17). The physical criteria that help identify a swipe pattern include:

- An irregular shaped stain
- With a contiguous boundary on one side and any of the following:
  – A feathered boundary

Figure 6.17 An example of a swipe pattern (Pattern J) from the death scene considered in Chapter 3. After the female victim was injured, she was moving in this this area depositing the blood onto the cabinet surface. (Photo courtesy of Chuck Merritt, San Diego County Sheriff's Office.)

– Striations (lines) across the body of the stain
– Diminished volume of blood across the body of the stain
– Accumulation of blood on the outer edges of the stain

Swipes can be helpful in recognizing that some object was bloodied and then in motion around another surface. In some instances, the direction of the motion for a swipe can be recognized by looking at the feathered edges or diminishing volume in the pattern.

Pattern Transfer

A pattern transfer is created when a bloody object comes in contact with another surface and produces a pattern in which a recognizable characteristic or image of the object is evident (Figure 6.18). Typical pattern transfers include finger and hand marks or feet or shoe marks, but any object has the potential to create a pattern transfer. The physical criteria that help identify a pattern transfer include:

- A regular margin stain.
- Demonstrating angular demarcations, curves, or other recognizable features, or an image of the object.
- They may be deposited in a series.

Pattern transfers are often overlooked, simply because the characteristics present in the pattern are not immediately associated to the object that created them. If recognized and an association is possible, the pattern transfer is very informative. It allows the analyst to recognize where specific objects have been and in what orientation they were during the contact. In the instance of distinct patterns that can be individualized in forensics, such as shoe, fingers, or palms marks, the pattern becomes even more important.

Figure 6.18 An example of a pattern transfer (Pattern K) from the death scene considered in Chapter 3. Hair and hair-like objects produce a distinctive pattern transfer with small, bifurcated ends (small V–shaped ends). Given the presence of female victim's head wound and the hairs deposited in the pattern, there is no question as to the source of this pattern transfer. (Photo courtesy of Chuck Merritt, San Diego County Sheriff's Office.)

Pool

Pools are produced when blood accumulates on a surface. The physical criteria that help identify a pool include:

- A clearly demarcated stain with regular margins
- An evident volume in the stain
- Without specific shape, but conforming to surface contours
- May demonstrate serum separation and or clotting

Pools generally have a limited value to the bloodstain pattern analyst other than indicating a blood source was positioned in such a fashion that allowed the pool to form. The amount of serum separation, where the serum (a straw-colored fluid) separates from the pool, as well as the amount of clotting evident in the pool, may suggest passage of time since the deposit (Figure 6.19).

Saturation

A saturation stain occurs when blood is deposited on or is in contact with an absorbent surface. Rather than forming a pool, the blood is wicked or absorbed into the permeable surface. Saturations often happen with clothing or on surfaces, such as sand or gravel. The physical criteria that help identify a saturation pattern include:

- A clearly demarcated pattern
- Without specific shape, but conforming to surface contours
- Absorbed or wicked into a surface

Like the pool, saturation stains have limited investigative value. More often than not, they mar other patterns of interest.

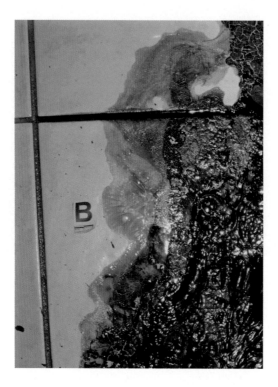

Figure 6.19 An example of a dried blood pool with evident serum separation (Pattern B) from the death scene considered in Chapter 3. This pool was associated to the male victim's head. (Photo courtesy of Chuck Merritt, San Diego County Sheriff's Office.)

Flow

A flow is the movement of liquid blood from one point to another usually under the effect of gravity. The physical criteria that help identify a flow pattern include:

- A clearly demarcated stain
- With generally regular margins, demonstrating movement along surface contours
- Margins lead from one point on a surface to another

Flows can be very informative. Typical flows always follow gravity (there are flow produced by air or accelerated motion), so if a surface containing a flow is disturbed, the orientation of the flow will likely help the analyst understand the orientation of the object when the flow was ongoing.

All of the described patterns appear in every major classification system, not just the taxonomic classification system. From one classification system to the next, the patterns may have slightly different titles or may be described in slightly different ways, but all exist in one form or another. The foundation of bloodstain pattern analysis is the ability to recognize these basic patterns and understand their mechanism of creation.

Complex Patterns

For the most part, the various patterns observed in a crime scene can be distinguished using these basic pattern types, but no classification system can account for every variation. The actions at scenes of crime are very dynamic. The analyst must recognize that a combination of actions might produce a pattern that has characteristics from several classifications. The simplest example of this is an individual dripping blood from his hand. If he remains stationary, the pattern begins as a blood-into-blood pattern; with slight movement, the pattern becomes a drip trail. If the individual swings his hand upward as he begins this movement, the result is a cast-off. Thus, the pattern produced would flow together, but would demonstrate qualities of each of the mechanisms. Recognizing this issue, the analyst uses the concept of a complex pattern to describe these circumstances. When presented with a complex pattern, the analyst simply identifies it as such and then identifies the underlying pattern types that are present.

Altered Stains

Some systems of classification treat altered stains as a distinct classification; in taxonomy, this is not the case. Alteration in the form of dilution, drying, or clotting can occur across the entire spectrum of stains encountered. Pools or flows might become clotted; smears or spatter may become diluted. Alterations, like the complex pattern, are simply recognized and described while evaluating the specific patterns involved. Alteration of stains can be of great importance to the analyst. Dilution may suggest subsequent activities or, in the case of clotting or drying, may suggest the amount of time that has elapsed since deposition.

Area of Origin Evaluations

Our prior discussion of directionality and impact angle are critical when considering impact spatter. Impact spatter, radiating patterns produced when a blood source is broken up at a point, have a source—an area in three-dimensional space where they originated (Figure 6.20). The analyst uses directionality and impact angle to identify where this breakup occurred. In the past, this area was often referred to as the Point of Origin; however, it is now generally described as an area. This change is due to the recognition of two things. First, the source is rarely a point source (a specific X, Y, and Z position). For instance, when an individual is struck with a blunt instrument and a laceration ensues, blood in the form of impact spatter may be projected from the entire injury. A 2-inch laceration is an area and not a specific point. Second, the techniques used to identify this area rarely have the ability to refine the location down to a true point.

Area of Origin (AO) evaluations are conducted using various techniques. Stringing is one popular way and consists of placing physical strings in the scene, oriented along the paths suggested by the directional angles and impact angles of the stain being evaluated. A second popular method is virtual stringing. Using forensic software, such as Backtrack Win and Backtrack Images, stains are evaluated for impact and directionality. The computer takes the resulting information and creates a virtual scene, with virtual strings. Additional methods for evaluating AO include graphing and the tangent method. Detailed descriptions of each of these techniques are available in *Bloodstain Pattern Analysis: With an Introduction to Crime Scene Reconstruction*, 3rd edition.

To string a scene, the analyst locates a number of well-formed spatter stains in the impact pattern. A well-formed stain is one where if the stain were halved along its long or short axis, the two halves would be generally equal (Figure 6.21). Typically the analyst will use at least 10 to 15 stains for the AO analysis; however, additional stains may be required. Just the same, if there are only a few stains available (a minimum of four), the evaluation

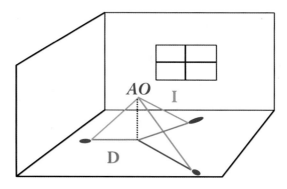

I = Defined by the impact angle of the stain
D = Defined by directionality of the stain
AO = Area of Origin

Figure 6.20 Area of Origin (AO) is defined by considering both the impact angle (the green line) and directionality (the blue line) for a number of individual stains in an impact pattern. Where these lines converge in three-dimensional space identifies the approximate position of the spatter event.

can be undertaken, so long as the analyst recognizes the limitation presented by the lack of stains.

The stains are evaluated for impact angle as described earlier in the chapter. Once the impact angle is established, a string is taped on the surface at the base of the stain and then oriented along the long axis of the stain. The string is then extended out to another surface at whatever the indicated angle of impact is, all the while keeping the string in line with the long axis of the stain. This technique is repeated for all of the stain being evaluated. As each string is added, a convergence of strings should become evident if the stains are related. When all strings are in place, the primary convergence for the strings is considered the area of origin (Figure 6.22).

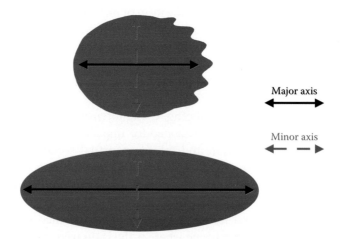

Figure 6.21 The stains chosen for impact angle analysis should be well-formed (symmetrical in shape) stains. If halved along either axis, the corresponding halves would generally be equal.

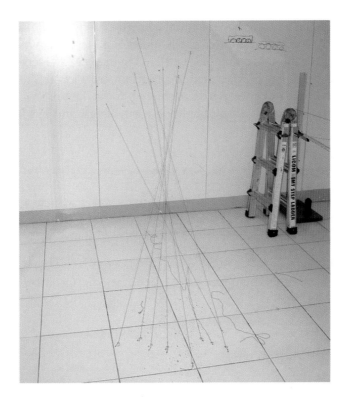

Figure 6.22 A training example of an area of origin analysis using the stringing method. Each string is placed based on the corresponding stain's impact angle and directionality. As more stains are analyzed and their strings positioned, a convergence begins to develop indicating the probable area of origin of the spatter event. (Bevel, T. and R.M. Gardner. 2008. *Bloodstain Pattern Analysis: With an Introduction to Crime Scene Reconstruction*, 3rd ed., Boca Raton, FL: CRC Press. With permission.)

AO evaluations can be significant to the investigation. They allow the analyst to limit the possible positions of the victim at specific moments. These limits may allow the investigative team to refute or corroborate specific claims by individuals involved in the incident. The value of AO evaluations will vary from scene to scene. Scene-specific conditions, such as how many stains are available for the analysis, whether the stains are on vertical or horizontal surfaces, or how widely radiating the pattern is, will ultimately hinder or help the evaluation. Thus, the information derived in one AO analysis may be able to significantly isolate the area of origin, while in another situation, it may only set broad parameters of possible and impossible. Due to the various scene nuances involved, only those properly trained in bloodstain pattern analysis and sufficiently practiced in the techniques should pursue AO evaluations.

Summary

In the end, a proper bloodstain pattern analysis will identify what kind of general events (impacts, cast-off, or spurts) were ongoing in the scene and where those events occurred. Additionally, information in the form of the sequence and flow of events may be forthcoming. When this information is combined with DNA evaluations and the information provided by the medical examiner, the bloodstain pattern analyst can then evaluate these general events in the context of that scene and in many cases identify a source event. Thus, an impact pattern may be identified to a gunshot or a blow to the head or a cast-off associated to the swinging of a weapon. Considered in the light of specific scene context, the bloodstain patterns shed significant light on what, where, and in what order bloodletting actions were occurring.

References

1. Balthazard, V., R. Piedelievre, H. Desoille, and L. Derobert. June 1939. *Etude Des Gouttes De Sang Projecte,* XXII Congres De Medicine Legale, Paris, p. 25.
2. MacDonell, H.L. 1982. *Bloodstain Pattern Interpretation,* Corning, NY: Laboratory of Forensic Science, Corning, pp. 44–53.
3. Willis, C., Piranian, A., Donaggio, J., Barnett, R., and Rowe, W. November 15, 2001. Errors in the Estimation of the Difference of Falls and Angles of Blood Drops, *Forensic Science International,* 123: 1–4.

Shooting Scene Processing and Reconstruction

7

MATTHEW NOEDEL

Introduction

Documenting and reconstructing scenes where a firearm has been discharged is a challenging and sometimes daunting task. Part of this complexity comes from the fact that there are hundreds of different calibers of ammunition used in thousands of different designs of firearms. The scene can be as simple as a single, nonexiting gunshot defect or as complicated as hundreds of gunshot defects involving handguns, rifles, and shotguns. Regardless of the situation, documentation, processing, and reconstruction of shooting scenes are accomplished by understanding the fundamentals of firearm evidence and taking a measured and consistent approach to the scene. The importance of shooting scene evidence in a crime scene reconstruction cannot be overemphasized. By evaluating shooting scene evidence (bullets, cartridge cases, cartridges, bullet defects, and weapons), the analyst can often limit the possible positions of a shooter or the victim and in some instances functionally place them in relatively discrete positions in the scene at the time of the gunshot.

Understanding Ammunition

Cartridges

A complete round of unfired ammunition is called a cartridge, which is typically made up of four components: a primer, a propellant (gun powder), a projectile (the bullet), and a cartridge case that holds the components together. It is important to use these terms correctly when working a scene and documenting evidence. If one were to locate and document an unfired cartridge but call it a bullet, this could result in confusion about what was recovered; as a bullet is the term specifically reserved for the projectile.

The Primer

The primer is a shock-sensitive, explosive compound traditionally made of barium, antimony, and lead. Due to recent environmental concerns, many manufacturers are beginning to use primer mixtures that do not include the heavy metals. These products are marketed as "lead free" primers. In either instance, primers are compounds that, upon compression

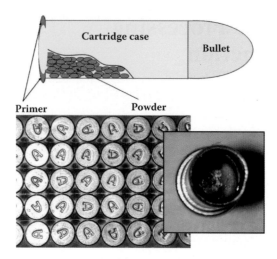

Figure 7.1 Rimfire cartridge—a round of ammunition where the primer is spun into the interior rim of the cartridge case.

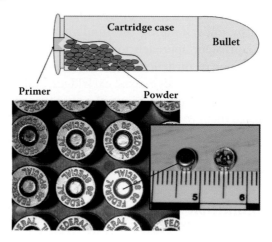

Figure 7.2 Centerfire cartridge—a round of ammunition where the primer is self-contained in a cup. The cup is then positioned at the center of the cartridge head.

or impact, explode to generate a spark. There are two basic forms of placement of the primer in the casing:

1. Rimfire cartridges are rounds of ammunition that have the explosive primer spun into the interior perimeter of the cartridge head (Figure 7.1). Nearly all modern rimfire cartridges are .22 caliber.
2. Centerfire cartridges are rounds of ammunition that have the explosive primer contained in a metallic cup that is positioned in the center of the cartridge head (Figure 7.2).

The Propellant

The propellant is the fuel for a round of ammunition. Smokeless powder is the most common form of propellant in modern cartridges (made of nitrocellulose and other components). When the powder burns, it rapidly generates a large volume of expanding gas,

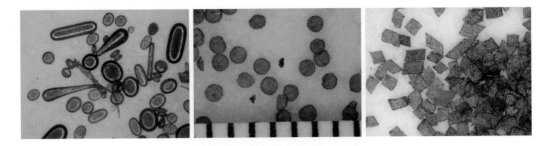

Figure 7.3 Three varieties of modern smokeless powder. The different shapes can vary the burn rate and pressure that a powder can generate.

which pushes the projectile out of the cartridge case and into the barrel. The shape of the individual granules (or particles) of powder can influence the rate that a propellant burns (Figure 7.3). A spark generated from the explosion of the primer is channeled so that it contacts and ignites the propellant. Pressures generated during the discharge of a cartridge can be on the order of 20,000 to 50,000 pounds per square inch (psi).

The Projectile

The projectile (the bullet) is a mass that is directed down the barrel of the firearm under the pressure of the expanding burning propellant. There are a variety of shapes and design features of bullets that will dictate how the fired bullet will perform once it leaves the firearm (Figure 7.4). Bullets can be constructed from a single material, such as solid lead or a combination of materials like a lead core wrapped in a copper or steel jacket.

The Cartridge Case

The cartridge case is the component that holds the primer, powder, and projectile together in the correct orientation for loading into a firearm. The "head" of the case is the position at the base of the cartridge. *Headstamp* is a term used to describe the data stamped into the cartridge head and often includes manufacturer, caliber, and other information (Figure 7.5). Headstamp information can identify the cartridge and may, in some instances, be used to associate related ammunition.

Figure 7.4 Three different projectile designs—a .38 special full metal jacket (FMJ), a .38 Special lead round nose (PbRN), and a .38 Special jacketed hollow point (JHP).

Figure 7.5 The head of the cartridge—the headstamp identifies the manufacturer: Aguila; the caliber: 12 (Gauge); and the symbol: MS for minishell.

Shotshells

A shotshell is a round of ammunition where the mass is either a single, large projectile (typically called a *slug*) or a collection of multiple, smaller projectiles (typically called *shot pellets*). Shot pellets are usually spherical, come in a variety of sizes, and can be constructed of lead, steel, bismuth, or other metals. A slug is constructed like a single bullet. Shotshells contain a primer, propellant, and a case like all modern ammunition, but usually contain additional components used to organize the projectiles that will be fired from the firearm.

These additional components inside shotshells are commonly referred to as *wads* (Figure 7.6). Wads may be constructed of simple disks of paper or plastic or consist of

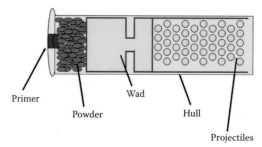

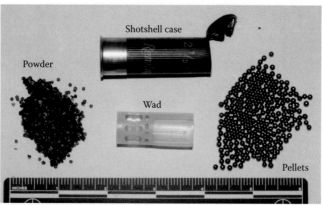

Figure 7.6 A schematic and disassembled shotshell.

Figure 7.7 Undamaged spherical shot (left) and shot damaged from impacting adjacent shot pellets during discharge (right).

complicated structures designed to perform multiple functions inside the shell. Because the propellant must be adjacent to the primer in order to be ignited upon impact, a wad (called an over-powder wad) is used to hold the powder in the proper position inside the shell. Upon discharge, the wad or wads become missiles themselves and are propelled from the firearm; their presence in the scene or victim can be a useful component of a shooting scene reconstruction.

Some shotshells contain a collection of small polymer granules called *buffer*. Buffer, when present, is designed to minimize the collision of adjacent shot pellets under the extreme pressure of discharge. Spherical pellets will be more predictable (thus more stable) in flight than deformed pellets (Figure 7.7). When a shotshell with buffer is discharged, the buffer is blasted out of the firearm and may be present in the environment of the shooting scene.

Caliber

The caliber of a round of ammunition defines the dimensions of the cartridge including overall length, case length, bullet diameter, case design, and other features. Caliber is often stamped on the head of the cartridge. Typically, matching the caliber of the ammunition to the caliber of the firearm is essential in obtaining the correct ammunition for a particular firearm. Be aware, however, that some calibers are so close in dimension that they may be interchanged in firearms designed for a different caliber.

Reconstruction Potential Associated with Cartridges

While processing a scene, it is important to document and collect unfired ammunition along with the fired components. Individual cartridges located in a scene may demonstrate where a person was located and the cartridge often has microscopic information useful for comparison. It is possible to compare microscopic information of the letters that make up the headstamp of fired cartridge cases to the headstamps of unfired cartridges recovered

Figure 7.8 Two common types of handguns. On the left a semiautomatic pistol (with associated magazine); on the right a revolver.

from a location to attempt to establish an association between two locations. Any boxes or individual cartridges located on scene should be collected as they can be used as a reference standard for future ballistic testing, often these unfired cartridges are the only source available of the same brand, style, or lot of ammunition needed for these additional tests.

Understanding Firearms

A firearm is a mechanical tool designed to direct and guide a projectile under high velocity and energy to a location forward of the shooter's position. The semiautomatic pistol and revolver are two of the most common types of firearms (Figure 7.8). Although there are hundreds of unique and individual design features that make firearms different, most firearms share some form of the following features.

Chamber

The chamber is the position in the firearm that holds a cartridge in the proper position to align with the barrel during operation and firing (Figure 7.9). The chamber must be sufficiently sturdy to handle the tremendous pressure generated from the expanding gases at the time of discharge. A cartridge discharged within the confines of the chamber is forced to channel the expanding gases in the direction of least resistance by pushing the bullet out of the chamber and down the barrel. Cartridges discharged outside of the confines of a chamber are free to expand in all directions and are unlikely to create the focused energy and high pressure that a firearm is designed to deliver.

Figure 7.9 Chamber areas of a semiautomatic pistol, revolver, and side-by-side shotgun.

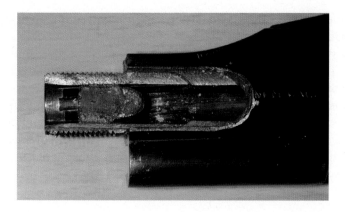

Figure 7.10 A cut-away firearm barrel showing a lodged bullet and the barrel lands and grooves.

Barrel

The barrel of a firearm is a tubular length of metal (typically steel) positioned such that when a cartridge in the chamber is appropriately aligned, the barrel accepts and then directs the expanding gasses and projectile(s) away from the point of ignition out of the firearm. Barrels can be smooth (as typically found in shotgun designs) or possess rifling (Figure 7.10).

Rifling is a set of *tracks* that are manufactured on the inside surface of a barrel; they force the projectile to spin as it travels through the barrel. The forced spin provides increased stability to the bullet after it departs the barrel. The tracks in a rifled barrel are further defined as *lands* (the raised portion of the track) and *grooves* (the lowered portion of the track). The number of lands and grooves, the width of each land and groove, and the direction of twist (right or left) are distinct features that the firearm manufacturer designates for each weapon it makes. Each barrel also has microscopic flaws produced by the manufacturing of the lands and grooves. These class and individual characteristics of the barrel are often translated onto the bullets fired from the weapon with a high level of reproducibility. When found on the bullet, they offer a mechanism and basis for laboratory comparison of fired bullets back to a recovered firearm.

Trigger

The trigger is a mechanism that when pulled initiates a sequence of operations that ultimately causes the firearm to discharge. There are two general methods called *action* that a trigger can go through to initiate discharge:

- Single action refers to an operation where pulling the trigger accomplishes only one thing—it fires the weapon by releasing a previously loaded spring tension. The spring must be preloaded by manually "cocking" the weapon.
- Double action refers to an operation where pulling the trigger accomplishes two functions—it first cocks the firearm (i.e., it loads the spring tension on the firing mechanism) and then, if the trigger pull continues, fires the weapon (releases the spring tension).

Generally, the amount of pressure on the trigger required for single action discharge is much less than the amount of trigger pressure required for double action discharge. Trigger pull pressure is often a consideration in reconstruction. Common single action trigger pulls are in the range of 4 to 7 pounds, while common double action trigger pulls are in the range of 8 to 12 pounds; however, the amount of pressure required to operate the trigger on any weapon is dependant on the actual condition of that firearm. The concept of a "hair trigger" is often discussed, a situation where a very light amount of pressure on the trigger is needed for discharge. While there is no defined amount of pressure that identifies a gun as having a hair trigger, generally a trigger pull pressure of less than 2 pounds is accepted by many as a reasonable cut-off level for a hair trigger.

Firing Pin/Striker

In order to initiate cartridge discharge, there must be some part of the firearm that can impact the primer with sufficient energy to cause the primer to explode. Usually the firing mechanism is a spring-loaded device that is released by the pull of the trigger. Many firearms have a hammer (which may be internal or external) that, when cocked, loads spring tension and when released by a pull of the trigger, falls forward releasing the spring tension. The action of the hammer falling can either directly impact the primer of a cartridge in the chamber or transfer the energy to a firing pin, which in turn is pushed into the primer of the cartridge.

Some firearms do not have a hammer. Typically, these designs have an internal "striker" or a firing pin that can be spring-loaded and released by pulling the trigger. When the firing pin strikes the cartridge, microscopic marks are translated from the firing pin onto the cartridge case. Laboratory examiners also use these microscopic marks to identify or associate fired cartridge cases recovered from a scene to weapons recovered in the investigation (Figure 7.11).

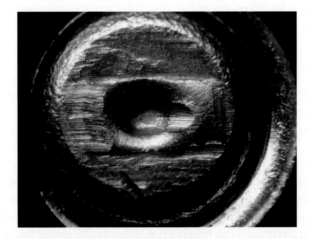

Figure 7.11 Microscopic details on a fired cartridge case. These microscopic marks are often reproducible from shot to shot and are useful for laboratory identification.

Firearm Safeties

A safety is any device that is designed to prevent a firearm from discharging. Safeties can be in the form of external levers or buttons or internal mechanical devices that engage and release automatically as the shooter operates the firearm. From a scene examination perspective, the documentation of the positions of safeties of recovered firearms can be very important. Not all firearms have safeties, and some firearms may have been modified to disable or remove their original safeties.

Firearm Caliber

The caliber of a firearm is dictated by the dimensions of the chamber and the diameter of the inside of the barrel (measured across the tops of opposing lands). On shotguns, the caliber is referred to as *gauge*, which is generally defined by the barrel diameter. Usually, the caliber of the firearm is stamped somewhere on the gun along with the serial number, make, and model. All of this information should be recorded photographically and in notes.

Reconstruction Potential Associated with Firearms

Beside laboratory comparisons of fired bullets and cartridge cases, recording the exact appearance of a firearm at a scene is essential in attempting to reconstruct the events. The position of the hammer, the position of the safeties, the contents (if any) of a chamber and the presence, absence, and location of bloodstains on the weapon are all examples of information that, if recorded, can make a tremendous difference in evaluating how a firearm was or was not used in a scene. Further, because firearms will typically require on-scene manipulation (i.e., unloading), their original condition is lost forever if one does not properly document these aspects early in the examination.

Before starting an on-scene firearm evaluation, one should thoroughly document everything about the firearm. Record the position of the firearm on the crime scene sketch relative to fixed points in the scene using standard scene processing protocols. These scene measurements allow the analyst to later relocate the firearm in the correct orientation and exact position where it was originally located in a scene.

Photographs and written notes should describe and document the positions of any levers or safeties observed on the firearm. After standard scene documentation and during collection of the weapon, take photographs from a variety of angles including straight on to incorporate the top, muzzle end, back end, and side of the firearm; then turn the weapon over and repeat the photographs. A completed series of photographs of this nature may answer questions about how the firearm performed. It is not uncommon that the analyst will find that features accidentally captured in a good series of photographs can answer questions, months or even years later, which were not at issue at the time of the examination, but have since become an issue.

An example can be seen in Figure 7.12. In this instance, the direction that the cylinder rotates on the revolver was captured in the photograph. The lead-in "scoop" adjacent to the cylinder stop indicates that this revolver rotates to the left (when looking from the shooters position). If the chamber position under the hammer and each chamber's content were correctly documented, one can reconstruct what shot would have been next without ever obtaining the firearm.

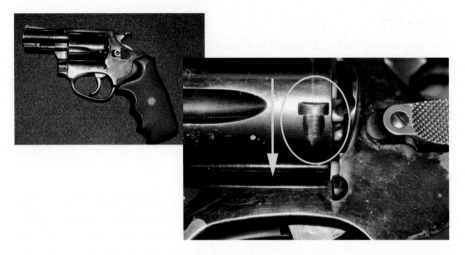

Figure 7.12 The stops on a cylinder can indicate which direction the cylinder is designed to rotate. Here, the lead into the stop is on the lower side of the notch identifying that this cylinder rotates to the left (from the shooter's perspective).

Accidental versus Unintentional Discharge

In reconstruction, it is important to differentiate between an accidental discharge and an unintentional discharge. As defined, the term accidental discharge is reserved for any firearm that can, because of mechanical wear, damage, design, or alteration, discharge without pulling the trigger. Unintentional discharge describes any process where a firearm is discharged by pulling the trigger where the operator of the firearm did not intend for it to be fired. True "accidental" discharges are more rare than "unintentional" discharges.

Handling Firearms at a Scene

The four basic rules of firearm safety should always be followed when handling a firearm on scene:

1. Always treat every firearm as if it were loaded.
2. Never put your finger on the trigger unless you are ready to shoot the firearm.
3. Always be aware of the muzzle end and what is beyond it.
4. Never point a firearm at something you don't want to destroy.

Ultimately a firearm on scene will have to be checked, unloaded, and made safe. When unloading these firearms, it is essential that the contents of the chamber or chambers are documented—even if the chamber is empty. When unloading a firearm, it is imperative that the operator keep the firearm pointed in a safe direction. In crime scene situations, what is truly safe is not always easily defined. For instance, in a middle-level apartment, a safe direction may not be easily located. In these instances, a stack of two or three bullet-proof vests can be used as a temporary backstop, thus it may be useful to keep several old vests in a scene response vehicle for such a purpose.

Unloading Firearms

In general, unloading a firearm involves two operations. First, the source of any new ammunition needs to be removed from the firearm. Second, documenting and then removing the contents of each chamber must be conducted. With thousands of different designs of firearms, no one process will work for every situation; however, semiautomatic firearms and revolvers will constitute a majority of firearms encountered in shooting crime scenes and the following guidelines should aid the crime scene analyst. **If you encounter a firearm that you are not familiar with or are less than confident in unloading—do not attempt to do so.**

Semiautomatic Firearms

Semiautomatic firearms have only one chamber to consider, but usually have a magazine associated. A magazine is a box that holds a stack of cartridges in the proper orientation for introduction into a pistol. In most instances, the magazine is detached and removed by depressing a latch or button somewhere on the firearm (Figure 7.13). In a crime scene circumstance, it is a poor practice to cycle each live cartridge through the firearm because:

- This requires the repeated manipulation of the firearm, thereby increasing the potential for an unintentional or accidental discharge.
- Cartridges are marked by the extractor and ejector during each cycle.
- This process requires that all of the mechanical features of the firearm work properly and the true condition of the weapon is unknown at that time.
- It is possible to break or damage parts of the pistol during this type of operation.

The typical steps to safely unload a semiautomatic pistol include:

1. Point the firearm in a safe direction.
2. Find the magazine release and remove the magazine from the gun (it is not necessary to remove any cartridges, if present, from the magazine itself).
3. Expose the chamber by pulling the slide rearward and document the chamber contents (even if it is empty). Warning: Anything already in the chamber will be removed during this operation and can be lost or contaminated, so perform this step with care (Figure 7.14).

Once the weapon is unloaded, the use of plastic cable ties can help lock the action open for ease of future inspection. The ties should not be placed through the barrel, rather secure them through the magazine well or some other position on the frame.

Figure 7.13 Two examples of different magazine release buttons.

Figure 7.14 The normal sequence to unload a semiautomatic pistol: drop the magazine; expose and clear the chamber; package all items.

Revolvers

Revolvers have a single cylinder that contains multiple chambers. Ultimately, it will be important to document the contents of each individual chamber (even empty ones). Different revolver designs have different mechanisms that enable unloading, but there is nearly always a release button or combination of operations that will allow the cylinder to be exposed or removed completely. A revolver that is cocked may require that the hammer be eased to the down position prior to unloading. Some revolvers require pulling the trigger while controlling the hammer to uncock the weapon. If this is the case, be sure to have an appropriate backstop and point the muzzle in a safe direction before attempting this operation.

The typical steps to safely unload a revolver include:

1. Point the firearm in a safe direction.
2. Before opening the cylinder, mark reference lines that identify which chamber was aligned under the hammer. Once the cylinder is opened, this information is lost if it wasn't previously identified.
3. Identify with notes and photographs the contents of each chamber. You can assign each chamber a number, typically starting with chamber #1—under the hammer.
4. Package each chamber's contents separately. It may be important for later reconstruction to know where in the revolver each cartridge or cartridge case was positioned (Figure 7.15).

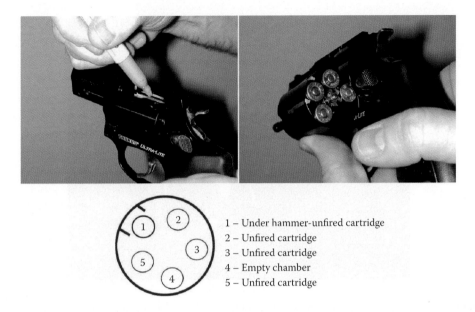

1 – Under hammer-unfired cartridge
2 – Unfired cartridge
3 – Unfired cartridge
4 – Empty chamber
5 – Unfired cartridge

Figure 7.15 To unload a revolver, mark the chamber that is under the hammer, expose the chambers, catalog the contents of each chamber (this gun has five chambers), and then package all items.

Once again, plastic cable ties can be used to hold the cylinder in the open position for packaging and subsequent storage.

Fired Cartridge Cases

Semiautomatic firearms have only one chamber; thus to deliver successive shots, the chamber must be emptied and reloaded after each discharge. The extractor is a part manufactured on most semiautomatic firearms that initiates this operation by hooking over the rim of a cartridge in the chamber. Some of the energy of the discharge is directed rearward (remember for every action there is an equal and opposite reaction), which allows the extractor to pull empty cartridge cases out of the chamber and force them against a fixed post called the ejector. The extractor and ejector work together to clear the chamber after each shot and automatically flip empty cartridge cases out of the firearm (Figure 7.16).

Fired cartridge cases in a scene typically represent the vicinity in which the case was expelled from a firearm. Using standard crime scene protocols, the position of each case should be documented relative to fixed positions in the scene such that the pattern and distribution of cases can later be mapped for any reconstruction effort. Each case should be collected and packaged separately. On scene a quick inspection and documentation of the headstamp may reveal useful information, such as caliber or brand. Every cartridge case located in the scene should be collected, as it may not be intuitive by looking at the fired cartridge cases, if more than one firearm was present or involved in the event.

Ejection Patterns

The extraction and ejection of fired cartridge cases are dictated by the mechanical design of the firearm and the orientation of the firearm maintained by the shooter. But, regardless

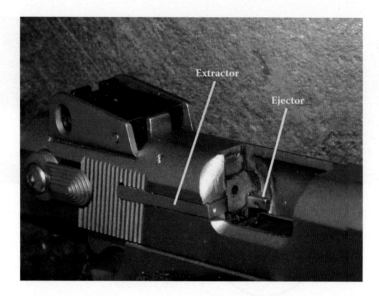

Figure 7.16 Close-up photographs of the extractor and ejector of a semiautomatic pistol.

of the physical design of the extractor and ejector, the person operating the firearm can easily change the firearm orientation, thereby changing the ejection pattern. It should also be noted that some firearms have a "slide stop" mechanism that locks the firearm open after the last cartridge has been delivered from the magazine and fired. If present, the slide stop feature interrupts the natural recovery of the firearm and the last shot may exhibit a significantly different ejection position than the prior "nonstopped" ejections.

It is very important to consider the environment into which cartridge cases are ejected and land upon. Hard smooth surfaces like streets or paved parking lots may allow ejected cartridge cases to bounce or roll a great distance from their initial impact point. Being cylindrical, if ejected onto these surfaces where there is a grade or changing elevation, the case can roll. Often this secondary movement is irregular and unpredictable. On the other hand, ejected cases that land in grassy or similar areas do not move in this unpredictable fashion and are more reliable for use in ejection pattern reconstruction than those that land onto unyielding surfaces. Intermediate objects in the vicinity of the ejection process (e.g., walls, car doors, people, or other adjacent objects) can alter the natural pattern and accidental movement of cases from on-going activity within a scene and may also alter the original pattern. Finally, ejection patterns may be influenced by the type of ammunition used and the condition (e.g., dry, well oiled, new, or worn springs) of the suspect firearm. For these reasons, ejection pattern testing should always use the actual firearm and identical ammunition to that used at the scene, and the results must be considered cautiously and in a proper context.

Determination of a recovered firearm's ejection pattern is a relatively simple examination. The analyst simply discharges a firearm from a fixed position and orientation and then records the impact locations of each cartridge case expelled. The record of the known ejection pattern (using the same firearm and same ammunition) can then be overlaid onto the previously recorded scene pattern or distribution and theoretical scenarios can be tested against both sets of information.

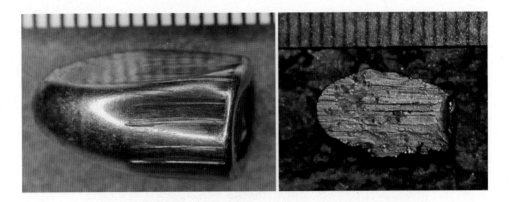

Figure 7.17 On the left is a fired bullet that hit a hard, flat, smooth surface. On the right is a fired bullet that hit a hard, flat, rough surface. The bullet on the left exhibits the left twist rifling information from the firearm from which it originated.

Fired Bullets

As it is the projectile(s) that create the damage to life and property, it is essential that all fired bullets or portions of fired bullets are recovered whenever possible. Bullets travel at high energy and high velocity, and as they pass through or against intermediate targets, they can pick up and retain valuable trace evidence including glass, tissue, fibers from clothing, paint, building material, or anything else they encounter. Also, the shape and performance of a fired bullet may provide information about that bullet's history.

Figure 7.17 shows two bullets. One hit a hard, flat, smooth surface. The other bullet hit a hard, flat, rough surface. Notice the appearance of the bullets; each bullet's surface retained information consistent with what it impacted. These observations are useful in evaluating a shooting environment. If the bullet in question indicates it hit a hard, flat, smooth surface, the analyst looks for such a location within the scene. Reading the bullet in this fashion can offer many clues that will aid in reconstruction. The examiner should be considering questions like: Why does this fired bullet have the appearance it does? Why did a hollow point bullet not expand? What did this bullet hit that caused it to break apart? Is there residual glass or other trace material that indicates this bullet's history? Failing to consider these issues is analogous to ignoring the presence of bloodstains in the scene.

Many bullets are designed with a hard copper jacket surrounding a soft lead core. Because these bullet designs have two different parts, when exposed to the physical forces of impacts, the jacket will often separate from the core (Figure 7.18). The examiner must recognize when this occurs and attempt to recover both portions of such a bullet. The jacket portion of the bullet will be the most useful for identification to a firearm, while the core will offer additional information about the type and caliber of ammunition that was used.

Recovering Fired Components

When recovering fired components from a scene, it is often necessary to cut into walls or other structures. Leaving fired bullets behind in the scene is not an option even when one believes the case is clear cut. Questions may arise days, months, or even years later that cannot be answered simply because the fired bullet was never recovered. When cutting into walls or structures to recover a projectile, care always should be taken to preclude hitting live electrical wiring, water pipes, plumbing, or other structures commonly found

Figure 7.18 Shown is a fired bullet where the jacket separated from the core. These two components represent only one shot, so they should not be counted as two bullets. Notice the material trapped as trace evidence on each component.

within walls. Be aware that these structures may not be in logical places behind the wall and always proceed carefully with the recovery.

When cutting through fabric (e.g., a car seat), cut three sides of a square a sufficient distance away from the hole and then fold the fabric back. This will allow you to replace the fabric into its original and proper position for documentation purposes and still explore beneath it for the projectile. When cutting into solid structures, consider cutting slightly irregular shapes and always mark and identify a direction (e.g., north, up, or similar reference). This will allow one to replace the cutaway area back into its original position if needed for additional examination. Finally, retain the cut-out portion of the bullet defect as evidence; it may be a source of trace or transfer evidence useful for future exam.

Perforation versus Penetration

When discussing bullet impacts, two terms are frequently interchanged inappropriately: perforation and penetration. In shooting reconstruction, perforation identifies a location where a projectile has gone completely through an object (e.g., a gunshot wound with an entry and exit). Penetration is the term used when the projectile impacts and remains in the last matrix it impacted (e.g., a gunshot wound with an entry only). A single bullet can both perforate and penetrate various targets. For example, a gunshot that passes through a car door and then impacts the driver but does not exit his body would have first perforated the door and then penetrated the body.

Shotgun Pattern Evaluation and Reconstruction

When a firearm involved in a shooting event is a shotgun, additional evidence and reconstruction potential may exist. As the shotgun is discharged, a wad and possibly buffer as well as the shot pellets or slug are all expelled from the firearm. These additional

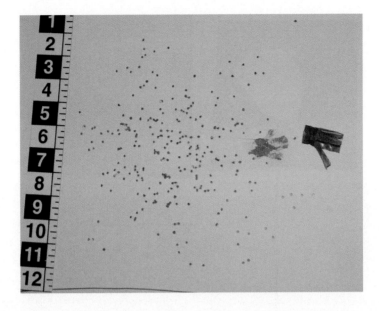

Figure 7.19 A shotgun pellet pattern from 10 yards. The large hole is where the wad went through the paper. The wad was recovered and placed adjacent to the damage it caused for this photo.

products should be searched for and their location documented. At close range, wads can be blasted into a wound or strike and leave a mark adjacent to the actual pellet or slug entry (Figure 7.19).

As will be discussed for gunshot residue patterns, shotgun pellets can spread out in a generally conical pattern in flight. At close range, the pellets have little time to spread out and the resulting pattern expected is small. The longer the pellets are in flight, the greater the distance of flight and the pattern has more time to spread out, resulting in a larger size. The combinations of ammunition and firearm utilized have a great influence on this pattern size. Figure 7.20 depicts a full length shotgun adjacent to the same make and model of a modified "shortened" shotgun. A shortened shotgun barrel provides less influence on the

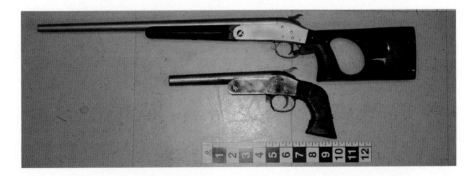

Figure 7.20 The weapon on top is an unmodified 410 shotgun; the lower weapon is a shortened version of the same model. The shorter barrel of the modified shotgun will change the characteristics of the shot patterns as compared to the unmodified firearm.

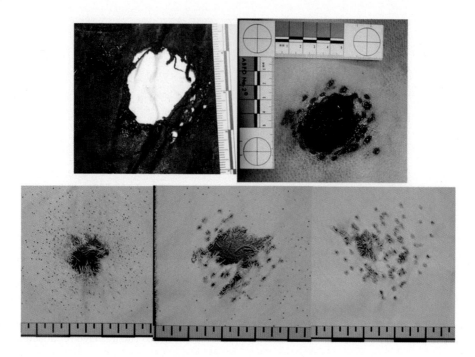

Figure 7.21 A bloody t-shirt and the underlying shotgun wound are shown in the top images. The shotgun was test fired into the targets (the lower images) at 1 foot, 2 feet, and 3 feet (left to right) and then compared to the fabric and wound.

shot than a full length barrel, and patterns from a shortened shotgun may not be equivalent to ones generated from a full length barrel (Figure 7.21).

When a shotgun pattern is encountered, the entire pattern should be documented, as well as the individual strikes. Angled shotgun patterns may have an elliptical appearance (Figure 7.22). Most wads initially carry a lot of energy and can travel at least 30 to 50 feet unless they hit an intervening object. When processing a shotgun pattern with no wad impact, back track toward the indicated origin of the shot to see if a wad can be located.

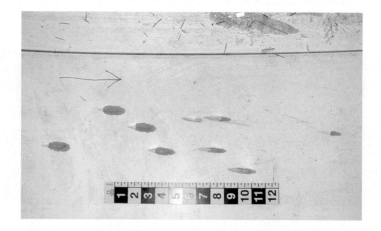

Figure 7.22 Ricocheted shot pellets exhibiting an elliptical pattern along with lead-in marks from each pellet. This shot originated from approximately 15 degrees above the surface.

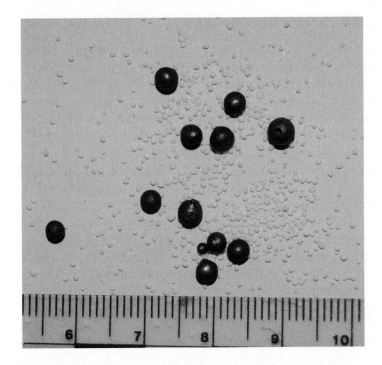

Figure 7.23 Shot pellets among buffer component, which is added to reduce the interaction of the pellets when fired.

Keep in mind that the shooter must be farther away than the wad location; so once the wad is located, the search must continue even farther back to locate the position of the shooter.

When buffer is present is a shotshell, it is expelled during the firing process. Buffer granules have greater mass than gun powder particles and, therefore, often travel farther (Figure 7.23). Like gun powder particles, buffer can also impact skin or tissue and leave a pattern of punctuate abrasions that look similar to stippling.

Recording Impacts and Ricochets

When a bullet impact site is located and validated as a bullet strike, it should be documented. Photographs are the most effective method of capturing and recording impact sites. In addition to the photographs, the position of each impact site must be located relative to a fixed point or baseline. A single bullet may create any number of defects in intermediate targets in addition to its final terminal impact. When multiple defects are associated with the passage of a single projectile, it is useful to name each defect site with a sequential designation (e.g., hole A exits at hole A1, reenters at hole A2, and ends in the wall at A3). Using this technique, all impacts named A are associated with that single trajectory and it will be easier to discuss and document in notes and reports.

While many bullet impact sites are difficult to evaluate, there are several basic reproducible features that can be considered in a shooting reconstruction. Because the character of bullet impact sites is dependant on many variables including bullet construction, impact site construction, influence of adjacent support structures, and other factors, the analyst must be careful and conservative in providing this assessment.

Evaluating Bullet Impact through Glass

Glass impacted by bullets has many reproducible properties that can be useful for a reconstruction. When a fired bullet perforates glass, the transfer of energy from the bullet to the glass surface causes a flexing of the glass on the exit side, as it is pushed before letting the bullet break through. This flexing "stretches" the glass on the exit side and often results in damage that has a beveled appearance and feel. Conversely, on the entry side, the fired bullet tends to make a clean smooth break. Therefore, when evaluating a bullet hole through glass, one can often define the entry versus exit side by finding the smooth (entry) versus the beveled (exit) side. This evaluation is not always possible. Because of the brittle nature of glass, definitively assigning an entry versus exit may not be possible if some of the glass shatters and falls away from the perimeter of the defect.

Fired bullets that travel through glass may have the jacket stripped from the core, and the nose of the bullet or its side may contain crushed glass and scratches on the surface. This damage usually requires low level magnification to see clearly, but visually appears as a white powdery material. Testing the perimeter of a bullet hole through glass will not always give positive results for copper or lead because much of the actual perimeter of a bullet hole may be displaced due to the brittle nature of glass.

The two common forms of glass encountered in scenes include laminated glass and tempered glass. Both forms are present in automobiles. Windshields are constructed of laminated glass, which are two layers of glass with a polymer sheet between them. This construction helps hold the windshield together when damaged. Because laminate glass is actually two layers, care must be taken if attempting to evaluate cracks in the glass, as a crack may be present on only one side of the glass (Figure 7.24).

Side and rear windows in vehicles are typically constructed of tempered glass. Tempered glass is designed to completely fragment into small squares upon impact. When a fired bullet impacts tempered glass, the entire panel of glass will fragment into small cubic pieces. Undisturbed glass may remain fractured, but in the frame. Secondary activity (e.g., opening a door or running over a curb) may cause the fragmented glass to fall out of the frame. Mylar-type tinting will often help hold a fragmented window together. When the initial

Figure 7.24 The view of the exit side of a bullet hole that went through laminated windshield glass.

Figure 7.25 Fractures radiating out from the impact site on a shot fired through tempered glass. The long narrow fractures will point back to the position of initial impact.

shot passes through the window, some of the translated energy is dispersed as radial fractures spreading out from the point of impact (Figure 7.25). If any of these radial fractures survive any secondary activity, they can be used to help establish the location of the initial impact. Because tempered glass fragments completely during the first impact, all subsequent shots through the fragmented glass cannot be sequenced except to say that they occurred after the initial shot. When working with shattered tempered glass, an effective technique is to reinforce the remaining glass with slightly overlapping strips of clear tape. While this process may not preserve all of the glass, it will hold most of it together. Using string to trace back along the length of the radial fractures, an approximate center may be located even when some of the tempered glass has fallen away (Figure 7.26). Figure 7.27 shows a

Figure 7.26 Even though the window has partially fallen in, the approximate area of initial perforation can be estimated by tracing the radial fractures back along their long axis.

Figure 7.27 This tempered glass car window received multiple shots and the pane ultimately collapsed. The window tinting held the glass mostly together. It was recovered and, from it, the first shot was identified and a template of the bullet damage was applied to the reconstruction of the shooting scene.

window shot five times but held together with Mylar window tinting. The glass could be recovered, laid out, and evaluated.

When presented with bullet defects in glass where the glass has not yet collapsed, a functional way of reconstructing the trajectory is to document the defects fully on scene, before the glass collapses. Often the window will be intact on arrival, but any minor manipulation or movement of the car may cause the window to subsequently collapse. Take photographs at 90 degrees to the window and include a scale. This photograph provides the landmarks for subsequent analysis. In this technique, a plastic sheet is cut to fit the door window. Using the photographs of the window prior to collapse, the defect is located and marked on the plastic. A hole is then cut in the plastic to allow introduction of a trajectory rod (Figure 7.28).

Bullet Ricochet

Fired bullets can perforate (go all the way through) an object, penetrate (enter and stay inside) an object, or ricochet off the surface they impact. Ricochets typically occur when the bullet is fired into a nonyielding surface at sharp angles. Depending on the properties of the surface and bullet, ricochet marks can be evaluated and may offer information as to the fired bullet's direction of travel. While ricochet is a very dynamic type of defect, it can usually be associated with low angle (~15 degrees and less) impacts.

Bullets that ultimately ricochet off of a surface can leave lead-in marks that represent the entry side of a ricochet. Lead-in marks are generated when the projectile first

Figure 7.28 Another method of reconstructing glass and bullet defects. Using a scene photograph (before the pane collapsed) to identify the position of a bullet defect, this clear plastic template was created. It was then inserted into the vehicle and the laser aligned with the terminal defect. When considered in conjunction with a gunshot wound to the victim's chin, a general understanding of the victim's position is possible.

encounters a surface and creates a small mark before burrowing deeper into the matrix (Figure 7.29). When painted metallic surfaces (e.g., automobiles) are impacted, visual cues may help identify the bullet's direction of travel. First, a feature known as a *pinch point* may be evident. When present, a pinch point represents the entry side of a ricochet on painted metallic surfaces (Figure 7.30). On some painted metal surfaces, the ricochet may leave "waves," cracks in the paint that recede away from the direction of travel (like waves following a boat traveling across the water).

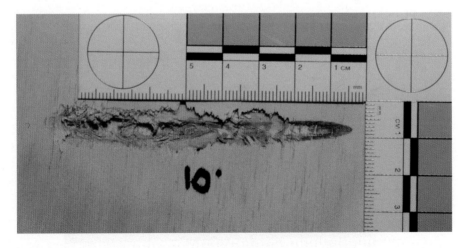

Figure 7.29 A ricochet from a .22 caliber bullet that originated from 10 degrees off the wooden surface. Direction of travel is from right to left and the elliptical black mark toward the right of the defect is a "lead-in" mark.

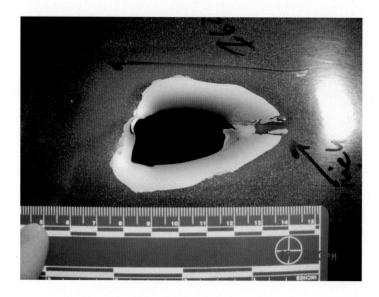

Figure 7.30 A perforation through painted automobile metal. The direction of travel was from right to left. The small island of paint on the right side of the defect is a "pinch point." This projectile was a 30-caliber rifle bullet. Notice how the size of the damage is significantly larger than the .30-inch diameter of the projectile.

Automobile metal is a strong surface for a fired bullet to overcome. Less brittle than glass, automotive metal tends to bend significantly before allowing a bullet to pass. This bending often results in a hole through an automobile body being much larger than the projectile that caused it (Figure 7.31). The analyst should not attempt to estimate the caliber of a fired bullet based exclusively on the size of hole left in car metal unless additional testing or supporting information is available.

At times, a metal tab called a *plug* can be torn from the car metal and ride with the fired bullet into the vehicle. Plugs are often mistaken as a piece of fired bullet, thus it may be helpful to check fragments with a low power magnet. Most bullets are copper or lead

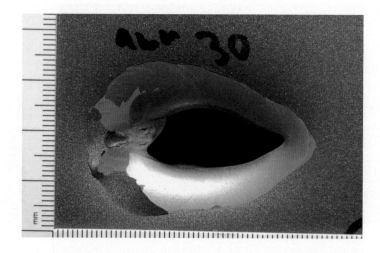

Figure 7.31 A painted metal car surface with a perforation and pinch point is shown. The pinch point is on the left side, thus this fired bullet was traveling from left to right.

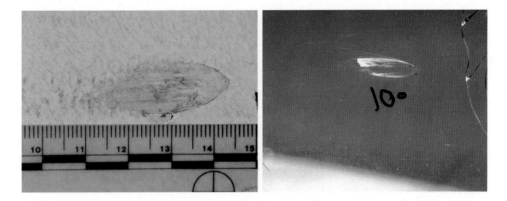

Figure 7.32 Pictured are two ricochet marks. On the left is a ricochet off painted concrete and on the right a ricochet off glass. Both shots were traveling from right to left. A tail on the lower edge of the left image supports that this bullet was spinning with a left twist at the time of impact, and a slight tail toward the top of the right image supports that that bullet was spinning to the right.

and will not adhere to a magnet; plugs from car metal are typically steel and will adhere to a magnet. In either case, one should document the position and collect the plug and any fragments that can be located.

Some bullet strikes leave a mark that shows both direction of travel and rotational spin. In these instances, the exit side of the mark is skewed toward the top or the bottom of the impact. Figure 7.32 shows two bullet strikes as a result of a left twist and right twist fired bullet. Determining the direction of barrel twist provides class characteristic information about the firearm that fired the bullet.

Bullet Impact Evaluation

From a scientific perspective, in order to identify a defect as having been caused by a fired bullet, supporting evidence beyond a visual assessment should be conducted. Some defects (like a cigarette burn through clothing) may look like a bullet hole, but in fact have nothing to do with the passage of a fired bullet. When a bullet perforates an object, it physically pushes its way through the barrier it has encountered. Many bullet impact sites can retain transfers that originate from the surface of the fired bullet (primarily copper or lead) and are deposited onto the perimeter or surface of the matrix impacted. Detection of these transfers, especially in association with the recovery of a fired projectile, will validate that the damaged areas being considered are due to a fired bullet. The following techniques are relatively simple field tests useful for the detection of copper and lead on suspected bullet impact sites.

Field Tests for Copper: Dithiooxamide (DTO) and 2-Nitroso-1-Naphthol (2-NN)

Dithiooxamide (DTO) and 2-nitroso-1-naphthol (2-NN) can each detect the presence of copper. The object being tested can dictate which one to use. When a copper jacketed projectile impacts a surface, trace residual copper may be left behind. This examination involves partially dissolving (with a solution of ammonia) residual copper from an impact site onto filter paper. Applying DTO onto the filter paper will result in a green-gray color when copper is present. Alternatively one can apply 2-NN to the filter paper and look for a pink color reaction when copper is indicated. These tests will not destroy (dissolve) lead if it is present in the impact site. If testing for both copper and lead, always conduct the copper test first.

Materials

Rubeanic acid (i.e., Dithiooxamide)

0.2% DTO in ethanol (0.2 grams DTO in 100 ml EtOH)

2:5 dilution of ammonia (20 ml NH_4OH diluted to a total of 50 ml with diH_2O)

2-Nitroso-1-Naphthol

0.2% 2-NN in ethanol (0.2 grams 2NN in 100 ml ethanol)

2:5 dilution of ammonia (20 ml NH_4OH diluted to a total of 50 ml with diH_2O)

Procedure

- Moisten filter paper with the 2:5 ammonia solution.
- Press and hold moistened paper directly onto surface to be tested (do not rub).
- Spray or apply DTO solution onto filter paper. A green/gray color reaction indicates a POSITIVE reaction for copper (can be difficult to see reaction against dark or dirty backgrounds).

or

- Spray or apply 2-NN solution onto filter paper. A pink/red color reaction indicates a POSITIVE reaction for copper.

Note: A test of known copper (from a reference bullet) should be conducted prior to testing an unknown impact site.

Field Test for Lead: Sodium Rhodizonate (NaRho)

This test can detect the presence of lead. Many bullets have lead cores that on impact release trace amounts of lead. Also, the surface of even copper jacketed bullets may have lead generated from the firing process or from residues trapped in the barrel from prior shots. This examination uses acetic acid to partially dissolve lead onto swabs or filter paper. Acetic acid can also dissolve and remove copper, so if testing for copper is to be conducted, the copper test must be attempted before the lead test. After transferring lead onto the swab or filter paper with acetic acid, applying a sodium rhodizonate solution onto the test matrix will result in a purple color reaction when lead is present. A second chemical (hydrochloric acid (HCl)) can be applied next. The purple color will change to a dark blue when lead is present.

Materials

Rhodizonic acid, disodium

15% acetic acid solution (15 ml concentrated acetic acid diluted to 100 ml with diH_2O)

5% HCl solution (5 ml concentrated HCl diluted to 100 ml with diH_2O)

A small amount or NaRHO is diluted with water to create a dark orange colored solution.

Procedure

- Apply a drop of 15% acetic acid to a cotton swab or filter paper.
- Press and hold the swab against the suspect area.

- Place a drop of NaRHO solution onto swab with sample. *A dark purple color with orange background constitutes a first level positive for lead.*
- Place a drop of 5% HCl solution onto the purple reaction: The orange color should clarify and the purple change to blue to confirm lead.

Note: A test of known lead (from a reference bullet) should be conducted prior to testing an unknown impact site.

Negative results obtained by these tests for copper and lead do not necessarily eliminate the defect as having been caused by a fired bullet. For these tests to work, a detectable transfer must have occurred at the time of impact, the actual bullet to surface contact area must be directly sampled, and the background debris must not obscure the target color reaction. For these reasons, a positive color reaction is good supporting information for a bullet strike, but negative results may not be used alone to eliminate a bullet strike.

Reconstructing a Fired Bullet Trajectory

Trajectory is a term that describes a fired bullet's path. Long-range shots exhibit a curved trajectory because the extended time of flight allows more time for gravity to influence the fired bullet. Over short distances (Figure 7.33) because the flight time is relatively short, the curvature or drop due to gravity is small enough that it can be essentially ignored and the trajectory can be assessed as a straight line. Bullet path determination should always be handled with care as intermediate objects—walls, automobile glass, bodies, paved surfaces, and the like—may cause changes in the bullet path away from a predictable straight line. These changes in direction can involve many complicated variables, so the best approach is to always consider *what* has been impacted when assessing trajectory.

The most accurate way to determine bullet path over short distances is to connect two impact locations separated by sufficient distance. Connecting these two points (via a laser

Bullet Drop as a Function of Distance Traveled

(Calculated from Sierra Infinity Five Exterior Ballistics Software).

Caliber	Bullet Weight*	Muzzle Velocity**	Drop at 15 feet	Drop at 90 feet
0.22 Long Rifle	40 grain PbRN	1080 fps	~0.04 inches	~1.39 inches
9 mm Luger	115 grain FMJ	1160 fps	~0.03 inches	~1.21 inches
0.40 S&W	180 grain JHP	990 fps	~0.04 inches	~1.63 inches
0.45 Auto	230 grain TMJ	850 fps	~0.06 inches	~2.21 inches
0.223 Rem	55 grain JHP	3400 fps	~0.0 inches	~0.14 inches

*PbRN = Lead Round Nose; FMJ = Full Metal Jacket; JHP = Jacketed Hollow Point: TMJ = Total Metal Jacket
**fps = feet per second

Figure 7.33 This table demonstrates the amount of bullet drop for different bullets over two distances. In situations involving short ranges of fire, a bullet can be considered as having followed a straight flight path, unless some issue of redirection is possible.

line or trajectory rod) provides a visual representation of the bullet path. Mathematically, a rod positioned through two points represents the hypotenuse of a right triangle where the other legs of the triangle can be constructed secondarily. Typically, the closer two points are together, the less accurate the trajectory reconstruction will be. Even when two well-established impact sites are connected, it is always advisable to report a range (plus or minus 5 degrees is appropriate) to accommodate surface abnormalities, measurement error, and other variables unique to any particular situation.

Trajectory Measurement Technique

Once two (or more) suitable bullet impacts have been located, documented, and measured so they can be functionally placed in the scene, photographed, and chemically tested, one can begin to record the angles involved. On scenes where total station or similar survey techniques are being used, measurements of the rod itself can be recorded by acquiring a reading at the base of the rod and at the tip of the rod. It is advisable to also record the angles directly. Not only does this provide a back-up measurement, it provides the examiner with data instantly. These data may assist with further examination and reconstruction of the scene (e.g., the trajectory may indicate where to look for other evidentiary items like shoe prints, cigarette butts, or cartridge cases).

Every trajectory has a horizontal and vertical angle. Considering these values independently is the easiest way to keep on track when documenting trajectories. The technique involves the use of trajectory rods, a "zero-edge" 180-degree protractor, an angle finder, and a carpenter's plumb bob.

Horizontal Angle

The horizontal angle is simply the North, South, East, or West component of the shot. To measure the horizontal aspect, connect two impact sites with a rod and place the center of a 180-degree protractor at the base of the rod. The protractor must always be held flat and level. Never pivot the protractor up or down to meet the rod when determining the horizontal—it is always measured with the protractor parallel to the ground and level. Next, the tip of the rod must be read against the protractor scale. While aligning the center point of the level protractor against the base of the rod, the plumb is held along the edge of the rod and the angle indicated at the intersection of the hanging plumb against the protractor is recorded as the horizontal angle (Figure 7.34).

A second technique for recording the horizontal angle involves using the plumb bob to translate the positions of the base and tip of the rod onto the level ground below. Place the plumb bob at the base of the rod and let the weight drop to the ground and mark that position. Next, place the plumb out toward the tip of the rod and mark that second position on the ground. Connecting the two points translated onto the ground represents the hypotenuse (horizontal angle) of a right triangle. Using a carpenter square, construct the opposite and adjacent legs of a right triangle. The intersection of the wall with the floor may provide a convenient reference for one of the legs, and the other can be filled in to complete the right triangle (Figure 7.35). If this technique is used, one can translate the angle onto paper that can be labeled and saved with scene notes. In both instances, photographing the protractor from directly above (or below) while the plumb is in place will document the angles for future reconstruction.

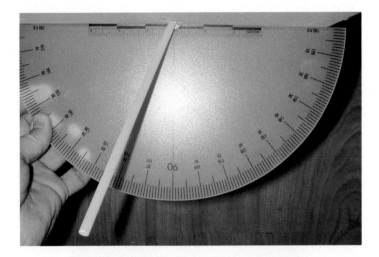

Figure 7.34 Recording the horizontal trajectory angle. Always hold the protractor level and translate the end of the rod to the edge of the protractor. In this image, the measure would be read on the inside of the rod and reported as either "from left to right at ~68 degrees" or "~22 degrees left of going straight into the wall."

Vertical Angle

The vertical angle is the up/down component of the trajectory. For this measurement, the protractor must be held straight up and down (aligning with a plumb bob will help) with the zero point of the protractor at the base of the rod. For vertical measure, the protractor should be "rolled" to meet alongside the rod and the angle read directly. Photographically, the image should be recorded with the plumb bob in the picture and the photo taken while the camera

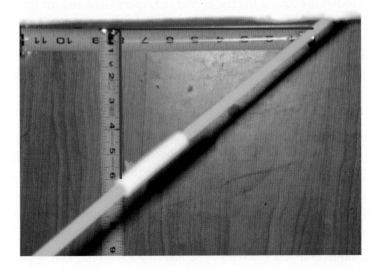

Figure 7.35 The horizontal angle aspect is always recorded on a level plane and one method is to translate the angle to the floor as in this photo; this allows for easier documentation. The photo is taken looking down onto the floor from above. The wall with the defect is at the top of the image.

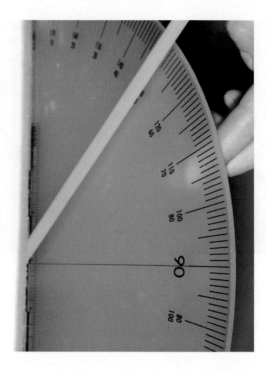

Figure 7.36 Vertical angle measurement recorded using a protractor. Reading the protractor on scene identified the angle as downward at approximately 40 degrees relative to level (–40 degrees). However, because the photograph was not taken properly (it is not taken parallel to the rod), actually measuring the angle from the photo will result in the incorrect angle of –55 degrees—a significant error.

is parallel to the rod. If the base of the rod is near the camera lens and the tip of the rod is far from the lens, distortion will result in the incorrect angle being recorded in the photograph.

A second and easier technique for recording the vertical angle is by laying an angle finder along the vertical aspect of the rod and simply reading and photographing the information directly from the device (Figure 7.36 and Figure 7.37).

Using a Laser to Define Trajectory

In many instances, it is difficult or impossible to insert a rod through two points because of the physical limitations of the object that has been shot. The use of lasers is an easy and accurate way to record these trajectories. The steps required include:

- Secure a laser onto a tripod (there are many commercial products for this).
- Position the laser line to pass through the multiple points and measure as you would with a rod (Figure 7.38).

In this technique, consider the laser to be just like a solid rod and document the horizontal angle by positioning the protractor level and moving a plumb bob around the perimeter of the protractor until the laser light hits the string holding the plumb. For the vertical angle rotate a protractor until it meets the laser light or simply place an angle finder on the laser itself and read the value.

Figure 7.37 Vertical angle measurement reading the angle directly from an angle finder is pictured. The angle is downward at approximately 23 degrees (–23 degrees).

The best circumstance for trajectory analysis is two or more in-line defects in which trajectory rods and or a laser trajectory are aligned. But this is not always the case. Additional situations that the analyst will encounter include:

- Deep penetrating defects in which a trajectory rod can be inserted or defects where obvious deflection occurred after entry into the surface
- Defects on surfaces in which no rod can be inserted

Figure 7.38 Lasers are often used in place of trajectory rods. The laser line is aligned with multiple defects and then photographed. The horizontal and vertical angle can be measured in the same fashion as when using a trajectory rod.

In the first situation, deep penetrating defects, the analyst proceeds with the analysis much as he did with multiple in-line defects. These types of defects are often found in vehicles, wallboards, or wood. If a bullet strikes a wallboard and then subsequently strikes a framing stud or similar intermediate target before exiting, this method will be useful as well. A trajectory rod is inserted into the deep penetrating defect using a centering guide. The centering guide is absolutely necessary, as it alone will align the rod to the penetration. Once seated, the angle is measured and documented in the same fashion.

In some instances impact angles can be calculated from the shape of the ellipse produced by the passage of the fired bullet through a surface. One must use caution when estimating trajectory angles in this manner as bullet deformation, substrate rigidity, bullet perimeter damage, and ricochet can all provide misleading information when considering only the bullet entry site. However, much like documenting and measuring an elliptical bloodstain, when the matrix results in a nondeformed ellipse, length to width ratios may be useful in recording entry angles. Much like documenting and measuring a bloodstain, the resulting angles are somewhat different from the horizontal and vertical angles measured in the physical process described in this chapter; nevertheless these two angles define the general path the bullet struck the surface at and do offer insight in terms of the overall reconstruction. Except in very specific circumstances, one should use extreme caution in attempting to determine caliber of projectile based exclusively on the overall dimensions of the resulting defect ellipse.

Photographing Laser Trajectories

Photography of laser lines is not difficult, but the analyst needs to understand the basics of photography. Typical laser photography requires darkness so as to not overexpose the image. Once the laser line is constructed, a camera is positioned to the side of the laser line and set to "bulb" (that is with the shutter open). The laser line is exposed to the camera by reflecting the laser light off of a white panel or poster board oriented toward the camera. The panel used to reflect the laser light must be moved between the impact point and the laser source to record the entire length of the laser line. This can be accomplished by having a person position the poster board with the laser dot centered on the panel and then have that person walk the distance between the impact site and laser position keeping the red laser dot on the panel. Secondarily, one must "paint with light" or otherwise fill in the darkened surroundings for reference purposes (Figure 7.39). Alternatively, a well-lit digital photo can be acquired first, and then without moving the camera, the laser line recorded and the two images overlaid using digital image software.

Shots into Vehicles

Because vehicles are a frequent target of gunfire, some special techniques will be discussed that help accommodate processing vehicles. Vehicles have many curved and irregular surfaces. These design features can make it difficult to locate useful reference points to measure from or identify. To overcome these irregular surfaces, a process to make and assign your own reference positions will be described. Often objects like a logo, hood ornament, inside rearview mirror, or inside brake light are engineered to be at the centerline of a vehicle. These natural landmarks are used as reference baselines to record the positions of bullet damage to vehicles.

Figure 7.39 This laser trajectory was photographed using a bulb setting and paint with light technique.

Establishing a Baseline for Vehicles

To provide external reference lines around a vehicle, one must first find two relatively parallel positions along one of the sides of the vehicle. A fixed measure, for instance 3 inches out from the center of the hub of the front and back wheels, can be marked on the ground. Connecting these two points constitutes a straight baseline that represents the side of the car. Extend this baseline several feet beyond the front and back of the vehicle. Once defined, this baseline can be made more visible by using masking or other tape over the line constructed.

Next, hang a plumb from the center of the front or back of the vehicle and mark that position. Connect the plumb position to the side baselines by extending a line all the way across the front or back of the vehicle. Use a carpenter's square to ensure the lines intersect at 90 degrees. Two legs of a rectangle should be defined on the ground—one across the front or back and one along one of the sides (Figure 7.40). If needed, the other two sides of the vehicle can be referenced in the same manner described completing a reference line around the vehicle.

Once the baselines are established, measurements of bullet strike positions on the vehicle can be identified by measuring "x" inches back and "y" inches over, relative to the external baselines.

Using a 360-Degree Scale for Vehicles

Because vehicles are mobile and may be hit at the front, back, or sides during the same event, assignment of angles of trajectory can get confusing. One method that may help resolve ambiguity about which trajectory is being documented is the use of a 360-degree reference. Rather than breaking the vehicle into 180-degree segments, the entire 360-degree scale will be used.

To use a 360-degree scale for trajectory measurement, zero degrees must be assigned prior to the measurements. For a vehicle, assigning the front as zero degrees is intuitive and is recommended because most people using a 360-degree process commonly understand that the front equals zero degrees. From that zero-degree assignment, all subsequent

Figure 7.40 Providing external reference lines for vehicles is also known as "squaring a vehicle." Mark an equidistant reference from two points on the side, connect the points, mark the front plane, and connect via a carpenter square.

trajectories will be based on the clockwise assignment of a 360-degree circle (Figure 7.41). If the front of the car is assigned zero degrees, a bullet trajectory striking from the rear at the back of the car would be 180 degrees, a bullet striking from the right into the passenger side would be 90 degrees, and a bullet striking straight from the left would be 270 degrees.

Once two points of a trajectory have been established, the trajectory rod will be pointing back to the location of the bullet origin. The vertical angle is measured in the ways previously described. When reporting trajectories from this type of process, one should use nomenclature, such as: "Shot A *originated from* approximately *x* degrees…." For example: *The bullet that caused trajectory "A" originated from approximately 228 degrees and was traveling downward at approximately 10 degrees.*

Recording Trajectory Angles

Consistent and clear recording of angles is essential in trajectory documentation. In notes, it is often very helpful to draw a sketch of the top view (horizontal angle) and the side view (vertical angle) of the trajectory you are recording so that should confusion arise later during reconstruction, the diagram (along with photographs) can clarify discrepancies in the record.

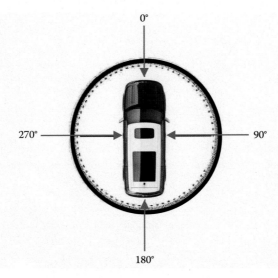

Figure 7.41 A schematic of the 360-degree assignment for angles.

Beyond written notes, photography is the best way to document established trajectories. Because photographs are two-dimensional representations of three dimensional objects, the correct orientation of photographs must be recorded or the photo may be deceptive.

For documenting the horizontal angles, a photograph straight down (perpendicular to) the level protractor should be taken. While parts of the actual rod may be out of focus, the photo will record the horizontal plane (north, south, east, west) from where the bullet originated. One way to evaluate if a horizontal photo has been taken correctly is to see if all numbers on the protractor are in focus.

For the vertical angle, the photograph should be taken perpendicular to the rod itself, i.e., all positions of the rod should be in focus. It is tempting to record a vertical angle from along an adjacent wall because these images can be visually appealing. The addition of a vertical reference (like a weighted string against the rod) will provide a reference from which the angle can be remeasured if needed.

Finally, demonstrative photographs are good for visual assessment and court presentation. These photos are taken for a completely different purpose than the ones used to record the angles. For demonstrative images, multiple probes inserted into a vehicle can show the general orientation of shots, but these cannot be used to remeasure the actual angles (Figure 7.42).

Reporting Measured Trajectory Angles

There are a variety of methods that can be used to report the measured trajectories. The only requirement for reporting is that everyone who reads the reported angles must be able to visualize the same result, and that result must be what was actually measured at the scene. One can test the report technique by showing the written results to an individual who knows nothing about the correct angles and having him sketch what that report looks like to him.

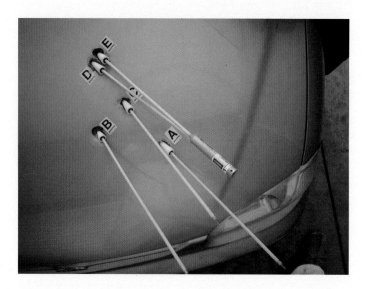

Figure 7.42 A demonstrative photo of multiple trajectory rods. Because of the perspective this photo was taken at, the angles in the photo cannot be used to calculate the true angles recorded at the scene. It simply demonstrates that the bullets were striking the vehicle on the right from a position forward of the driver's door.

Horizontal Angles

While facing a bullet hole surface (such as a wall) the position to the left of the bullet defect can be assigned as zero degrees and the position to the right of the defect can be assigned as 180 degrees. This is what a 180-degree protractor placed against the wall would show. Results are recorded and reported as from left to right exactly as they are read from the protractor:

- Bullet "A" originated from approximately 126 degrees (from left to right) and downward at approximately 22 degrees.

While saying that bullet "A" described here was from "left to right" seems counterintuitive (because the origin was from the right side of the protractor), this technique assures that there is only one number available for each trajectory (that is an angle between zero and 180 degrees). Everything at a horizontal angle greater than 90 degrees is originating from the right side of the 180-degree scale.

A second way to report the horizontal trajectory discussed above is to say:

- Bullet "A" was traveling from right to left and originated from approximately 54 degrees out from the wall.

Either of the techniques offered here or any modification can be employed as long as it is clear to the reader of the notes, documentation, and report exactly what angle is described and that angle cannot be misinterpreted.

Vertical Angles

Vertical angles are more intuitive to understand than a horizontal angle and can simply be described as "x" degrees upward or "x" degrees downward. Some examiners abbreviate by using plus or minus signs, such that 20 degrees downward would be −20 degrees, and 16 degrees upward would be +16 degrees. Again, as long as it is clear and there is no ambiguity to the reader of the report, the method is valid.

Gunshot Residue Examination

There are two different examinations associated with gunshot residue, and these two tests are often confused. The first is also known as muzzle effluent—it tests for the products that follow the bullet out of the barrel; the other test is for primer residue, material originating from the primer of the cartridge.

Muzzle Effluent

Muzzle effluent is comprised of the products within the ignited and expanding gases that follow the projectile out of the firearm. These products are most typically nitrites (a combustion product of nitrocellulose), smoke, and soot (vaporized lead and debris from the high temperatures of discharge), and particles of unburned or partially burned gun powder. Because these products are very light weight (nonmassive), they generally cannot travel great distances (typically no more than 4 or 5 feet), but can be seen with the naked eye if the surface impacted is not overly complicated or bloodstained.

When an intervening object is in line and relatively close to the exit end (muzzle) of a firearm, the intervening object has the potential to retain a pattern of the muzzle effluent and gun powder particles (Figure 7.43). When a firearm is in contact with an object, the effluent energy and velocity is at its greatest and may be blasted directly through the exterior layer and into a wound or underlying layers. As the muzzle to target distance increases, the light weight and mass of smoke, soot, and particles quickly slow them down and they spread out as they mix with the ambient air. The farther away an intercepting surface, the larger the diameter of the resulting pattern becomes. Ultimately the distance between muzzle and target is so great (approximately 4 to 5 feet), the particles run out of forward

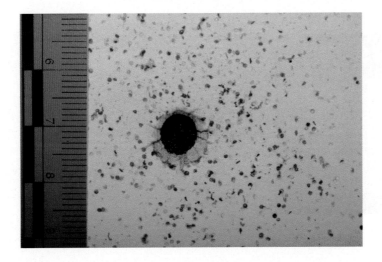

Figure 7.43 Shown is a pattern of gunpowder particles surrounding a bullet hole. This test shot was delivered onto paper from a .45 caliber pistol at 6 inches away. The multicolored disks are partially burned gun powder particles.

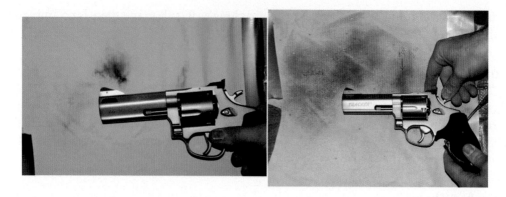

Figure 7.44 A revolver fired adjacent to the wall left residue defining the distance between the cylinder gap and muzzle. At right, the sodium rhodizonate reagent was used to develop the vaporous lead in the pattern.

energy and simply fall to the ground. By comparing the shape and distribution of patterns observed in a scene to reference patterns generated at a later time, an estimation of firearm to target distance can be determined.

At times, objects adjacent to the discharge of a firearm can intercept residues that are forced out of the opening in the firearm. With revolvers, because there is a gap between the cylinder and the barrel (to accommodate opening the firearm), gunshot residues may be forced from the cylinder gap and the muzzle. If an object is immediately adjacent to the firearm, it may be possible to develop a profile that defines the dimension of the firearm barrel (Figure 7.44).

Stippling is a term used for a pattern of punctuated gun powder impact wounds that occur when a firearm is discharged close to uncovered skin. To generate stippling on skin, the particles of gun powder must have sufficient energy to wound or damage the skin when they impact. A stippling pattern is usually associated with close range gunshots and when present identifies the entry side of a gunshot (Figure 7.45).

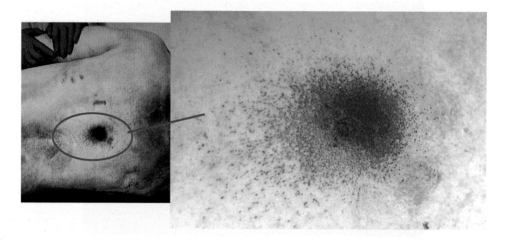

Figure 7.45 Pictured is a stippling pattern comprised of hundreds of small punctuate wounds surrounding a bullet entry indicating a close range for the gunshot wound to the back.

Clothing often retains gunshot residues useful for muzzle to target distance determination; therefore, care must be taken to protect and recover clothing whenever possible. When a victim is transported from a scene to an emergency treatment facility, it is very important to recover the clothing left at the scene or removed while at the hospital.

Primer Residue

Another product associated with gunshot residue testing originates from the explosive priming mixture. Upon detonation of the priming mixture, microscopic particles of fused barium, antimony, and lead can "leak" out of openings of a firearm. These products can land on the hands of a shooter or adjacent objects at the time of discharge. They are not visible to the naked eye and require a scanning electron microscope (SEM) to see and detect them. These products are easily dislodged from the surfaces on which they land and finding them does not necessarily identify that a person has fired a gun.

Testing for primer residue typically involves using sticky tape to sample the area in question. By "dobbing" a stub with an exposed sticky side over the surface in question, these particles (if present) will stick to the surface of the stub. The entire stub can then be inserted into an SEM and searched for the particles in question. Interpretation of the meaning of a positive or negative result for these particles is subjective; finding these particles cannot identify a shooter and the absence of these particles cannot eliminate a shooter. Each result must be considered in context with the event being investigated.

Processing Shooting Scenes

With the wide variety of technical, common, and slang terms associated with firearm evidence, it is important that proper communication is established. For example, if a person says, "I recovered a slug from the driver's seat," you may be well advised to clarify if they have recovered a fired shotgun slug (correct term) or do they mean a fired bullet. Similar confusion can exist when one says that "there was a bullet sitting on the table." Do they mean a fired bullet (i.e., projectile) or do they mean a cartridge, the complete round of ammunition? A third example is differentiating a bullet jacket from a bullet core; the scene investigation must account for the potential for bullet cores to have separated from a bullet jacket. Also there must be a clear distinction between "fired cartridge cases" and "cartridges." Reconstruction will rely on the accurate communication of these terms.

Shooting scenes often seem overwhelming at first. When considering how best to process a scene consider mentally working backwards from a theoretical future "trial" to where you find yourself on scene in the present. When trying to decide, for example, whether to collect or leave a particular piece of evidence, consider if it may be useful for reconstruction or court presentation years later. If fired cartridge cases are on scene, one should attempt to find a fired bullet for each case recovered. Every fired bullet that

Vehicle Processing Worksheet

Case Number_____

Date_____

Year_____Make_____Model_____

VIN_____

Color (ext)_____Color (int)_____

Plates (state/number)_____

Doors_____Hatchback   Y   N

Damage/Descriptions_____

_____

_____

_____

_____

Defect #_____   Location_____ _ _

Description_____

_____

_____

Test for Copper_____N/A   Test for Lead_____ _N/A

Horizontal Angle_____   Vertical Angle_____

Projectile Recovery_____

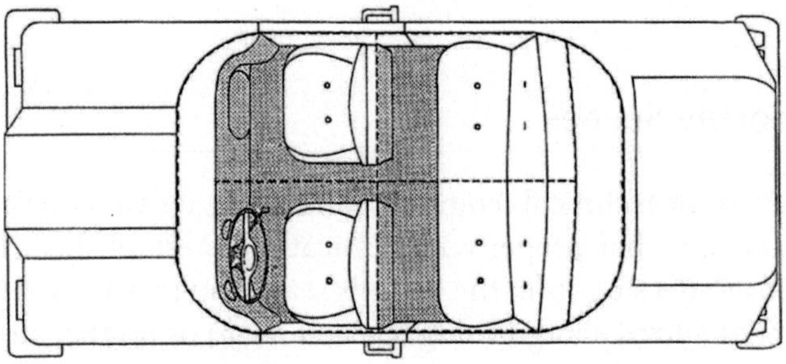

Figure 7.46 A sample worksheet for processing bullet defects and trajectories in a car.

you can find should be recovered because fired bullets left in a crime scene cannot be evaluated and will forever represent missing information in the scene. Remember, while working on scene you may not know what the future explanation or explanations for the event will be, so you must collect all relevant evidence to have the potential to reconstruct at a later time.

Deceased victims should be carefully evaluated in association with the medical examiner to attempt to ascertain if any fired bullets exited the body. A careful evaluation of the clothing at the scene may help with shot accountability and may help preserve other valuable data, such as bloodstain evidence or gunshot residue deposits. Remember, a fired bullet may be present in a saturated blood pool or embedded in a floor or crawlspace beneath the accumulated blood pool. If it can be determined that the body has not been repositioned, and an exit wound exists, this potential should be investigated.

In situations where a firearm is on scene or available for evaluation (such as in an officer-involved shooting or suspected suicide), an accurate count of unfired cartridges and firearm capacity may help assure that you have accounted for each shot delivered. While you may not be able to determine the total number of cartridges originally in a firearm, this evaluation should give you a maximum number of shots available.

Lastly, when clothing is present and worn by a deceased victim, take care to not further contaminate the appearance of that clothing. Patterns of bloodstains or gunshot residue that are visible as the victim is observed on scene may be obscured or obliterated by rolling or preparing the body for removal. With the assistance of the medical examiner, preserve this clothing by removing it prior to rolling the body or cutting and removing the important area to prevent secondary contamination from occurring. If cutting the clothing from the body, do not use potential bullet holes (or stab slits) as the starting point for your cut; make the cut irregular so the clothing can be reassembled via physical match and clearly document that you have conducted this process.

By reducing a shooting scene to simple individual components, one can process each aspect and combine all of the smaller observations into a complete reconstruction. For each shot you must process, imagine the mechanisms that must have occurred for the shot to occur, and look for evidence of each mechanism. Challenge yourself to track each shot from ignition in the firearm through to the final resting point of the bullet and repeat this process for each shot you must process. Accounting for each aspect of each shot will lead to a successful shooting reconstruction. Figure 7.46 to Figure 7.48 are

Trajectory Processing Worksheet

Case Number_____

Date_____

Defects #_____   Location_____

Damage/Descriptions_____
_____
_____
_____
_____

Test for Copper_____N/A   Test for Lead_____N/A

Horizontal Angle_____   Vertical Angle_____

Projectile Recovery _____
_____
_____
_____
_____

Figure 7.47 A sample worksheet for documenting each trajectory.

Firearm Processing Checklist

Case Number_____

Date_____

Location of
Firearm_____
_____

          Revolver   Semiautomatic Pistol   Rifle   Shotgun

             Other_____

Safety position_____

Condition of the Chamber_____

Magazine Inserted_____

Revolver Indexing (Sketch cylinder and casings positions)

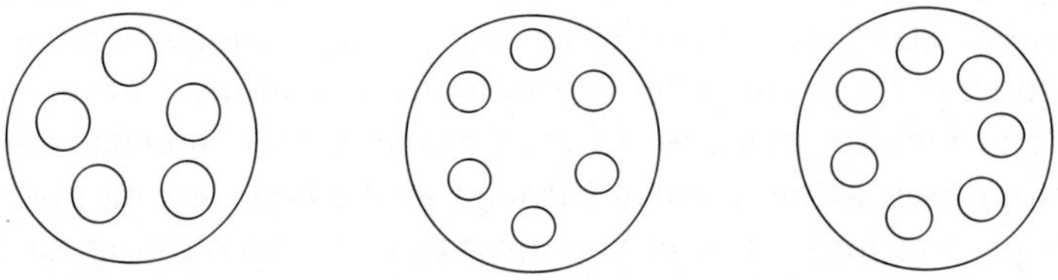

Additional notes:

_____
_____
_____
_____
_____

Figure 7.48 A sample worksheet for evaluating firearms.

Shooting Reconstruction Equipment List

General
Sharpie pens (silver and black)
Tape Measure
Calculator (with sin functions)
Packaging material
Bright light (300 Watt halogen or equivalent)
General Tools (for disassembly to recover bullets)
Reciprocating Saw (for cutting into structures) and blades
Masking Tape
Camera
Ladder
Gloves

Trajectory
Trajectory Rods
Centering Guides
Zero Edge Protractors
Plumb Bob
Level
Angle finder
2 ft × 2 ft right angle (Carpenter Square)
Tripods
Laser
String
Traditional Compass

Field Testing Bullet Strikes
Sodium Rhodizonate and associated chemicals -(test for lead)
2-NN and associated chemicals -(test for copper)
DTO and associated chemicals-(test for copper)
Acetic Acid
Ammonium Hydroxide
Ethanol
Hydrochloric Acid
Swabs (Q-tips)
Reference Copper and Lead
Graduated Cylinder
Sprayers/Applicators

Figure 7.49 A basic shooting reconstruction kit might include the items listed here.

examples of basic shooting scene worksheets that are an effective method of capturing all pertinent data. A list of the basic shooting scene specific supplies and equipment is listed in Figure 7.49.

Summary

Ultimately, if the analyst is to understand and functionally reconstruct a shooting scene, he must incorporate three basic elements. The first is any terminal ballistics provided by the medical examiner or scene impacts. This information will allow the analyst to understand generally in what orientation the bullet struck and passed through the victim or object. The second element is the information derived from the scientific examination performed by the firearms examiner. This information may provide clues as to distance of fire, and certainly allow correlation of bullets, casings, and weapons. Finally the analyst must consider the exterior ballistics as described in this chapter, where specific trajectories are defined from the various defects found in the scene. Only by considering all of this information can a reasonable explanation for the shooting event be defined.

Each situation will present its own limitations based on the data available and the context in which the firearm evidence is found, but using whatever information is available, some conclusion may be possible. In the best circumstances, the analyst may be able to define a relatively specific position for the shooter and certainly exclude other positions. In worse case scenarios, the analyst may only define general direction of fire or perhaps nothing at all with regard to the shooter's position. Depending on the data available, in a best-case circumstance, the analyst may be able to define the victim's position in conjunction with a specific scene trajectory. In other situations (e.g., when there is only terminal ballistic information), it may be impossible to limit the victim's position at all. Each scene is different, and each scene demands consideration of all of the available evidence.

Chapter Author

Matthew Noedel holds Bachelor of Science degrees in Microbiology and Medical Technology with a minor in Chemistry from the University of Montana. He received a third bachelor's degree in forensic science from California State University at Sacramento. Noedel began in the field of forensic science as a toxicologist and chemist and conducted lab work on such notable cases as the Exxon Valdez shipwreck and the Dorothea Puente serial murders in Sacramento, California. In 1990, Noedel joined the Washington State Patrol Crime Lab and by 1992 was a member of the Crime Scene Response Team (CSRT) where most notably he assisted in processing some of the homes and vehicles owned by Gary Ridgeway, the Green River Killer. In 1995, while with the CSRT, Noedel was assigned to the Firearm and Tool Mark section of the crime laboratory where he examined hundreds of firearm cases, including thousands of pieces of physical evidence related to shooting events. As a primary crime scene responder, Noedel was also responsible for much of the training and mentoring of new crime scene examiners.

Noedel founded the company Noedel Scientific in 2005 and continues to provide forensic examination, training, and consultation in shooting and other crime scene reconstructions. He is a Distinguished Member of the Association of Firearm and Tool Mark Examiners (AFTE) and certified by that organization in firearm, tool mark, and gunshot residue examination. He was the editor of the *AFTE Journal* from 2003 through 2008 and continues to serve as an assistant editor for the journal. Noedel has been the president of the Northwest Association of Forensic Scientists (2008), a member of the International Association of Bloodstain Pattern Analysts, and is currently a board member of the Association for Crime Scene Reconstruction.

The Forensic Pathologist, the Body, and Crime Scene Reconstruction

8

SCOTT A. WAGNER, MD

Introduction

The forensic pathologist (FP), whether working as coroner or medical examiner, is duty bound to find the truth in the circumstances, cause, and manner of death. A death scene investigator (DSI) refers to an individual trained, and preferably certified, working as an indispensable part of the medical examiner/coroner (MEC) system. All individuals of the MEC system are part of the death investigation team providing expertise about the body to law enforcement, the legal system, and the public. When working with homicides, the facts learned from examining the body at the scene and at the autopsy provide key event segments in crime scene reconstruction. An FP is a physician (MD or DO) who has specialized in pathology (the study of injury and diseases of the human body) and further subspecialized in forensic pathology. The expertise, concern, and the very focus of the FP is the body.

The FP is trained in evaluating injuries (even in living victims) and diseases for forensic purposes and can often provide information to event segments involving chronology: namely, *termini ante, peri,* and *post quem* regarding the death and injuries of an individual. For example, once a victim is stabbed in the heart, what actions are possible, probable, or likely? If the person has severe heart or lung disease, how can the chronology of events change? What was the sequence of the wounds? Has the body been moved? Is the death a homicide or natural death? These and many other questions can be answered by the FP.

Theory and Approach to Death Scene Investigation

The body is often the largest and most important piece of evidence at crime scenes involving death. Examination of a body at the scene requires special training and should only be performed by an FP, certified death investigator, or other person specifically trained in death investigation. Autopsies should only be performed by an FP. Death investigation starts when the body is discovered, and working backward, the life is "reconstructed," similar to crime scene reconstruction. An old axiom in forensic pathology is that: "One takes the victim as he finds him." This simply means that one starts from the undeniable fact that the person is deceased, and works back to the point where the person was alive, collecting and analyzing findings along the way. No assumptions are made because facts are determined as the result of the examination of this specific victim, with his unique set of circumstances, medical conditions, and injuries. Facts are collected about the scene, then the body, and assembled like pieces of a puzzle; then opinions are rendered regarding the injuries and ultimately the cause and manner of death is determined.

Just as in crime scene analysis, the death is "reverse engineered" to find the true, underlying cause that, if removed from the situation, would find the person still alive. For example, an individual is found shot in the head. The autopsy shows a gunshot wound through the skull causing laceration of brain tissue and hemorrhage. Analysis shows that but for the gunshot wound causing massive brain laceration and bleeding, the person would be alive. The cause of death is the disease or injury that sets into motion the chain of events leading to death, or gunshot wound of the head in the example. The mechanism(s) or proximate cause(s) of death is/are the major biochemical or pathophysiological problems initiated by the cause of death, or laceration of the brain and hemorrhage in this example. The manner of death classifies the death for medical–legal purposes and is designated homicide, suicide, accident, natural, or undetermined (unclassified).

The time-honored crime scene principle "nothing just happens" has a corollary in death investigation. No person just "dies," and in homicide, no one is killed without a trace, as every contact leaves a trace. Our current technology, methods, techniques, and even "luck" might be inadequate to detect or even prove homicide beyond a reasonable doubt, but the facts and evidence of homicide are there nonetheless, hidden for the time being. The autopsy itself is limited. For example, because the autopsy cannot detect cardiac arrhythmias, a person dying of a sudden, lethal arrhythmia might have a normal appearing heart (and negative toxicology), and will be certified as "no anatomic cause of death." In this and other similar cases, however, violent death is nearly always ruled out, because circumstances, injuries, and toxicology do not indicate violence. The autopsy is not the entire investigation either, and is only part of a complete investigation of the crime scene. Subtle homicides are often only detected by close collaboration of all members of the crime investigation team, coordinating scene investigation, witness statements, forensic science, and a complete autopsy with full toxicologic examination.

Homicides

Homicide is a medical–legal term and is defined as a person or persons killing another human being, either by commission or omission. Murder, manslaughter, and reckless homicide are strictly legal terms referring to the degree of action in the homicide. Certifying a case "manner of death, homicide" by a medical examiner or coroner, does not mean the perpetrator committed murder, or will even face legal charges. The policeman shooting the school sniper is an example of "justifiable" homicide. Shootings and stabbings are often the obvious homicides, and some doubt the value of a full investigation and autopsy in a case where the cause of death is "obvious." For example, a common question is, "Why, in the case of a witnessed homicide of a single gunshot wound of the head, is an autopsy necessary"? Here are but a few reasons for an autopsy in such a case:

- To confirm the cause and manner of death: that which is "obviously" true to a lay person's observation, occasionally proves to be false by examination of an expert.
- To gather event sequences for crime scene reconstruction (CSR) to confirm or refute the purported chain of events leading to the death.
- To provide photographic evidence for court proceedings.

- To obtain the bullet and match it to a purported gun.
- To track a bullet through the body, e.g., the bullet might not have entered the brain (nonlethal), and the person was strangled instead by a second perpetrator.
- To obtain trace evidence.
- Witnesses might die or change statements; therefore, independent confirmation of statements is needed.
- To obtain specimens from the deceased for toxicology studies.
- To gather medical data for expert medical testimony.
- The forensic pathologist is a witness for the deceased. Direct examination by the forensic pathologist allows him or her to explain direct observations, such as injuries, to the court.
- To correlate the injuries and other observations on the body and the evidence with witness statements.
- To generate a report for the defense and its experts to review.
- Because the court and the jury have the expectation that such an exam should take place, i.e., doing a complete autopsy in homicides is a legal and medical standard in the United States.

One can see that the purpose of the autopsy is much more than simply determining the cause and manner of death. The body contains a wealth of evidentiary value and information for event segments; therefore, investigation of a homicide or potential homicide requires a full medical–legal autopsy so no reasonable investigative question remains unanswered, even when the cause of death is "obvious."

Five Basic Questions Posed by the Death Investigation

1. Who: Identity of the victim and the perpetrator(s).
2. What: What killed the victim?
3. Where: Where was the victim injured? Where did the victim die?
4. When: When was victim injured? When did the victim die?
5. How: How was the victim injured? How did the victim die?

These questions were outlined in the classic book, *Pathology of Homicide*, (Charles C Thomas Publishers, 1974) by Lester Adelson, MD and still hold true today. One should note that "Why" is notably absent. This is an important question, but not part of the standard death investigation; it is a question for others, such as psychologists, psychiatrists, courts, and even society. However, the aim is to provide the facts so that those who ask the question "Why" can have accurate information at hand.

Forming Preliminary Opinions: Be Suspicious but Objective

Upon receiving the first call and information about a death scene, one should formulate a working opinion about the nature of the case so that the proper resources are at the scene. Opinions are based on facts and as information is gathered, the facts can change. One should not be closed minded at any time, i.e., drawing a conclusion before all the information is available. Committing to a firm opinion too early in the investigation will stop objectivity. If the death investigator becomes biased and loses objectivity, this will show up in the conclusions of the investigation and even on the witness stand. Investigators who have participated in many scenes know that some small piece of evidence that seems insignificant at the scene can become huge at the time of trial. In a death investigation, attention to detail and objectivity are basic essentials.

The burden of proof is on the prosecution in criminal cases. For a death investigation team, this means that enough evidence is collected in a criminal case to prove guilt in a court of law beyond a reasonable doubt. Homicide, suicide, and accidents for that matter, must be proven to the standard of reasonable scientific probability or reasonable medical certainty. However, one must be suspicious and objective at the same time. The MEC is not law enforcement. The detectives have a different role, which is to find probable cause to arrest a suspect and assemble a motive and *corpus delecti* (body of the crime). The DSI should not try to do the detective's job, but should provide objective analysis of the evidence and information for the detective and other members of the prosecution team.

The role of the MEC is to find truthful, objective answers to the questions surrounding the death. One has only one first chance at the scene, and the information is easier to get and can be more accurate early in the investigation. Pertinent questions to be posed at the death scene are listed below.

Detailed Questions to Be Considered at the Scene:

- Identity and home address of the deceased.
- Reason the person is at the location at the time of death. Does the person belong there? (For example, person at a stranger's house.)
- Is the person dressed appropriately for the scene? (For example, shorts and a t-shirt outside in winter.)
- Begin investigating the person's background and medical history. Ask friends and family. If at a home, review files, business cards, medication bottles, etc.
- Begin to form a range of the time of death. When was the last time the mail or the newspaper was picked up? When was the person last seen or spoken to? Check cell or home phone. Check for the signs of death (see Signs of Death later in the chapter).
- Perform cursory examination of the body.
- Is this the only scene? Has the body been moved? Has the scene been altered or sanitized? (For example, if fingernails are missing from the fingers and are not at the scene, this could be a second or a sanitized scene (Figure 8.1).)
- Is the body position appropriate for the scene? Inappropriate livor or rigor indicates the body has been moved (Figure 8.2).
- How does the environment factor in the death and state of the body? (For example, multiple deaths in house in the winter could mean carbon monoxide poisoning. If the body is on a heat register, this could speed decomposition.)

The Body and the Death Scene

The body is often the largest piece of evidence at a death scene. The evidence or crime scene technician at the scene is usually the principle evidence collector, although any law enforcement personnel might also collect evidence. Generally, evidence should not be collected directly from the body at the scene unless that evidence is unstable, in danger of

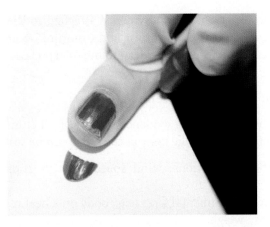

Figure 8.1 Broken fingernail from a homicide victim. The broken nail was found at a second crime scene, where the victim was most likely assaulted. Finding and matching this missing nail implicated a suspect in this strangulation homicide.

disappearing, or being significantly altered in transport. Lighting and other conditions are often poor at the crime scene, possibly resulting in inadequate recovery or even loss of evidence. The decision to collect evidence directly from the body at the scene is a judgment call and should be done in consultation with personnel in charge of the scene. This can include transferred evidence or evidence of unknown source, such as a small hair or nail fragment, which should be copiously photographed before removal. In blood pattern analysis, the pattern can be destroyed by placing the body in the bag; therefore, key items of clothing should be collected in such cases. In most cases evidentiary items, such as clothing, should remain on the body for collection at the morgue, which affords better lighting

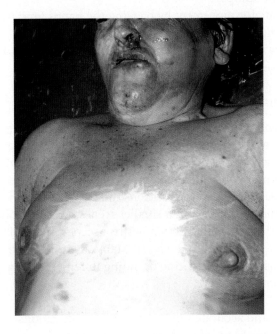

Figure 8.2 Anterior livor mortis. Cleared livor mortis on the front of the body and the folded arms indicate this body was found face down and turned over.

and a controlled environment to collect evidence attached to the body. Any substantial examination of injuries should also only occur in the morgue because clothing, blood, and poor lighting can obscure the wounds and lead to misinterpretation.

Examination of the Body at the Scene

After the body and the surrounding evidence have been documented, the body can be examined. The steps of examining the body at the scene can be summarized as follows:

- Note the location, conditions, wind speed and direction, temperature, and humidity.
- Note significant environmental facts (e.g., body on a heat register).
- Check given sex, weight, and height against direct observation of the body. Driver's license and other IDs are often inaccurate.
- Starting where the body lies, examine from head to toe (preferably prone, or front of body facing up). This exam should be repeated after the body is moved if the body was in an awkward or contorted position.
- Remove any trace evidence that could be lost in transport. In most cases, evidence on the body should remain on the body until the autopsy.
- Do not undress the body at the scene or remove any medical devices from resuscitation
- Begin scene assessment of the body.
- Assess rigor, livor, and algor mortis, as well as decomposition.
- Evaluate for signs of trauma and disease.
- Be sure to photographically document the body before, during, and after the exam.
- Note any significant findings or questions and discuss those with the pathologist prior to or at the autopsy.
- Prepare the body for movement by bagging the hands (and head as some prefer) and by wrapping the body in a clean white sheet.
- DO NOT allow the body to be transported face down. This can cause livor to fix in the face as well as "smashing" the face and nose.

Photographic Documentation of the Scene and the Body

The camera is an essential tool of the death investigation. To use a photograph in a court, it must be a "true and accurate representation" of what the investigator views at the scene. The DSI should have access to a digital camera and, at a minimum, know how to use the basic features. While many jurisdictions employ technicians to perform standard crime scene photography, there are numerous reasons the DSI will find the digital camera likely the most useful tool in his or her bag. At smaller scenes, DSI might be the only individual with a camera. Also, the MEC offices often desire a second set of pictures, focused on the body and the evidence connected to the body. Many investigators find that having digital images handy can assist in report writing by aiding in remembering significant details.

Uses of digital photography:

- Provides a true and accurate representation of observations
- Documents the positions of evidence and the body
- Documents the steps of removal of evidence and the body

- Allows immediate review of the photograph's quality
- Refreshes the memory, days or even years later
- Allows experts, colleagues, and jurors to review the evidence
- Digital format allows ease of enlarging the image
- Ease of storage and sharing of digital images

Focusing on the body, the DSI should tell a photographic story about the body at the scene. Photos are taken before any objects are moved. Overall photos of the relationship of the body to the environment and evidence should be shot. Then focus toward the body and evidence around the body. Photos should then be taken depicting all four sides of the body (including the back). When possible, the photographs should be taken at right angles to a body or object, to avoid a *perspective illusion* in the photo. Perspective illusion causes objects in the foreground to appear larger than those in the background, when an object is photographed at anything other than a 90-degree angle. As the photographic documentation proceeds, one should review the photos periodically for quality.

Polaroid photography is useful for identification photos because the print can be made on the spot and shown to family members. These photos can deteriorate over time, and should be scanned and made into a digital file if long-term storage is needed. Video documentation is another useful tool, especially in complex death scenes. The body, evidence, and other objects can be viewed from multiple angles. Because a video consists of 30 frames per second, the mind assembles this group of images into a three-dimensional view of the object. Also, by panning and zooming in and out, a video can provide a perspective of the scene and body location hard to match with still photography. Digital video is widely available and easily stored.

In any type of visual identification, be it photos or videos, one should generally avoid shots of an investigator performing a task. Investigators are not actors nor are they accustomed to appearing on camera. Camera angles, shadows, and perspective artifacts can distort the facts and detract from the main goal of visual documentation: to provide a *true and accurate representation* of the facts.

Many investigators keep a photo log, recording the location, date, condition, case number, photo number, and notes about the photos. Photos should be made with some type of designation of the date and time the photos are logged. This can be accomplished simply by burning the files to a compact disc and signing and dating the disc. Many programs automatically designate the time a photo was taken and the date modified. In any event, these steps will allow the investigator to demonstrate the photos were not altered after being taken.

Position of the Body at the Scene

Victims may be found in contorted or apparently uncomfortable positions on the floor, commonly the bedroom or bathroom. As a general guideline, the more contorted the body, the more sudden the death. The person appears to have "fallen in his tracks." However, this does not mean the decedent lying apparently comfortably in bed did not also die suddenly. Bodies found in awkward positions that compromise breathing can die of positional asphyxia. The chest wall must be able to rise and fall for respiration to occur. If one is wedged too tightly in a position, the chest wall cannot rise and fall. Consider also that the covering of the mouth and nose, such as in an intoxicated person lying face down, can cause obstructive asphyxia and suffocation. For these reasons, it is essential that the body position is documented either by photography or by description of witnesses when the body has been moved.

Blood at the Scene

Both natural and unnatural deaths can produce abundant blood at a scene. Traumatic deaths that involve arterial or venous bleeding, such as stabbing, can produce abundant blood at the scene with spattering often high on the walls or ceiling. When recognized, the spattering should be examined by experts in this area. Gunshot wounds can cause extensive external bleeding, but some wounds can cause minimal external bleeding and massive internal bleeding. In short, the amount of blood perceived at a scene does not necessarily indicate the severity of the trauma within the body. The scene should be correlated with the autopsy findings to determine the event sequence. For example, information at the crime scene suggests that the victim was shot to death, but very little blood is present at the scene. Subsequent autopsy in this case can show a deep wound, such as in the abdomen, with abundant blood in the abdomen. This example illustrates the necessity of correlating the scene and the autopsy to provide the proper context and event sequence.

Certain natural deaths can produce abundant blood at a scene, mimicking a violent death. Alcoholics can bleed from varices in the esophagus. The varices are dilated blood vessels produced when blood travels around the liver, hardened by cirrhosis. Stomach ulcers can cause fatal bleeding. Lung tumors or tuberculosis can produce bleeding from the lung. This bleeding can be quite extensive when the victim coughs up blood, which can be seen in the toilet, bathtub, towels, and sinks. Even severe nosebleeds can cause a fatality in the right conditions.

At times, other fluids can be mistaken for blood, such as the purged fluid that exudes from the mouth and nose in decomposing bodies. This fluid is brown and malodorous. Any doubts about the origin of the fluid can be answered at the autopsy.

Vomitus

One common problem in the investigation of sudden death is the interpretation of the presence of vomitus on the face. Many investigators have learned incorrectly that the presence of vomitus indicates that the deceased aspirated or choked on the vomitus, and that this represents the cause of death. Vomiting is often an involuntary action that is present in deaths of many causes. Vomitus contains acid powerful enough to cause chemical burns on the face, making it appear that a caustic chemical had been ingested. Aspiration of large amounts of vomitus material can cause death, and if the person initially survives, can develop severe pneumonia, which can be fatal as well. The goal of the investigation is to find the cause of the vomiting, which will aid in finding the cause and the manner of death.

Vomitus is routinely seen in a number of deaths (which the author calls *terminal vomiting*), including deaths involving profound unconsciousness, such as drug- or alcohol-induced coma and brain injury or disease. Cardiac deaths often produce vomiting. In fact, virtually any death can produce vomiting, likely because there is a period of profound loss of consciousness and loss of neuronal control of visceral reflexes. Noting vomitus in multiple locations around the scene can be an indication of an illness causing vomiting, rather than terminal vomiting.

Physical Examination of the Body at the Scene

Scene Assessment

The body is assessed or examined head to toe at the scene. The aim of this examination is to gain some insight into the nature of the death. Wounds can be blood covered and the lighting poor, so firm conclusions cannot be drawn from this exam. Keep in mind an autopsy will likely be performed. At the autopsy, a more detailed examination will be made at the morgue, where the body can be undressed, the lighting is better, and the environment is more controlled.

A scene assessment of the body can provide law enforcement and others of the death investigation team with a working cause of death, or at least several possibilities. It should be made clear that this information is preliminary and subject to a full autopsy and further investigation. Often, the MEC or DSI is asked specifics about wounds, etc. Any conclusions made after a scene investigation can be taken literally, so most death investigators are cautious and make it clear that *all opinions are working opinions.*

The Body, the Four Signs of Death, and the Time of Death

When first touching the body, the four signs of death should be evaluated because, once the body is moved, the rigor mortis will be changed or "broken." After rigor, algor, and livor mortis are assessed, the remainder of the scene assessment of the body can begin.

The determination of time of death, or the interval between the time of death and when the body is found (i.e., postmortem interval), can only be estimated unless there are irrefutable bits of evidence (e.g., death in hospital), credible witnesses, or a watch breaks and freezes the time of the traumatic incident. The longer the time since death, the greater the chance for error one has in determining the postmortem interval. There are numerous individual observations using the body and investigative information, which, when used together, provide the best estimate of the time of death. In order to create the best estimate of the postmortem interval, the examiner must check the following: rigor mortis, livor mortis, body temperature, and decompositional changes. A thorough scene investigation is necessary. The scene environment is the single most important factor in determining the postmortem interval. Keep in mind that in most cases, the post mortem interval is only a best estimate of the time of death, for which only a range of times can be given.

Rigor Mortis   Rigor mortis literally means "the stiffening of death." It is a chemical reaction in which a stable complex of adenosine and myosin of the muscle fibers causes stiffening in a flexion position (bent). It is a chemical reaction that comes and goes. In checking for rigor, the jaw, arms, and then the legs are straightened out of the flexion position and the resistance is assessed. Rigor mortis is typically reported as:

- Not yet present
- Beginning in the jaw
- Beginning in the extremities
- Full rigor
- Beginning to dissipate
- No longer present

Because rigor mortis is a chemical reaction, there are many variables on the rate of formation depending on the environment, size of the person, and condition of the person at death. Other rigor mortis facts include:

- Muscles begin to stiffen within 1 to 3 hours after death at 70 to 75°F, developing fully after 9 to 12 hours.
- A high fever or high environmental temperature will cause rigor to occur sooner.
- Rigor mortis will occur more quickly if the decedent was involved in strenuous physical activity just before death.
- Rigor mortis is detected first in the jaw, face, upper and lower extremities, in that order. The examiner must check the jaw, then the arms, and finally the legs, to feel if the associated joints are movable.
- The body is said to be in complete (full) rigor when the jaw, elbow, and knee joints are immovable. This takes approximately 9 to 12 hours at 70 to 75°F environmental temperature.
- The body will remain stiff for 24 and up to 36 hours at 70 to 75° before the muscles begin to loosen, usually in the same order they stiffened.
- Rigor is retarded in cooler temperatures and accelerated in warmer temperatures.
- When the body stiffens, it remains in that position until the rigor passes or the joint is physically moved and the rigor is broken (or decomposition occurs).
- The position of a body in full rigor can give an indication (together with livor) whether or not a body has been moved after death (Figure 8.3).

Livor Mortis (Blood Settling)   Livor mortis is the gravity-dependant settling of blood after death. After death, with the stoppage of the heart, gravity takes over and the blood settles in the lowest parts of the body. If these areas are pressed, the lividity will clear or "blanch." Because blood is pigmented, it eventually leaches out of the blood vessels, breaks

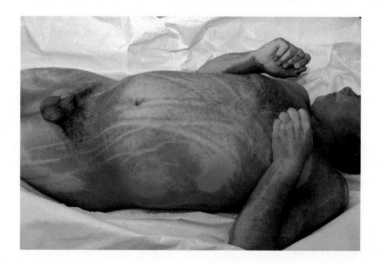

Figure 8.3 The rigor and livor pattern tell a story. This body was found face down on a wrinkled sheet in rigor with the hands up as shown. Turning the body over reveals the arms figured in a flexed position and pressure-cleared livor including long vertical lines from the wrinkles in the sheet.

down (hemolyzes), and then "stains" the tissues after a period of time (called fixed lividity). Livor mortis is recorded as follows:

- Absent
- Blanching in the dependant (down) areas
- Partially fixed in the dependant areas
- Fixed in the dependant areas
- Covering most or all of the body (e.g., bodies found in water)

If a body is moved before lividity is fixed, lividity will shift, causing two patterns. This phenomenon can allow the investigator to detect whether a body has been moved. Intense lividity can be mistaken for contusions by nonexperts. Any questions regarding lividity and contusions can be resolved at autopsy. Lividity does not involve hemorrhage into the skin, as does a contusion. Below are additional facts regarding livor mortis:

- Livor mortis is a purplish red discoloration in the tissues that can be seen as early as 30 minutes after death, and becomes more visible over time.
- Blood will settle in the blood vessels, then tissues (when "fixed") in the gravity dependant (lowest) areas of the body.
- Dependant areas that contact the surface the body is resting on will show "clearing of livor." Also, the bony areas beneath the skin will compress the skin against the surface and prevent the blood from settling in the tissues (Figure 8.4).
- Livor mortis is noticeable approximately 1 hour after death and becomes "fixed" in about 8 to 10 hours.
- When livor is fixed, the color will not blanch under pressure and will remain in those areas even if the body is repositioned.
- Even if the body is moved after lividity is fixed, there may be a slight discoloration in the new dependant areas even though the blood remains fixed in the original position.

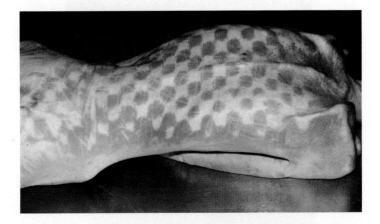

Figure 8.4 Patterned livor mortis. Because livor mortis can be cleared with pressure, objects pressing against the skin when livor forms can cause a pattern. This individual was lying on an "egg crate" foam mattress. The foam tips of the mattress touch the skin and clear the livor, while the cups of the mattress allow the livor to form.

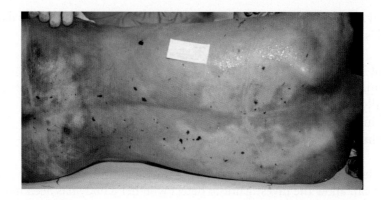

Figure 8.5 Pink lividity. Pink lividity can be seen in frozen bodies or in cyanide poisoning.

- Fixed livor seen on a nondependent location indicates that a body has been moved after death.
- Livor mortis will be visible until the body becomes completely discolored by decomposition.
- Carbon monoxide poisoning will cause the livor to be bright red. Cold, freezing, refrigeration, and cyanide poisoning causes red-to-salmon pink lividity (Figure 8.5).
- Livor mortis can be more difficult to evaluate in dark-skinned individuals because the color contrast makes the purplish red color difficult to see.
- Intense lividity in dependant areas, such as the head or the extremities hanging downward, can cause rupture of the capillaries and petechial hemorrhages (point-like hemorrhage) (Figure 8.6).

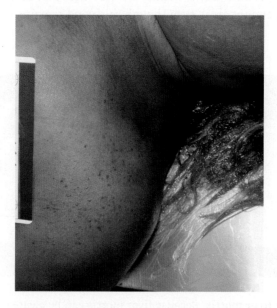

Figure 8.6 Petechiae and livor mortis of the upper body. Petechiae and livor mortis are seen in the upper body of this victim of suffocation and strangulation because the body was placed upside down after the homicide.

Body Cooling (Algor mortis)   Algor mortis is the loss of heat after death. Even though measuring the loss of heat of a body is the most common scientific method for estimating the time of death, there are many variables further complicating this estimate. "Normal" temperatures vary widely in individuals. Exercise and fever can raise temperatures. Postmortem, the body does not cool at a linear rate. Body type (mainly the amount of body fat), clothing, and age also change the rate in which a body loses heat.

Measuring postmortem temperatures remains controversial today for the above reasons. Some offices simply use a gloved hand and report the body warm or cold to touch, while some take a rectal or ear temperature. Others make a small incision at the scene and take at least two liver temperatures. Each method has its merits and drawbacks. Warm and cold to touch is subjective and can vary with an individual. It can be impractical to pull down the pants or to incise the abdomen at the scene. One should check local practices for postmortem temperature reporting.

Additional facts regarding algor mortis are as follows:

- After death, the body cools from its normal internal temperature to the surrounding environmental temperature.
- Measuring body cooling is not always an accurate method of predicting the postmortem interval, e.g., after a 12-hour postmortem interval.
- At an ideal environmental temperature of 70 to 75°F, the body cools at approximately 1.5 degrees Fahrenheit per hour in the early postmortem period.
- If a decedent's body temperature were higher than normal because of individual variation, infection, or physical exercise, 98.6°F (37°C) is not an accurate starting point.
- The outside environment determines the rate of cooling. Cooling occurs more quickly in the cold and may occur slowly or not at all in hot climates.
- If body temperature is measured at the scene, it should be taken on at least two separate occasions before the body is moved.
- A rectal or liver temperature is the most accurate measurement.
- The environmental temperature should be recorded.

Eyes

If the eyes remain open after death, the corneas (the central, clear covering over the eye) will become cloudy within 2 to 3 hours. If the eyes are closed, cloudiness might take up to 24 hours. Eyes that remain open in a dry environment will become blackened in the sclera (covering over the whites of the eyes). This is called *tâche noire* (black drying), and can be mistaken for bruising.

Clothing

The type of clothing may help indicate what the person was doing and the time of day at death. The type of clothing should be correlated with the person's schedule and habits, i.e., if one finds a man in pajamas who worked third shift and slept during the day, this would have a different meaning than a first-shift employee who slept at night. This data should be used with caution and as a guideline because one's attire can vary widely. Thick clothing will hold heat in the body, potentially changing postmortem heat loss.

Determining Time of Death by Scene Investigation

Information from the scene, other than that associated with the body, may also be critical in estimating the time of death. All clues from a house or an apartment must be analyzed. Was the mail picked up? Were the lights on or off? Was food being prepared? Were any major appliances on? Was there any indication as to the kind of activity the individual was performing, had completed, or was contemplating? How was the person dressed? What do the witnesses say about the person's habits? When was the last time the person was known to be alive? Was the phone used? These questions allow the DSI to "climb inside" the deceased in the scene environment to understand what the deceased was doing just before death.

Forensic Entomology and Time of Death

Insect larvae and other insects associated with the body can be used to estimate the post-mortem interval. An entomologist will be able to determine, not only the type of larvae, but also its developmental stage. From egg to adult insect, each stage has a specific time duration, which enables an entomologist to state how long the insects have been present (Figure 8.7). The species of insect present and the habits of the insect are also of import, e.g., carrion beetles prefer decaying material. Remember, this time estimate is based only on the time larvae were present on the body. Thus, if a body was moved from indoors to outdoors, the true postmortem interval estimate based on insects will be skewed. Larvae and insects of varying ages can be saved in alcohol or saved live with tissue media. In significant cases, where time of death is important, the author recommends contacting and, if possible, summoning a forensic entomologist to the scene.

Beetles, larvae, and other insects can bore into the body and cause holes in the skin that can resemble injuries, such as gunshot wounds. Insects seem to be drawn to areas that are injured, such as a gunshot wound of the face. Exposed areas are also more susceptible to insect activity.

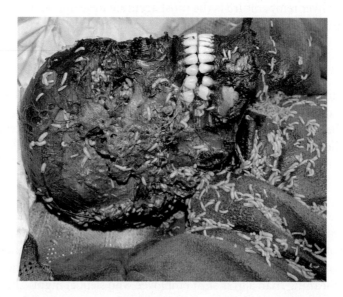

Figure 8.7 Fly larvae. Forensic entomologists are very effective using the time for fly larva development and other insect data to estimate the post mortem interval.

Forensic Botany and Time of Death

Flora discovered under or near the body may be helpful. A botanist may be able to examine the specimen, classify the type of flora and time of year it would normally be present, and determine how much time elapsed to reach that particular growth stage.

Decomposition

Decomposition is the fourth sign of death behind rigor, livor, and algor mortis. Decompositional times can vary widely depending on the climate. Hot, subtropical areas can produce advanced decomposition in as little as 24 hours, as compared to a northern climate where the same amount of decomposition might take one week or longer. Decomposition begins when a musty, rancid odor first appears. Once the investigator smells this, the odor is not easily forgotten. This odor is from processes called autolysis and putrefaction, and the changes are largely due to bacteria from the body breaking down tissue. Decompositional changes then progress from greenish discoloration of the abdomen to skeltonization. The progression of changes is listed below:

Changes in the Body during Decomposition:

1. The first change is a greenish discoloration of the abdomen, and then the discoloration spreads throughout the body.
2. As discoloration occurs, the body will begin to swell due to bacterial gas formation, which is promoted in warm weather and retarded in cold weather. Tissues swell and the eyes and tongue protrude.
3. As the body becomes bloated, the epidermis begins to slip and form blisters, and the blood begins to degrade.
4. Degrading blood produces "venous marbling," where hemolyzed blood "tattoos" the tissues producing outlines of the blood vessels.
5. Purging develops. Decomposed blood and body fluids, appearing dark brown and smelling malodorous, come out of the body orifices, largely due to gas propelling the fluid along the path of least resistance. Note: This should not be mistaken for blood from an injury.
6. Lastly, skeletonization may take weeks or months depending on the environment. Many bodies are discovered in partial skeletonization.
7. Exposed portions of the body decompose faster. The visceral part of the body also tends to decompose faster (i.e., abdomen, chest, and head). When a body part is exposed because of injury, that part tends to decompose faster. Insect activity accelerates this decomposition.
8. Decompositional changes are dependant upon temperature, humidity, insect activity, and condition of the body at death (e.g., patients with infections can decompose more rapidly).
9. By way of example, if a person dies at home and the temperature is about 70°F, it is not unusual for the first signs of decompositional changes to appear in 24 to 36 hours.

Other Decompositional Changes

Adipocere   Fat tissue beneath the skin begins to saponify (turn into soap), particularly in moist environments. A hard wax-like material forms, which takes a minimum of a few

Figure 8.8 Mummification. Hot, dry conditions produce a drying of the tissues resulting in a dark, leathery appearance. In this case, the fingertips are mummified due to the furnace being turned up to a maximum level by the perpetrator, presumably to speed decomposition. The environmental humidity can be very low in such conditions.

weeks to develop. Once adipocere forms, the body tends to exist in a relatively preserved state for many months. Unlike normal decompositional changes, there is no green discoloration or significant bloating. The exterior of the body remains white to brown and the outermost layers of the skin slip off.

For bodies totally submerged in cold water, adipocere will be evenly distributed over all body surfaces. Adipocere is not exclusive to bodies found in water. For example, bodies found in plastic bags or wet grave sites, which provide a moist environment, may also undergo this change. There may also be a differential development of adipocere depending on whether or not areas of the body are clothed.

Mummification   Mummification occurs in hot, dry environments. The body dehydrates and bacterial proliferation may be minimal. The skin becomes dark, dried, and leathery. The process occurs readily in the fingers and toes in dry environments regardless of the temperature. Most mummified bodies are found in the summer months or in hot, dry climates. Mummification can occur indoors in the winter, especially if the heat is turned up, creating a hot, low humidity environment (Figure 8.8). It is possible for an entire body to mummify in only a few days to weeks in the right conditions. Once a body is in this state, it can remain preserved for many years.

Identification Methods

Collection of Evidence at the Scene

Identification is one of the key functions and responsibilities of the MEC office. Establishing positive identification is important for a number of reasons. The goal is to produce a death certificate with the proper person's name. Most important is the next of kin. Denials of the death, as part of the grieving process, can be strong initially, especially for those out-of-town family members. One can only imagine the problems that can arise if the wrong body is at the funeral. To receive death benefits, life insurance policies, and to proceed with the probate of wills, a positive identification is needed. Rarely, individuals fake deaths for various reasons, such as to collect life insurance monies.

In criminal homicides and other criminal proceedings, the identity must be known in order to try the case. Rapid identification of the deceased allows the detectives and other investigators to interview witnesses, family, and associates of the deceased quickly, while the crime is fresh.

One must continually be aware of any situations where misidentification can occur. The potential for misidentification is ever present at the scene of multiple fatalities and disasters, such as traffic fatalities where the remains are commingled. Care must be taken by taking as much time as needed to be certain of each identification and by using a second or supporting method if there is any doubt.

Visual Identification

This nonscientific method is the easiest and most common way of performing an identification (ID). The family, or even close friends or neighbors, view the body and confirm the identity. This can also be done by taking a digital or a Polaroid photo of the body. The DSI can help confirm the identification by looking at a picture or picture ID of the deceased. The driver's license is very good for this because height, weight, and eye color are noted. If the deceased is in surroundings (e.g., home, car, job, etc.) that are familiar and appropriate and the face is in good condition, the investigator can become comfortable with this method of ID. However, there can be pitfalls to this method.

Laypersons can become upset or uncomfortable at the sight of the body and might not look at the face. They might agree too quickly with the ID to simply get away from the body. People do not appear the same in death as compared to life. Witnesses can be deceptive, or claim to know the person. In cases of moderate decomposition or extensive facial injuries, it might not be possible to make a good visual ID, so other methods must be used. In the final analysis, the MEC is responsible for the ID of the decedent, so if there is any doubt, other methods must be used.

Other Visual Methods of Identification

Scars, tattoos, birthmarks, moles, dentures (often they have the dentist or the person's name etched within), other marks, jewelry, clothing, and other personal items can be used to support, or if unique enough, confirm the identification. These items are particularly useful when there is slight doubt in facial identification. It is always better to use several points of ID when using visual methods, e.g., facial, two hip replacement scars, and three unique tattoos on the body. One should keep in mind that all tattoos and nonmedical scars are not unique. Unless the person has been incarcerated, there is probably not a good description of these marks. Therefore, one has to rely on family and friends for the description. Also, jewelry and clothing can be traded, changed, or stolen, so caution is advised in using clothing alone as an ID point.

"Softer" Forms of Identification

This includes information based on association and exclusion. For example, a person was burned up in a house fire. The person that lived there did not show up for work and is missing. This person fits the height, weight, and sex of the person living there. This information is important for an additional ID, but should be backed up with more information if possible.

Scientific Forms of Identification

Scientific methods involve specific criteria agreed upon by experts to establish ID. These scientific methods are generally too time consuming or costly to perform in each death, nor are they necessary in each death. However, in cases involving homicides, severe decomposition, charred bodies, severe facial injuries, unusual or suspicious deaths, and multiple traffic or transit fatalities, at least one scientific method should be used to confirm the ID. Scientific forms of identification include:

- DNA analysis
- Fingerprints
- Dental identification
- Comparison of antemortem and postmortem x-rays
- Confirming a specific medical prosthesis

DNA Analysis   Since deoxyribonucleic acid (DNA) analysis became available in the middle 1980s, it has revolutionized identification procedures and criminal justice. Positive blood type analysis in the past could only be given in terms of a certain percent of the population. Currently, a positive DNA sample can statistically narrow down the identity of an individual to one in billions to a trillion. DNA analysis is not the answer for identifying all individuals and solving all crimes. The public may expect every crime and even every death investigation to include some sort of DNA analysis. Due to the expense, time, and the need for samples from parents or other relatives, DNA is only used for identity in those cases when other forms of identification are not adequate.

Each person has a unique (unless there is an identical twin) collection of DNA within the nuclei of all cells. Mitochondrial DNA is the exception. Mitochondria are small organelles found in all cells, containing a small amount of DNA different from the large amounts found in the nuclei of cells. Mitochondrial DNA is passed *unchanged* from the mother to all her children. DNA is a long molecule with many sequences containing only four amino acids. In DNA analysis, the DNA is extracted from the sample, and then short sequences of DNA (short tandem repeats or STRs) are replicated into many copies. These copies of short DNA sequences are then measured producing a *profile*. The profile of the unknown person or evidence sample is compared to the standard sample.

When all of the DNA sequences (DNA profiles) are identical, the results are reported as a "match." The result is also given weight in terms of how probable or how frequent a given DNA profile is found in a given population. This probability calculation gives the investigator or juries an idea of how much weight to assign to a given result.

Polymerase chain reaction (PCR), and the newer STR methods are much quicker and require less DNA than the older restriction fragment length polymorphism (RLFP) testing. The STR method is superior to the other methods because the fragments are small and easily amplified so that analysis can be performed on a very small amount of DNA or with degraded samples. In 1998, the FBI set up the Combined DNA Index System (CODIS), a database for DNA profiling of individuals based on 13 different STR loci. Mitochondrial DNA is used as a last resort, when the DNA is severely degraded. Mitochondrial DNA is more robust, and there are more copies in the cell than nuclear DNA.

Many MEC offices routinely store samples of blood indefinitely in all cases, on commercially available cards, so that the DNA can be analyzed if any future questions arise regarding identity, criminal involvement, or paternity.

Fingerprints   This method of identity has been in use for over 100 years, and no two fingerprints have been shown to have identical ridge details, not even in identical twins. Fingerprinting is a quick, inexpensive method of identification. Many local police have fingerprint experts on staff or close by. Currently, the Automated Fingerprint Identification Systems (AFIS) is available online to law enforcement. The prints are scanned into the system, and, by computer, can achieve results in minutes to hours as compared to the manual methods taking weeks to months. Printouts of potential matches from the system are extremely detailed, but need final confirmation by a fingerprint expert.

The fingerprint identification method is useful as long as fingerprints are available for comparison. Generally antemortem fingerprints are available for those individuals who were or are in the military, in some government positions, in custody of law enforcement, holders of some licenses, and others (about 10% of the population). If no fingerprints are on file, personal items, such as toothbrushes, hairbrushes, and the like can be used to make a postmortem comparison.

All homicides, suspicious deaths, and identity "problem" cases should have a full set of classifiable prints taken. The victim must be fingerprinted to *exclude* his or her prints from those found at the scene. Some advocate a set of prints in all cases seen by an MEC office. Fingerprints can be lifted from all but the most severely burned or decomposed individuals.

Dental Identification   Comparing the dental examination of the body to antemortem dental records and/or x-rays by a forensic odontologist is a very reliable method of identification, but less so than fingerprints. As with fingerprints, some records, either charts and/or x-rays, must be available for comparison. Comparing antemortem dental charts is much less accurate than x-ray comparison. The charts can be old and out of date, causing inaccuracies. X-rays can show fillings, tooth root morphology, and sinuses, among other features. The forensic odontologist can give an opinion of a "match" when an acceptable number of features or points of identification correlate.

X-Ray Comparisons and Medical Devices   If antemortem x-rays exist, certain comparisons with postmortem films may aid in identification. The sinuses of the skull can be useful to compare because the sinus configurations are thought to be unique. This author recommends another point of identification as well if sinuses are compared. Calcified regions or strictures in the body can form unique patterns and be found in unique areas. These include granulomas in the lung, calcified heart valves, and blood vessels. Previous fracture with orthopedic hardware in place can be specific for an individual if it is the type of device that carries a specific serial number (e.g., artificial hip or knee). These serial numbers can be found in the medical record of the surgery. Other medical devices with serial numbers include breast implants, pacemakers, insulin pumps, and penile prostheses.

The Medical–Legal Autopsy

The autopsy answers the final question: Why did life pass from the body of this individual? The autopsy is a complete evaluation of an individual's death and the circumstances surrounding that death. It includes a full examination of the inside and the outside of body, as the autopsy is called the "ultimate physical examination." This examination includes:

- Complete evaluation of the circumstances of death and the medical history.
- Collection and documentation of trace evidence on and around the body.

- Photographing and cataloging of injuries.
- Detailed examination from head to toe.
- Internal examination, including the dissecting of organs and tissues.
- Microscopic examination of organs and tissues.
- Laboratory and toxicological examinations of body tissues and fluids.
- Written report detailing the pertinent findings, negative findings, and conclusions including the cause and manner of death.

The complete autopsy is really a consultation where the pathologist becomes immersed in the known facts of the death investigation. When pathologists agree to do an autopsy consultation, they use any means available to them or known to them to answer the questions posed by the death investigation. While the major portion of this consultation is the autopsy itself, the pathologist will use additional tests, experts, consultations, and research to report the facts of the autopsy and to render an opinion. The investigation of death and the autopsy can take the pathologist into virtually any field in medicine, engineering, science, law enforcement, law, and many other disciplines.

Phases of the Medical–Legal Autopsy

A comprehensive medical–legal autopsy has three phases:

1. Premorgue analysis
2. Morgue analysis, or the autopsy, *per se*
3. Postmorgue analysis

Premorgue analysis is knowledge of the death scene, witness statements, environmental conditions at the scene, and the known circumstances surrounding the death. This information is gathered before the autopsy itself. The "morgue analysis" phase includes examination of the body and the associated trace evidence. The postmorgue analysis phase occurs over the ensuing weeks to months and includes analysis of microscopic slides of tissues sampled during the autopsy procedure. Toxicologic, microbiologic culture, chemical, and other laboratory results are reviewed in this phase as well. Often, additional investigative information is received during this time period. The facts obtained from all three phases of analysis are assembled like the pieces of a puzzle to form a picture or snapshot of the person just before death. The forensic pathologist views this picture or puzzle of assembled facts to render an opinion, most importantly the Cause and Manner of Death. The pertinent assembled facts and opinions are included in a written autopsy report. Occasionally, pieces of the puzzle are missing. In such cases, the forensic pathologist must use his or her experience and training to fill in the missing pieces to render an opinion.

Because opinion is formed by the facts at hand, if the facts change, so can the opinion. For example, initially a gross autopsy in a case of sudden, unexpected death, might show severe coronary disease. Days later when the toxicology analysis is reported, and high levels of multiple drugs are found, the Cause of Death, must be changed to Multiple Drug Toxicity. Thus, the opinion given by the pathologist is only based on the facts that are known to him. If the facts are insufficient, the pathologist may have "no opinion," and the Cause and Manner of Death ruled Undetermined.

Jurisdiction and Permission for Autopsies

In medical–legal autopsies, the fundamental function of the autopsy is to establish the cause and manner of death. For MEC offices, the autopsy is done to complete a death certificate and to register the vital statistics. A treating physician, coroner, medical examiner, or health officer can certify a death without an autopsy. Autopsies are expensive, so the jurisdictional authority or MEC office must be selective about choosing cases for autopsy. A coroner, medical examiner, judge, and, in some areas, a public health officer can order an autopsy without the permission of the next of kin. In most jurisdictions, if the next of kin desires an autopsy, this is given some weight in making the decision to request an autopsy. Due to budget concerns, MEC office might not be able to accommodate all families who request an autopsy. The family can obtain a private autopsy by engaging a pathologist to perform the examination, usually at a fee.

Misconceptions of the Autopsy

A common misconception is to think of the autopsy as a simple dissection of organs. In truth, the organ dissection is only a part of the complete examination the pathologist performs. More than a simple medical procedure focusing on the organs, the autopsy is a comprehensive consultation with the pathologist as part of a complete death investigation. The autopsy is not like a lab test, where a body is sent in like a blood sample, and a result is then printed out. The pathologist uses the circumstances, scene information, trace evidence, external examination and internal examination, and microscopic and toxicologic exams, among many other things, to render opinions regarding the injuries, diseases, and the cause and manner of death.

The autopsy is not the entire death investigation either, where the body is sent for autopsy for a cause and manner of death, before any real death investigation had been performed (as the author has seen). The death investigation starts when the body is found, and then examination of the body and the autopsy should be the later steps in the process of a sound death investigation. At times, the autopsy can reveal more information, making a second look at the scene necessary, but not the first thorough look. This does not mean the scene should be held because of a cursory original investigation. (For more information on the process of the autopsy, see the references listed at the end of the chapter.)

Traumatic Injuries

Blunt Force Injuries versus Sharp Force Injuries: The Importance of Terminology

Forensic pathologists commonly distinguish blunt force and sharp force injuries when describing wounds. When describing these wounds, the words used to describe the injuries, such as contusion, laceration, abrasion, stab wound, incised wound, etc., carry great weight because they have a specific meaning and context. Precise description and meaning of wounds is important for several reasons. Erroneously describing an incised wound as a laceration tells the investigator to look for a blunt object rather than a knife or other sharp object. Common definitions for wounds allow for communication between investigators. In legal proceedings, it is important to use standard terminology and a reproducible description of findings.

Blunt Force Injuries

Blunt force injuries are visible changes of tissue caused by a scraping, hitting, crushing, shearing, tearing, or similar blunt force. The appearance and severity of the injury is dependant on the *amount* of force applied, the *object* used to transmit the force (e.g., narrow versus broad), the *part of the body injured* (bony area versus soft), and the *condition* of the tissue injured (muscular and fit versus fragile and diseased). Blunt force injures can be sustained if the object strikes the body, if the body strikes the object, or a combination of both. Blunt force injuries are called:

- Contusions
- Abrasions
- Lacerations
- Avulsions
- Crush Injuries
- Fractures

Features of Blunt Force Injuries

These blunt force injuries often appear together. For example, lacerations are nearly always accompanied by abrasions. Crush injuries may show all types of blunt force injury. Blunt force injuries often result in a loss of tissue that is transferred to the object causing the injury. This might be a small amount of tissue in a simple laceration or large amount of tissue in an avulsion injury. Objects will also transfer material to the wound (for example, wood splinters from a board). All blunt force injuries should be examined for transferred material.

Contusions   A contusion, commonly known as a bruise, is a hemorrhage into skin or tissues caused by a blunt force that tears blood vessels. The leaking of blood discolors tissues, resulting in a purplish red or dark red discoloration. Because this is a visual process, certain factors alter what can be seen (Figure 8.9):

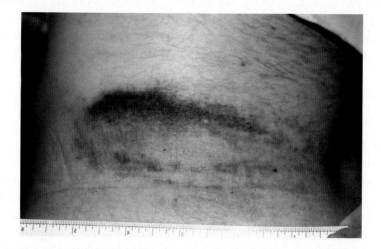

Figure 8.9 Contusion. This contusion is on a living person who was thrown into the wire rigging of a sailboat. The central clearing of the contusion is where the wire struck the skin. The blood is "milked" and forced from the central area of contact to the periphery. The contusion is about four days old (by history) and a golden brown hue can be seen in the center of the lesion (see text regarding healing contusions).

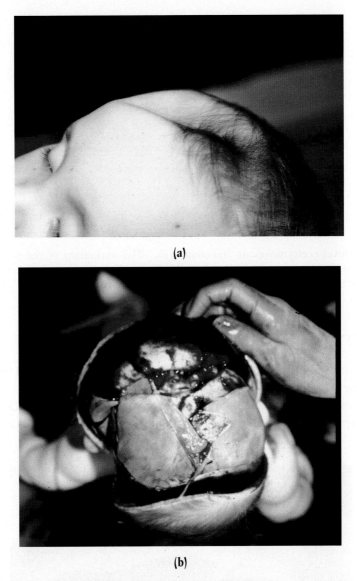

(a)

(b)

Figure 8.10a,b Depressed skull fracture with no visible contusion. (a) A depressed skull fracture can be seen clearly, but no contusion is visible. (b) When the scalp and galea are reflected back, extensive contusion hemorrhage can be seen. This illustrates the value of autopsies in children because contusions can be hidden.

- Deep contusions might not be seen except at autopsy.
- Contusions are harder to see in people with a dark complexion.
- Elderly, malnourished, and ill individuals are more likely to bruise.
- Children may be more likely to bruise on the surface, but deep bruises may be difficult to see without an autopsy (Figure 8.10a,b).
- People with cirrhosis, liver failure, and bleeding disorders will bruise more easily, as do those on certain medications (e.g., Coumadin®).
- The site of hemorrhage does not always correlate with the injury because blood drains along the path of least resistance, e.g., "raccoon eyes" in a skull fracture (Figure 8.11).

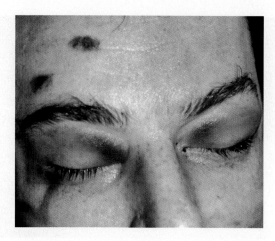

Figure 8.11 Orbital ecchymoses or "raccoon eyes." The darkening of the soft tissue around the eyes is due to blood accumulating in the soft tissues. This finding alerts the pathologist to search for fractures in the base of the skull, most likely the frontal bone or orbital roofs.

Special types of hemorrhage into tissues include:

- Hematoma: Literally a "blood tumor" or a large collection of blood in or around the tissue (Figure 8.12).
- Ecchymoses: Large, confluent areas of hemorrhage under the skin (Figure 8.13).
- Petechiae: Small, pinpoint or slightly larger hemorrhages in a tissue (Figure 8.14).

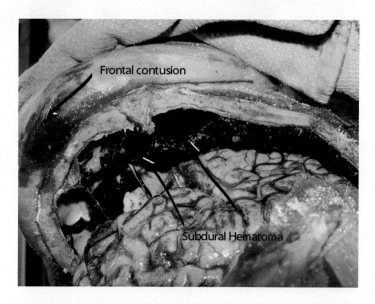

Figure 8.12 Subdural hematoma. A large hematoma can be seen between the brain and the dura, shown by the arrow. The pressure of the hematoma can affect the function of the brain, resulting in coma and death. This hematoma was produced by the deceased falling and striking his forehead. The small veins bridging the dura and the brain happened to be torn during the fall, resulting in hemorrhage.

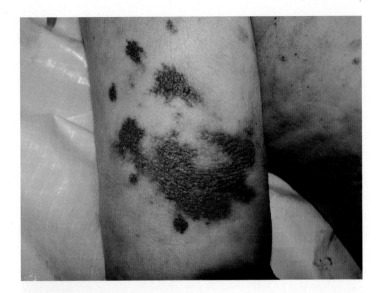

Figure 8.13 Ecchymoses. Ecchymoses are confluent, visible areas of hemorrhage under the skin. These lesions are commonly seen in the very ill or elderly, especially in patients with poor, thin skin or those taking blood thinners like Coumadin®.

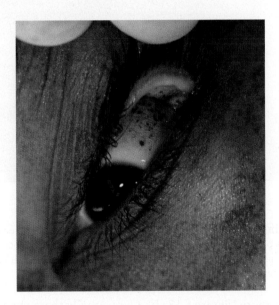

Figure 8.14 Conjunctival petechia. Small point-like hemorrhages in the conjunctiva, or clear membrane of the eye, are often seen in asphyxial deaths. These petechiae are due to hemorrhage of small vessels in the conjunctiva caused by the increased vascular pressure seen in asphyxia.

Color Changes in Contusions—Generally, contusions change color after a period of time. Estimating the age of a contusion by the color is not reliable or predictable, and should only be given in general terms. Soon after it occurs, the contusion is red-purple or dark blue (minutes to hours). In the next few days, the color tends to be dark purple. After about five to seven days, the body then breaks down the hemoglobin in the tissue, turning the contusion green to dark yellow/brown, and then to pale yellow. Resolution can be from

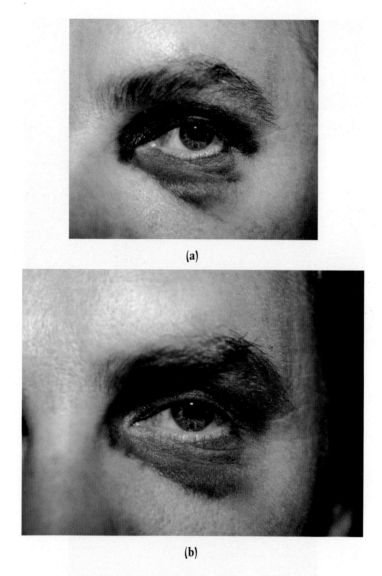

(a)

(b)

Figure 8.15 a,b Healing contusions. (a) Photo was taken three days after the author was struck in the orbit and (b) this photo was taken five days after being struck. Note that the greenish rim around the central purple hemorrhage seen in (a) has began to turn golden brown or yellowish brown as seen in (b) after only two days.

10 days to a month or more (Figure 8.15a,b). Occasionally these changes will occur out of order and are highly variable.

Abrasions   An abrasion is the denuding of skin or tissue caused by a blunt or rough blunt object. An abrasion is also commonly known as a "scrape." There are four major types of abrasions:

1. Abrasion (usual type): Due to an object contacting skin or tissue parallel to its surface (Figure 8.16).
2. Sliding abrasion: More linear and intense than a usual abrasion, it is caused when movement or sliding is involved. The abrasion lines show the direction of sliding (Figure 8.17).

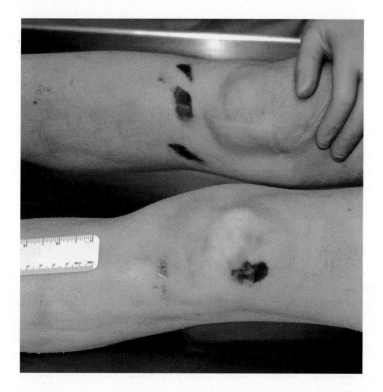

Figure 8.16 Usual abrasions. Abrasions are the pattern in the skin caused by a blunt object denuding skin. This victim of a motor vehicle crash shows usual abrasions on the knees, commonly known as "scrapes."

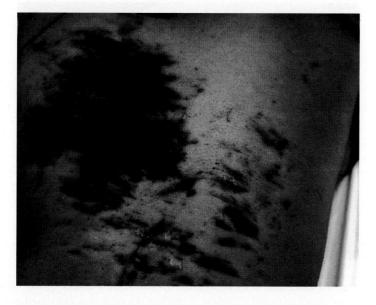

Figure 8.17 Sliding abrasion. This victim was thrown out of a moving vehicle. The long axis of the abrasions show the direction the body moved across the pavement.

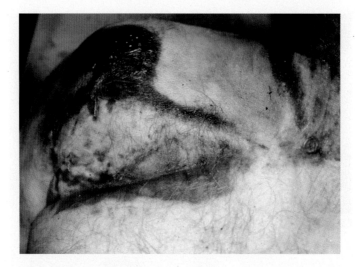

Figure 8.18 Pressure abrasion. The shoulder shows a yellow indentation below a purplish thermal burn. This victim's shoulder was wedged in a roller mechanism, whose shear force crushed the shoulder. The pressure flattened and thinned the skin so that the yellow fat beneath shows through the skin at the indentation. The mechanism was also hot, producing the thermal burn on the upper part of the shoulder.

3. Pressure abrasion: When a heavy object or force compresses tissue in a mostly perpendicular direction (Figure 8.18).
4. Pattern abrasion: Often the combination of several abrasion types forming a pattern reminiscent of the blunt object that contacted the skin (Figure 8.19).

Because abrasions involve the scraping away of skin, this skin can be transferred to the object causing the abrasion.

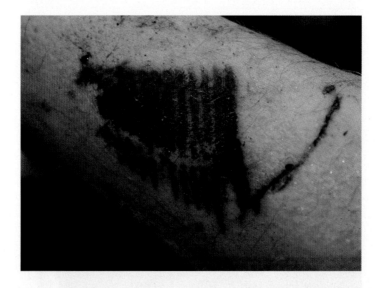

Figure 8.19 Patterned abrasion. This individual struck a solid object in his vehicle at a high rate of speed causing this patterned abrasion of the leg. Automotive aficionados will recognize this as a General Motors-type brake pedal. Studying patterned abrasions can be useful in that they can leave an outline of the object that caused the injury.

Figure 8.20 Laceration of the scalp with marginal abrasion. Blunt force striking the skin with sufficient force tears the skin resulting in tissue bridging, undermined margins, and a marginal abrasion.

Lacerations (Tears)   A laceration is the tearing or splitting of skin caused by a blunt force object carrying force. Lacerations show at least three characteristics and are often associated with a contusion (Figure 8.20).

1. Undermined and jagged margins
2. Tissue bridging
3. Abraded margins

Do Not Confuse a Laceration with a Cut—Lacerations can be straight or jagged in shape. A common mistake is to call a straight laceration a cut (Figure 8.21). A cut is really an incised wound, which is a sharp force injury, i.e., the tissue is cut, not torn. This is a very important distinction. The author recalls one case where the police were looking for a knife (because the laceration was straight) when the murder weapon was a baseball bat. Lacerations can be straight, but will usually have undermined (and jagged) margins, tissue bridging, and abraded margins. The laceration in Figure 8.21 is classified as a laceration because it shows these three criteria, not because it is straight. The laceration is straight because the victim fell against the straight edge of a table during a seizure.

Configuration of Lacerations—The configuration of lacerations largely depends on the area of the body injured and the presence of underlying bony structures. Other important factors include the size, shape, surface, angle, and force of the object contacting the skin. The same object and force striking the soft, boneless region of the abdomen will cause a much different injury around the mouth area (Figure 8.22).

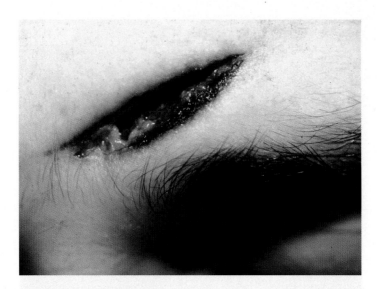

Figure 8.21 Laceration of the forehead. This laceration can looks like a cut because it is straight. Careful observation, however, reveals tissue bridging, undermined margins, and marginal abrasion.

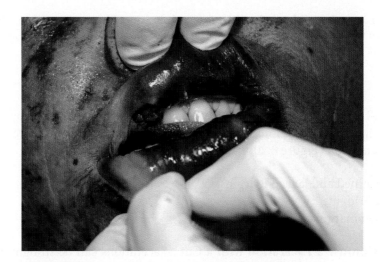

Figure 8.22 Laceration of lip due to underlying teeth. The configuration of a laceration is dependant on underlying bony structures. In this figure, the lip was lacerated as it became "sandwiched" between the fist that causes the contusion and laceration and the teeth below. A similar blow to a soft area, like the stomach, would likely not have cause a laceration.

Avulsions   Avulsion is the tearing away of tissue. In an avulsion, tissue is hanging from, or completely missing from the body. The remaining margins show laceration-like borders, except the tearing is often deep, involving bone, tendon, muscle, and other tissues (Figure 8.23). The scene should be searched for the avulsed tissue, and this tissue should be collected. If the tissue is found later, it could reflect badly on the MEC office. If the tissue cannot be found, one should think about where it might be, such as a second scene. Essentially, this missing tissue is evidence.

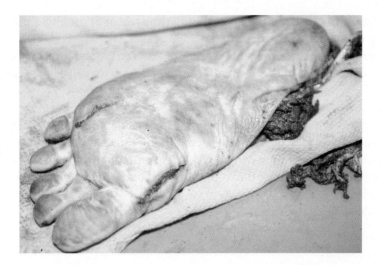

Figure 8.23 Avulsion of the foot. Airplane crashes impart tremendous force to tissues, causing shearing and shredding of the entire body. Intact body parts can be difficult to find in high speed airplane crashes.

Crush injuries   Crush injuries involve tremendous forces and large objects. The object(s) causing the injuries are usually not difficult to find due to the shear size. Characteristics of crush injuries include:

- Combination of all blunt force injuries
- Deep injuries to tissues, such as laceration of organs
- Accidental deaths, such as automobile crashes, and industrial accidents
- Fracture of bones

Fractures   Fractures of bones generally require a large amount of force. Exceptions include the elderly with osteoporosis, where fractures can even occur spontaneously with normal activity, such as walking. Children and young adults have pliable bones that bend, but do not break as easily. In the extremities and elsewhere, children tend to get greenstick fractures, where the bone bends like a young, green sapling. Bone fractures are caused by direct and indirect trauma [DiMaio and Dana, 2006]. Direct fractures are classified as follows:

- Focal: A small to medium force striking a focal bone.
- Crush: A large force over a large area, often breaking the bone into multiple pieces (comminution) and causing soft tissue injury.
- Penetrating: An object striking bone with great force in a concentrated area, e.g., a bullet.

Indirect fractures are caused by a force acting outside or away from the bone. Types of indirect fractures include:

- Rotational fracture: The bone is twisted, causing a fracture, such as abusively twisting the arm or leg of a child.
- Traction fracture: The bone is literally pulled apart.

- Angulation fracture: The bone is traumatically bent at an angle until it snaps, leaving an angular fracture line.
- Compression fracture: The bone is compressed, causing fracture. In osteoporosis patients, the weight of the body can cause a vertebra to collapse or "compress."

Sharp Force Injuries

Sharp force injuries are generally made by a sharp object cutting the skin (except for special incised wounds, like ice pick wounds), commonly called a "cut." This is as opposed to a laceration, which is caused by tearing the skin. A common mistake is to call cuts "lacerations." This wrong classification of the wound can lead to the police looking for a baseball bat instead of a knife.

Types of sharp force injuries:

- Stab wounds
- Incised wounds
- Hesitations marks or wounds
- Defense wounds or "cuts"
- Puncture wounds
- Chopping wounds

Stab Wounds   A stab wound is a cut of the skin or other tissue that is generally deeper than it is wide, caused by a sharp object like a knife, piece of glass, shiv, or similar objects. Because stab wounds involve deep arteries, veins, and organs, the mechanism of death in these cases is often hemorrhage. The configuration of a knife stab wound depends on the sharpness of the blade. Most blades are sharp on one side and dull on the other, creating a V-shaped mark on the sharp end and a blunt or pyramid-shaped wound on the other end (Figure 8.24).

Abrasions in and around the stab wound are caused by features on the knife. "Hilt" marks are caused by the handle and the attached (finger) guard. Other features, such as serrations or other adornments on the knife can leave abrasions (Figure 8.25).

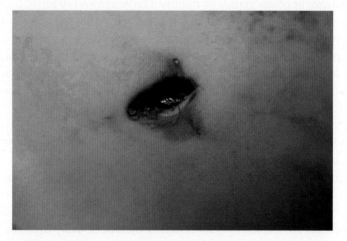

Figure 8.24 Stab wound. This wound displays a pointed end at the 9 o'clock portion of the wound. The other end of the wound shows a more blunted area. Small dots are seen at 12 o'clock and 4 o'clock where the wound was stitched together at the hospital. The sharp edge of the knife caused the 9 o'clock or sharp part of the wound, while the opposite end was caused by the blunt edge of the knife.

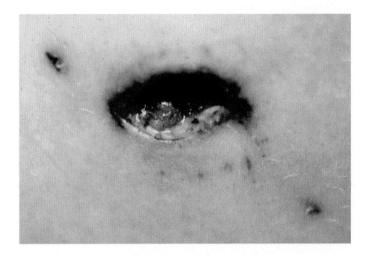

Figure 8.25 Stab wound with hilt mark. Stab wounds are deeper than they are long. This stab wound demonstrates that the full length of the knife was thrust into the body. The abrasion on the wound, and the radial marks surrounding the wounds were caused by the hilt, or end, of the knife. The two outside abrasions were caused by the finger guards of the knife. These characteristic marks could be used to exclude or include unknown knives in an investigation.

Unlike gunshot wounds, where a bullet can be matched to a specific gun, knives can only rarely be matched to a specific wound. Cases where the perpetrator's fingerprints or the deceased's blood are on the knife allow matching to a specific knife. Also, if the knife, scissor, or other sharp instrument tip hits bone, it can break off and be matched up by tool marks to the purported sharp instrument (Figure 8.26a,b). Knife length and width

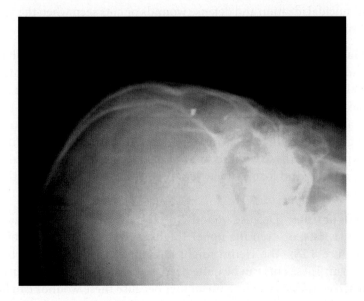

Figure 8.26a Scissor fragment in skull. Radiographs are not only for gunshot wounds. In this x-ray of a stabbing victim, a small metallic fragment can be seen in the middle of the figure, a white dot near the top. This victim was stabbed with a scissors, part of which broke off in the skull. The small fragment was removed at the autopsy (see Figure 8.26b). Knife tips can break off when hitting bone as well. The broken fragment can be matched to a purported weapon.

Figure 8.26b Metallic fragment removed at autopsy. This is the scissor fragment removed as described in Figure 8.26a.

cannot be reliably predicted by wound measurements. Tissue is very stretchable, so even a short blade can penetrate deeply. A long knife might not have been fully inserted. However, if multiple stab wounds are present, an experienced pathologist can give a range of possible knife lengths. Absent some specific information, such as DNA, the pathologist can usually only opine that the wound(s) are "consistent" or "not consistent" with a purported knife.

Incised Wounds   Incised wounds generally are longer than they are deep. As a sharp force injury, the tissues are cut, leaving sharp, clean edges unless the knife is dull or has attached ornamentation on the blade. Incised wounds are often present with stab wounds in a fatal knife attack. The most characteristic of these wounds is the hesitation wound seen in suicides and suicidal ideation and defense wounds or cuts seen when the victim attempts to ward off a knife attack.

Hesitation Marks or Wounds   Hesitation marks are commonly shallow incised wounds on the wrists and neck, though other areas, such as the antecubital fossa (inside of the elbow) can be involved also (Figure 8.27). These areas are sensitive parts of the body, so each cut is painful. When the person gets up enough nerve, another cut is made. Lack of determination and/or knowledge of anatomy means the cuts are not deep enough to hit vital arteries or veins, such as the radial artery in the wrist. In the author's experience, these wounds are not usually successful in causing death. The victim either survives (and forms linear scars), or resorts to another method of suicide, such as a drug overdose.

Defense Wounds or Cuts   Defense wounds are cuts, usually incised wounds of the hands, arms, shoulders, wrists, or even the upper thighs, sustained as a result of fighting off a knife attack (Figure 8.28). The victim might attempt to grab a knife or block the knife blows with the arm. These cuts can be quite deep, severing tendons and muscles. The word "defense" in defense wounds can be a misnomer because these wounds can be sustained if the deceased was the aggressor and simply lost the fight.

Puncture Wounds   Puncture wounds are usually deep wounds with a punctate (point-like) entrance wound on the skin. Nails, awls, ice picks, and screwdrivers are typical weapons. Often, the side of the weapon will cause an abrasion that at least partially surrounds

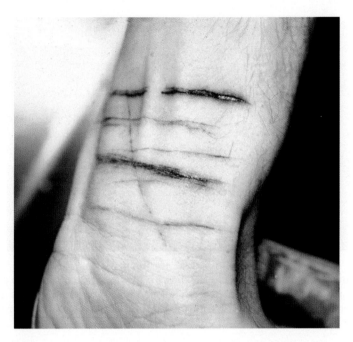

Figure 8.27 Incised wounds of the wrist (hesitation cuts). Incised wounds are longer than they are deep. These characteristic incised wounds of the wrist, seen in suicide attempts, are also called hesitation cuts.

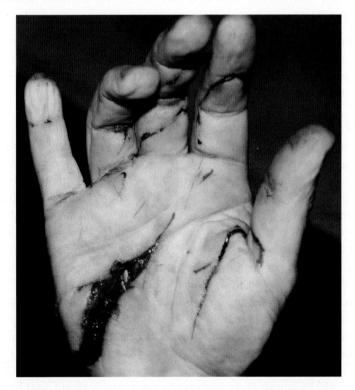

Figure 8.28 Incised wounds of the hand (defense cuts). Defense cuts are a special type of an incised wound encountered when the victim attempts to fight off a knife attack. The deep cuts seen here tell us the story of the violence inherent in the attack and the determination of the victim to prevent the attack.

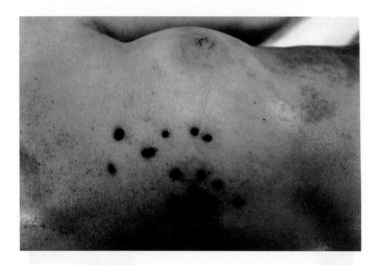

Figure 8.29 Puncture wounds of the chest. The victim was killed with an ice pick. The multiple stab wounds are located around the heart. The purposeful placement of the ice pick wounds around the heart display the determination of the perpetrator, i.e., these are not randomly placed puncture wounds.

the wound. To cause death, many such wounds must be concentrated in certain area, such as the heart (Figure 8.29).

Chopping Wounds   Chopping wounds are produced by weapons with at least one sharp edge, such as a machete, hatchet, axe, or meat cleaver (Figure 8.30a,b). These instruments are large and have weight, which can cause blunt force injuries as well, such as contusions and bone fractures.

Firearms and Gunshot Wounds

Firearms   Firearms fire a bullet or other projectile with tremendous kinetic energy that when contacting the body, the kinetic energy is transferred to the skin, soft tissues, and organs. This energy produces a laceration of the tissues, including blood vessels, resulting in hemorrhage (the primary mechanism of death in many gunshot wound deaths). Other effects of gunshot wounds depend on the region of the body or organ system that is shot. Bullets striking the brain can cause laceration of vital parts of the brain, leading to near immediate death. Gunshot wounds of the lungs can cause an air leak (pneumothorax) and subsequent death if untreated. The ferocity of gunshot wounds is such that the victim can survive the initial gunshot wound, only to die months later due to an infection or blood clot.

For many reasons, the firearm is unique among devices that can cause death. Unlike knives and blunt objects, a person can be killed without close contact. If a pattern is visible on the skin or clothing, an accurate estimate can be made of the firing distance. If the projectile (except for smoothed bore guns) can be found, the exact weapon can be identified. A person can shoot himself or be shot by another person and the wound is identical. For this reason, the author recommends performing autopsies in all suicides by gunshot. Also, to further document the purported suicide, the bullet can be retrieved for comparison to the gun.

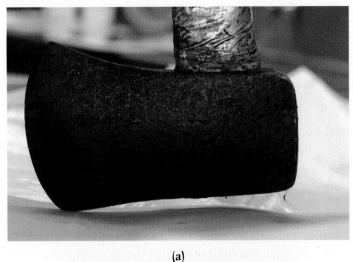

(a)

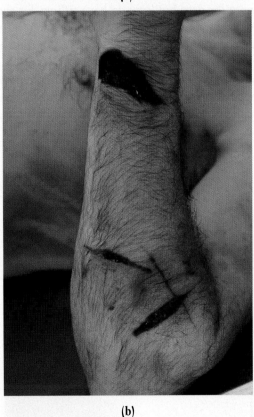

(b)

Figure 8.30a,b Chopping injuries: Axe and axe wounds. (a) Axes, swords, machetes, and other such weapons have sharp edges and weight. These weapons can cut, tear, and break bones. (b) The cuts are often long and deep. An axe can cause blunt force injuries and sharp force injuries. The wrist wound depicted here shows abraded margins such as a laceration.

The common types of civilian firearms are:

- Revolver
- Pistol
- Rifle
- Shotgun
- Machine guns

The pistol and revolver are commonly called handguns. The revolver most commonly holds six rounds (unfired bullets) in the central cylinder. The cylinder turns as the gun is fired. The pistol is loaded by a magazine or "clip" that may hold from 7 to 15 or more rounds. Rifles and shotguns are designed to be fired from the shoulder. Rifles vary greatly in the caliber and type of round that can be fired. Bullets from high-powered rifles often fragment in the body, dispersing energy and causing a characteristic "lead snowstorm" on x-ray (Figure 8.31). Handguns and rifles have riflings, which cut unique "lands and grooves" in the bullet, specific to the gun that fired the weapon. Shotguns are smooth bored guns that generally shoot shot (or BBs). Some shotguns, particularly those for deer hunting, do have riflings for shooting a large projectile called a slug. The riflings make the gun more accurate by causing the bullet to spin.

Handguns and rifles fire ammunition or cartridges composed of a primer, gunpowder, or propellant, and a bullet or projectile. When a firing pin of a weapon strikes the primer, the resulting explosion ignites the gunpowder. Gunpowder, vaporized primer, and metal from a gun may be deposited on skin and/or clothing of the victim. In addition, elements from the primer may be deposited on objects in close proximity to a discharged weapon.

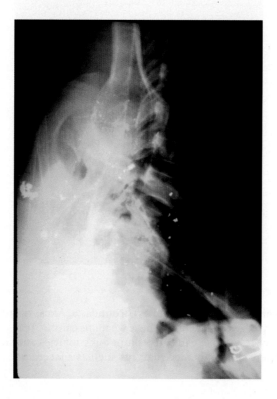

Figure 8.31 **"Lead snowstorm."** This lateral film of the neck shows metallic flakes in a complete path through the neck area. This person was shot with a high-powered rifle.

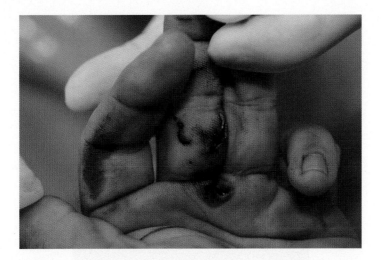

Figure 8.32 Gun-induced laceration and soot deposition of the hand. The mechanism of the pistol produced a laceration of the hand. Soot was also deposited on the hand and fingers. These findings indicated the gun was in the hand of the victim and supports the theory of suicide (also see Figure 8.33).

Gunpowder comes out of the muzzle in two forms:

1. Completely burned gunpowder, called "soot" or "fouling," can be washed off the skin (Figure 8.32).
2. Particles of burning and unburned powder can become embedded in the skin or bounce off and abrade the skin. The marks on the skin are called "tattooing" or "stippling."

Gunshot wounds

Inspecting the skin or the clothing for the characteristic patterns of burned and unburned gunpowder allows the wound to be classified by type:

- Hard contact (close contact)
- Contact (loose contact)
- Near contact
- Intermediate range
- Distant (undetermined range)

Hard contact—The muzzle has been pushed tight or "hard" against the skin, forming a tight seal between the muzzle and skin, causing the heat, soot, and bullet to go into the wound. The result is most often charring of the wound edges (due to a heat of about 1400°F) and an abrasion of the wound margin. In bony areas where the skin is stretched, such as the forehead, the wound margins can tear, forming a stellate (star-like) pattern. Soot is then heavily deposited inside the wound. Back spatter may be present on the weapon or shooter (Figure 8.33).

Contact (loose contact)—The muzzle is incompletely or not quite touching the skin, so a slight rim of soot surrounds the wound. This soot can be washed away and no stippling is seen. Less abrasion is present compared to a hard contact wound (Figure 8.34).

Near Contact—The muzzle is not touching the skin at all, but is within less than about 1 inch. A wide rim of soot and seared skin surround the entrance bullet hole, much wider

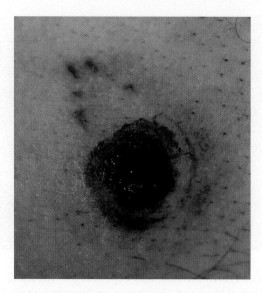

Figure 8.33 Hard contact entrance gunshot wound. The patterned abrasion at 10 o'clock, and the red abrasion ring around the wound was produced by the gun barrel and sight contacting the skin when the gun was fired. Around the wound is heavy soot, the black material depicted inside and around the wound. The finding of a hard contact wound on the chest of this individual supports the theory of suicide.

than with a contact wound. No stippling is seen, or the wound must be classified as intermediate range (Figure 8.35).

Intermediate Range—Seeing stippling or powder tattooing of the skin is diagnostic of this wound (Figure 8.36). These wounds occur at muzzle-to-target distances of approximately 6 inches up to 3 or 4 feet, depending on the weapon used and the type of

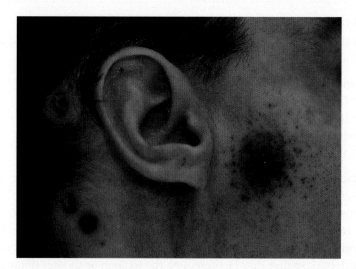

Figure 8.34 Loose contact gunshot wound. The gunshot wound at the lower left hand corner of the photo shows surrounding soot. The gun muzzle was held slightly away from the skin causing soot to go into and around the wound. The wound in front of the ear shows a soot pattern that is wider and begins to break up causing stippling, otherwise known as an intermediate range wound. The other two wounds behind and below the ear show no soot or stippling, so the range is classified as "undetermined" for these two wounds.

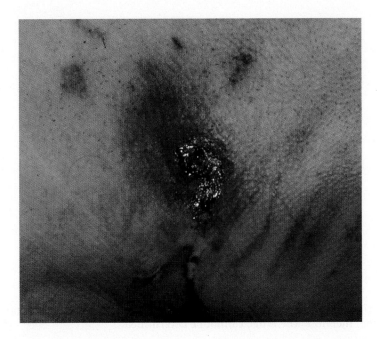

Figure 8.35 Near contact wound. The term is used by some authors to describe a pattern between a contact and intermediate range wound. A wide rim of soot surrounds the wound because the barrel is not touching the skin and is likely less than 1 in. away. If stippling is seen, the wound must be classified as an intermediate gunshot wound.

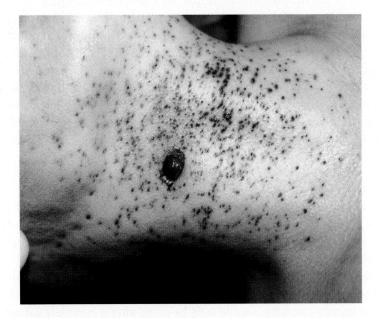

Figure 8.36 Intermediate range gunshot wound. Any gunshot wound with stippling (small dots surrounding the wound) is referred to as an intermediate range gunshot wound. Unburned portions of gunpowder tattoo the skin. The stippling must be measured in all directions. The firearms examiner can then fire test patterns with the same gun and ammunition at known distances. These patterns can be compared to the unknown pattern on the body, and the distance estimated.

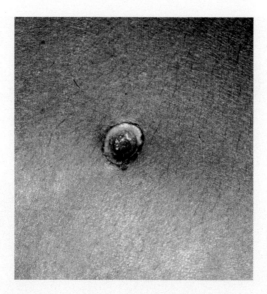

Figure 8.37 Undetermined range gunshot wound. This gunshot wound has no surrounding soot or stippling; therefore, the range cannot be determined.

ammunition. There is no soot deposition or charring, only stippling or powder tattooing of the skin. Stippling is imbedded in the skin and cannot be washed off. An estimate of the range of fire can be given if the diameter of the stippling on the body (or clothing) is compared to that of the weapon when test fired by a firearms examiner.

Undetermined Range (Distant)—No soot or stippling is seen. The wound has a small "abrasion collar" produced by the bullet scraping the skin circumferentially as the skin is perforated. In such wounds, the actual range of fire is likely distant, greater than 4 feet (depending on the weapon and ammunition). However, if the true range is less than 4 feet and there is an intermediate target, such as clothing, the wound will often appear without soot or stippling. Therefore, the range cannot be determined (Undetermined) just from examining the wound on the body. In such cases, there should be search and examination of other objects, such as clothing, for soot, stippling, or other evidence that can aid in determining the range of fire (Figure 8.37).

Exit Wounds

Exit wounds vary greatly in appearance. They can be irregular, stellate, slit-like and rarely, round (Figure 8.38). Round exit wounds can resemble entrance wounds before they are cleaned. Exit wounds do not have an associated circular abrasion at the entrance hole. While exit wounds are generally larger than entrance wounds, some exit wounds are the same size or smaller. The DSI should be very cautious giving an opinion about entrance and exit wounds at the scene where the lighting is often bad and the wounds are bloody. Opinions about gunshot wounds should only be given after a complete autopsy.

Shored Exit Wounds—These are exit wounds with associated irregular abrasions that are caused by the skin contacting a hard surface (e.g., floor) or a tough article of clothing (e.g., leather coat).

Graze and Tangential Wounds—When a bullet strikes the skin at an angle insufficient for penetration into the deep subcutaneous tissue, the skin is torn and abraded. The tears often point in the direction the bullet traveled (Figure 8.39).

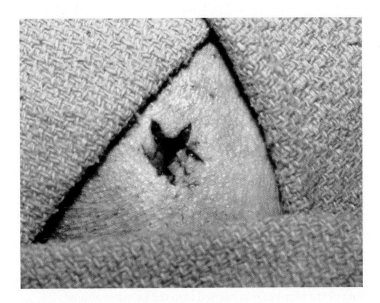

Figure 8.38 Exit wound. This exit wound is stellate in configuration. No soot or abrasion can be seen around the exit wound. This exit wound was caused by a .22 caliber bullet.

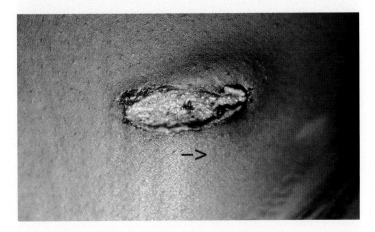

Figure 8.39 Graze wound. As the wound tangentially contacts the skin, it is abraded and torn. The tears point to the direction the bullet travels over the skin.

Secondary Target Wounds and Trace Evidence—If the bullet goes through any object before hitting the victim, parts of this object may be carried into the wound. For example, if the victim is shot through a blanket, a portion of blanket may be in the wound or stuck in the surrounding skin (Figure 8.40). Glass and clothing are common secondary targets.

Shotgun Wounds—Shotguns fire shot that produce a dispersed pattern, the width of which depends on the choke of the gun (Figure 8.41). The shotgun wound produces additional wounds that give information regarding the range of fire. While the soot and stippling patterns are similar to those described above, the spread of the shot and the wounding pattern also can aid in estimating the range of fire. Portions of the shotgun shell

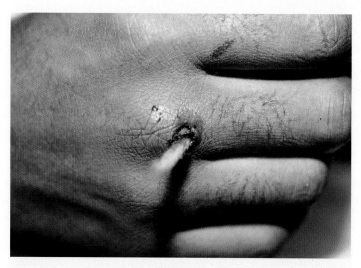

Figure 8.40 Intermediate target in a gunshot wound. This person was shot while holding up a blanket. The filling of the blanket was carried into the gunshot wound.

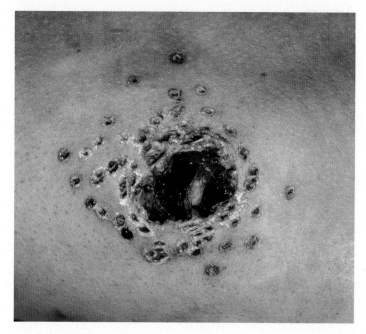

Figure 8.41 Shotgun wound. Shotgun shells contain multiple small BBs, called shot. As the shot comes out of the barrel of the gun, it stays together for several feet, then starts to separate. As these individual shot break up and hit the skin, characteristic individual satellite shot injuries can be seen around the main hole.

packing (wadding) can also be found in the wound, up until a range of fire of about 5 to 6 feet. Patterns of shotgun wounds can be generally described as follows:

- *Contact to about two feet:* A single, round entrance hole is seen with all shot and wadding found within the wound.
- *Two to four feet:* The shot begin to disperse and a single irregular, scalloped "rat hole" is seen. Wadding is usually found in the wound.

- *Four feet to about ten feet:* The shot disperse farther with satellite holes surrounding the central hole. The wadding is probably not in the wound, but might cause an abrasion if it strikes the skin.
- *Ten feet and beyond:* The shot have dispersed such that a central hole is no longer seen—only individual entry wounds of each shot.

Shotguns that fire slugs may or may not be rifled. Once a slug enters the body, it usually does not exit. Riflings are only seen on those shotguns that are used to fire a slug. If the shotgun shell is found, firing pin tool marks can be matched to the shotgun in some cases.

Miscellaneous Firearm and Gunshot Wound Facts *The caliber of the weapon cannot be predicted by the size of the entrance wound*—Wound size can vary depending on the energy of the bullet, the type of bullet, and the region of the body struck.

All gunshot wound cases should be x-rayed—Even if there is an exit wound, x-rays should be performed. Part of the bullet, like the jacket (which can contain riflings), can and often does remain in the body. The body should be x-rayed with the clothing on, because clothing can trap bullets (Figure 8.42). Cartridge casings have been found in the hair at autopsy (Figure 8.43a,b).

Terminal Ballistics—There are three forms of ballistics: (1) *External*, the study of trajectories caused by scene defects; (2) *Internal*, the study of firearms analysis (e.g., range determination); and (3) *Terminal*, the study of wound tracks and trajectories within the body. In CSR, all three forms of ballistics are combined to define the trajectories to reconstruct the shooting.

Figure 8.42 Bullet in a sweater. Some articles of clothing can trap bullets. For this reason, the clothing should be x-rayed and carefully searched, so as not to lose a bullet or other trace evidence.

Figure 8.43a,b Cartridge casing in the hair. The hair should be examined carefully for evidence. As shown here, (a) a missing cartridge casing was found, and at about 8 o'clock, (b) a bullet jacket can be seen in the clothing.

Description of Wound Tracks (Terminal Ballistics) by the Forensic Pathologist   At the autopsy, after the body is examined initially, the wounds are cleaned carefully, and analyzed for visual patterns. Each wound is photographed, measured, and diagrammed by the pathologist. The wound track (terminal ballistics) is determined and then described by the pathologist in detail, starting from the outside of the body, going through, following the wound until the end. The bullet and other associated evidence is recovered by the pathologist and then photographed, taking care not to damage the riflings on removal (some mark the bullets).

Note: All descriptions are given in anatomic position in relation to the body, not the observer. Anatomic position simply refers to the body facing the observer, with the palms facing upward. Descriptions are given from the point of view of the victim or on the victim's body, i.e., the observer's right is the victim's left. This concept is easy to remember if one thinks of putting himself or herself in the point of view or "crawling inside" the victim, or thinking of the wounds on one's own body. The path of the wounding or "wound track" through the body is then described. When the wound track "event" or "internal ballistics" is combined with the trajectory "event" or "external ballistics" from the scene, an event analysis can be put together regarding reconstruction of the path of the projectile from the time it leaves the firearm until its final terminus in the body or beyond.

Strangulation

There are two types of strangulation: ligature and manual. Ligature strangulation is nearly always homicidal; however, a tie or similar article can become caught in machinery or other objects and pull the ligature tight enough to cause death. The latter types of cases are often obvious at the scene. Manual strangulation commonly involves more and varied trauma of the neck.

Ligature Strangulation In ligature strangulation, a weight other than the bodies' weight is used to compress the neck vasculature. In the majority of cases, the perpetrator manually tightens the ligature (Figure 8.44). There may be marks on the neck from the victim's own hands, attempting to resist. Petechiae seem to be more prominent than in other ligature deaths.

Manual Strangulation Manual strangulation refers to applying pressure to the neck by the hands or forearms, usually compressing the vessels of the neck causing injury, unconsciousness, or death. When extreme pressure is exerted on the neck, or in young victims, the airway can be compressed. Abrasions and contusions of the neck, jaw, tongue base, and even the mouth are often seen (Figure 8.45). Facial and conjunctival petechiae are often seen and the face is congested. The neck and tongue should be carefully dissected by the pathologist and usually reveals muscle hemorrhage, hyoid and thyroid cartilage fracture, and other soft tissue hemorrhage. Semilunar fingernail-like abrasions can be present.

Figure 8.44 Ligature around the neck from suicidal hanging. The ligature furrow is easily seen in this figure and the rope has caused a patterned abrasion of the neck.

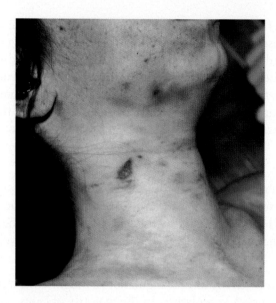

Figure 8.45 Manual strangulation. Multiple contusions and abrasions are seen at the base of the jaw and in the neck. Neck dissection showed extensive hemorrhage of the soft tissues and muscle of the anterior neck and base of the tongue.

The Autopsy Report

The main opinion of the FP is the cause and manner of death, which should be prominent on the report. Of equal importance, is a summary of the injuries, usually on the front page under the heading, "Anatomic Findings" or "Anatomic Diagnoses" or a similar phrase. Deeper in the report is a more detailed description of the major injuries. For example, a man who was pistol-whipped in the head and then shot in the chest by another person underwent an autopsy. The front page of the autopsy would include:

Anatomic findings:

1. Entrance gunshot wound of the right midchest:
   a. Range not determined
   b. Wound track directed right to left, front to back, and head to toe
   c. Wound track involves the skin just lateral to the nipple, chest wall, fifth rib, right upper lung lobe, pericardium, right heart ventricle, left lower lung lobe, and corresponds to:
      i. Bullet recovered in the posterior 10th rib, and given to Mr. Sherlock Holmes of the Baker County Forensic Services Agency
2. Laceration, right forehead with subgaleal contusion
   Cause of death: Gunshot wound of the chest
   Manner of death: Homicide

As shown above in item 1, the facts are laid out describing the bullet path in three dimensions and the trajectory through major tissues and organs. Deeper in the autopsy report, one should find a "description of injuries" that in this example case would read as follows:

Description of Injuries—In the right chest at a distance of 20 in. (50.8 cm) from the vertex and 10 in. (25.4 cm) from the midline is an entrance gunshot wound. There is no evidence of surrounding soot or stippling. The wound is elliptical and measures 1/2 × 1/2 in. (1.3 cm × 1.3 cm). There is a circumferential collar of abrasion that measures 1/8 in. (0.32 cm) in thickness. The wound is located 1 in. (2.5 cm) lateral to the right nipple. The wound track is directed right to left, back to front, and head to toe. The wound track involves the skin just lateral to the nipple, soft tissue, chest wall, fifth rib causing fracture and hemopneumothorax, right upper lung lobe tearing several large pulmonary vessels, pericardium causing hemopericardium, right heart ventricle (through and through), and continues posteriorly and downward into the left lower lung lobe tearing several large vessels and causing hemopneumothorax, and corresponds to a bullet recovered in the left posterior 10th rib. This bullet is photographed and given to Mr. Sherlock Holmes of the Baker County Forensic Services Agency.

On the right forehead is a 1 × 1/2 in. (2.5 × 1.3 cm) comma-shaped laceration, just over the right eyebrow. Beneath this laceration is a 1 × 1 in. contusion (2.5 × 2.5 cm). No skull fracture or cerebral contusion is present.

The above example report contains a great deal of technical data that can be difficult for someone who does not have a detailed spatial knowledge of anatomy. Pictures, diagrams, and three-dimensional models all help one understand the trajectory. One should not hesitate to meet with the FP if the trajectories are not clear from the description given. Until the external ballistics at the scene are matched up with the internal ballistics on the body, the event sequence cannot be reconstructed.

Reconstruction of a Bullet Trajectory

In this case, if no information is available about the position of the shooter, many trajectories are possible. The shooter can move and hold the gun in many different ways and the victim can twist, bend, jump, and turn, to name a few possibilities. However, the one undeniable fact is the path of the bullet through the body. The more facts discovered about the position of the shooter and the victim, the better the reconstruction of the shooting. For example, if it can be established that the shooter is standing 10 feet away, on equal ground with the victim, a likely position of the victim at the time he was shot is facing the shooter from his right side and somewhat bent over.

Conclusion

This outline of forensic pathology has attempted to touch on some major ideas and theories in the field. In-depth discussions of death scene investigation, wounding, toxicology, the autopsy, and other subjects are beyond the scope of this chapter, so we direct the reader to the references below. Every forensic expert is a professional with deep knowledge of his or her subject. FPs obviously use medical and anatomic terms that are like a foreign language to some. Those writing crime scene reports should seek out the FP and consult as one professional to another if there are any questions involving terminology, descriptions, or opinion. One or two misinterpretations of a finding, such as a bullet trajectory, can lead to a flawed crime scene reconstruction.

References and Suggested Reading

Adelson, L.A. 1974. *The Pathology of Homicide*, Springfield, IL: Charles C Thomas Publisher.

Brogdon, B.G. 1998. *Forensic Radiology*, Boca Raton, FL: CRC Press.

Clark, S.C., M.F. Ernst, W.D. Haglund, et al. 1996. *Medicolegal Death Investigator*, Big Rapids, MI: Occupational Research and Assessment, Inc.

Collins, K.A., and G.M. Hutchins. 2003. *Autopsy Performance and Reporting*, 2nd ed., Chicago: College of American Pathologists.

Cotran, R.S., V. Kumar, and T. Collins. 2003. *Robbins Pathological Basis of Disease*, 7th ed., Philadelphia: W.B. Saunders Co.

DiMaio, V.J.M., and S.E. Dana. 2006. *Handbook of Forensic Pathology*, 2nd ed., Boca Raton, FL: Taylor & Francis.

Di Maio, D.J., and V.J.M. Di Maio. 1989. *Forensic Pathology*, New York: Elsevier.

Di Maio, V.J.M. 1990. *Gunshot Wounds: Practical Aspects of Firearms, Ballistics and Forensic Techniques*, New York: Elsevier.

Dix, J. 2000. *Color Atlas of Forensic Pathology*, Boca Raton, FL: CRC Press.

Dix, J. 1999. *Handbook for the Death Scene Investigator*, Boca Raton, FL: CRC Press.

Dix, J., and M. Graham. 2000. *Time of Death, Decomposition and Identification: An Atlas*, Boca Raton, FL: CRC Press.

Ellenhorn, M.J. 1997. *Medical Toxicology, Diagnosis and Treatment of Human Poisoning*, 2nd ed., New York: Elsevier.

Froede, R.C., ed. 2003. *Handbook of Forensic Pathology*, 2nd ed., Chicago: College of American Pathologists.

Geberth, V.J. 2006. *Practical Homicide Investigation*, 4th ed., Boca Raton, FL: Taylor & Francis.

Hanzlick, R. 1997. *Death Investigation Systems and Procedures*, Boca Raton, FL: Taylor & Francis.

Haglund, W.D., and M.H. Sorg, eds. 1996. *Forensic Taphonomy: The Post Mortem Fate of Human Remains*, Boca Raton, FL: CRC Press.

Karch, S.B. 1993. *The Pathology of Drug Abuse*, Boca Raton, FL: CRC Press.

Ludwig, J. 2002. *Handbook of Autopsy Practice*, 3rd ed., Totowa, NJ: Humana Press.

Mortiz, A.R. 1956. Classical Mistakes in Forensic Pathology, *Am. J. Clin. Path.*, 26, 1383.

Rohen, J.W., and C. Yokochi 1993. *Color Atlas of Anatomy*, 3rd ed., New York: Igaku-Shoin.

Spitz, W.U., ed. 2004. *Mediolegal Investigation of Death*, 4th ed., Springfield, IL: Charles C Thomas Publisher.

Stimson, P.G., and C.A. Mertz, eds. 1997. *Forensic Dentistry*, Boca Raton, FL: CRC Press.

Wagner, S.A., et al. July 1991. Asphyxial Deaths from the Recreational Use of Nitrous Oxide, *J. Foren. Sci.* 37(4): 1008–1015.

Wagner, S.A. 2000. *The Autopsy, Chapter One: Unraveling Life's Mysteries*, video tape, DVD, 30 min., Wagner Research, LLC., distributors: CRC Press, Boca Raton, FL.

Wagner, S.A. 2004. *Color Atlas of the Autopsy*, Boca Raton, FL: CRC Press.

Wetli, C.V. 1984. Investigations of Drug-Related Deaths: An Overview, *Am. J. Foren. Med. Pathol.* 5(2): 111.

Wetli, C.V., R.E. Mittleman, and V.J. Rao. 1999. *An Atlas of Forensic Pathology*, Chicago: ASCP Press.

Wetli, C.V., R.E. Mittleman, and V.J. Rao. 1988. *Practical Forensic Pathology*, New York: Igaku-Shoin.

Chapter Author

Scott Wagner, MD, is a board certified forensic pathologist and the director of the Northeast Indiana Forensic Center in Fort Wayne, Indiana, and assistant clinical professor of pathology at Indiana University School of Medicine. He is author of the books *Color Atlas of the Autopsy* and *Death Scene Investigation: A Field Guide*, and is the producer of the video *The Autopsy, Chapter One: Unraveling Life's Mysteries*.

Writing Crime Scene Reconstruction Reports[*]

9

Introduction

In order to be of value, it is important the analyst reduce his beliefs and conclusions to a written format. As simple as this might seem, writing reconstruction reports can be quite difficult. This difficulty stems from two basic issues. First, the reconstruction is a compilation of information from various sources and reports. It is not based on a single individual's efforts. The analyst must have a thorough understanding of these reports and must interrelate specific facts from all of them in order to reach any conclusions in the reconstruction. Second, the reconstruction derives its actual form through a reasoning and logic process; thus a reconstruction is very much a mental product conceived in the mind of the analyst. Logic and reasoning are individual skills, and it is often difficult for the analyst to point out small subtleties in the evidence and evidence relationships. In trying to achieve this, it can become easy for the analyst to lose focus and difficult for others to grasp the analyst's underlying decision-making process.

A reconstruction is very much a puzzle unraveled in the mind of the analyst and then put to words on paper. For others to believe its final form and conclusion, they must be confident they understand "how" the analyst arrived at the individual decisions that support the conclusions.

Far too often in investigative reports, this final form of conclusion is a simple statement such as:

> Smith raped Jones at knife point, resulting in two stab wounds. At the conclusion of the assault Smith then shot Jones while she was lying on the floor.

Although such a concluding statement may well be accurate, it leaves the reader sorting through every document related to the report in order to try and understand "how" the investigator reached that particular conclusion.

Even after reviewing all of the related documents, the "how" may not always be evident. Reasoning is very much an individual mental process. We can never be confident that one

---

[*] Significant aspects of this chapter first appeared in Chapter 10 of *Bloodstain Pattern Analysis: With an Introduction to Crime Scene Reconstruction* 2nd ed., Bevel, T. and R.M. Gardner 2002. Boca Raton, FL: CRC Press.

reader will see the same significance in each piece of information or put the same bits and pieces together in the same manner. In some fashion, the reconstruction report must elaborate on the analyst's reasoning and lead readers step by step through that process. Only then can readers of the report properly evaluate the conclusion and determine if they agree or disagree.

Certainly if they disagree with a report of this latter nature, both parties can then point to specific issues and recognize at what point their opinions diverge. What should not occur, although it often does, is an off-the-cuff dismissal of an opinion regarding some action. If two forensic experts are viewing the same evidence, then there is little rationale for completely polarized viewpoints.

The discussion of Event Analysis in Chapter 3 provides a backdrop for preparing the reconstruction report. Remember, each event segment is a specific action defined by supporting evidence and scene context. For each of these claimed actions, the report should list the facts that support that action. A basic format might look something like this:

> EVENT # 1
>   Event Segment #1A
>   Supporting Evidence (Cross Reference)
>   Event Segment #1B
>   Supporting Evidence (Cross Reference)

Essential Report Elements

Whatever format is used to create the reconstruction report, there are several essential elements that should be included in the report. These include:

- A statement of purpose with a disclaimer
- A list of references
- The body of the report, with specific references
- A flow chart

Statement of Purpose

Either on the lead sheet of the report or in the initial pages, the analyst should have a standard statement of purpose. It should define the purpose of a reconstruction and include a disclaimer indicating that the report conclusions are based on the data available at that time. Every objective analyst understands that additional information may be forthcoming at some point in time after the report is prepared. This additional information has the potential to alter previously held opinions, so the disclaimer makes this clear to the reader. The following is a functional statement of purpose and disclaimer:

> Crime scene reconstruction (CSR) is the use of scientific method, physical evidence, reasoning, and logic to gain explicit knowledge of a series of events that comprise a given crime or incident. The goal of a crime scene reconstruction is to identify the sequence of events. The analyst's opinion is based on all available evidence and relies on his/her education, experience, and training. While all events and segments may not be identified, those that are reflected are the best explanation given the data. Should additional information become available, the analyst will consider its importance and may choose to revise the analysis.

References

A reconstruction report is developed only after reviewing multiple sources of data. This includes scene examinations, evaluation of physical evidence, and other forensic expert opinions (e.g., reports from DNA, fingerprint, or trace experts). The analyst should list these primary sources up front in the report, so the reader is aware of what relevant sources were both known and utilized by the analyst. The following is an example:

The following documents and references were utilized as sources of information for this report:

- Redacted Kent PD (KPD) Criminal Investigation Report Case 00-XXXX
- Crime Scene Photos Kent PD
- Crime Scene Sketch(s) Kent PD
- WA State Crime Laboratory Report 100-XXXXXX
- King County ME (KCME) Autopsy Report 00-XXXX Autopsy photographs.
- Physical examination of items recovered from XXXX S XX Street Kent, WA
- R.M. Gardner photos
- Bloodstain pattern analysis report, R.M. Gardner, dtd. 21 Jun 2004

Body of the Report

Ultimately the analyst must articulate his conclusion in some format to the reader. In this chapter, we will demonstrate two basic report formats that serve the analyst's needs. These two formats include:

1. Event Analysis: outline format
2. Event Analysis: narrative format

Regardless of the format used for the report, a critical part of the body of the report are specific references to the facts supporting the analyst's conclusions. Remember that each action or event segment is based on one or more specific facts from the scene and evidence. These facts may come from any number of supporting documents to include specific photographs. Although the basic documents were listed in the previous Reference section, this was a general reference, indicating only that the document was considered in making the analysis. As specific facts are listed in the body of the report, a direct reference should be included. This allows the reader to find the specific facts claimed in the report. This reference is generally listed in parenthesis following the stated fact. Consider the following example:

Event Segment B1: The attacker initiated the assault from the north side of Mr. X.

1. No pattern transfers, swipe marks, or wipe marks were found on the south side of the sheets or comforter at the level of the area of attack. (RMG photo 229)
2. Spatter was present on the top sheet, to the far south side (the area exposed in the scene); this spatter was undisturbed. (RMG photos 302, 303, 306, BSPR pp. 5–6)
3. There were evident smear patterns on the top of the comforter, north side directly beneath the area of attack. (RMG photos 279, 287, KPD photos 23 and 25, BSPR p. 3)
4. There are multiple contact patterns present on the north side of the comforter. (RMG photos 279, 287, 283, 284, BSPR pp. 25)

5. Pattern transfers consistent with the knife were located on the fitted sheet, tip oriented to the south. (RMG photos 333, 334, 337, 349, BSPR pp. 8–9)
6. Mr. X received two deep wounds to the upper back, left side. (KCME p. 4)

The supporting facts used to conclude that the attack began on the north side of the bed are backed up by direct references to specific evidentiary photographs (e.g., RMG photo 229), specific crime scene photos (e.g., KPD photos 23, 25), a specific page of the bloodstain pattern report (e.g., BSPR pg. 3), and a specific page in the medical examiner's report (e.g., KCME p. 4). If a reader questions these facts or wishes to review them for any reason, the reference allows him to go directly to the case documentation and find what he needs.

Body of the Report: Outline Format

In the outline format, each event is described in the upper hierarchy of the outline. Supporting event segments are listed at the next level in sequential order. Beneath the event segment, supporting facts and the cross references are listed. The following is an outline report format example:

References: For purposes of this example the following reports were utilized:

CS: Crime scene report
MR: ER medical report
BP: Bloodstain pattern report
VS: Victim statement
SR: Serology report

Event Analysis

A: Disturbance occurs within the bathroom. No major bleeding injuries occur here.
 1. Beer bottle broken in the tub, possibly used as a weapon.
  a. Minor scalp injury consistent with victim's claim of head injury. (MR,2)
  b. Broken bottle glass in and around tub (CS,2)
 2. No major injuries sustained here.
  a. Complete lack of spatter or blood in this area. (BP,1 CS,2)
 3. Victim in the tub/shower at the time of the assault.
  a. Liquid stains present near the entrance to the door. Possible sources are water or alcohol. Officers on scene do not record smelling alcohol, thus water is the most likely source. (CS,3)
  b. Victim claims she was showering and was wet. (VS,1)

Using this portion of the report, the reader understands that Event A was a disturbance in the bathroom. This event included three distinct event segments:

1. The event began with the victim in the shower.
2. A bottle was broken during the event.
3. None of the bleeding injuries occurred here.

To establish the occurrence of this event, the analyst called upon specific information from four documents. This included Page 2 of the medical report, Page 1 of the bloodstain analyst's report, Pages 2 and 3 of the crime scene report, and Page 1 of the victim's statement.

A continuation of the outline example follows. Note that in the report the capitalized letter represents the event, the number represents the event segments, and the small letters represent the supporting evidence.

Event, event segments (continued)

B: Altercation moves to main room. Bleeding injury sustained, but not a major one.
  1. Victim ends up outside bathroom, no indication of standing on her own.
     a. Victim claims being pulled out of the room and falling to the floor. (VS,2)
     b. Large stain on the floor, liquid intermixed with blood. No spatter or droplets present in the pattern. (CS,2 BP,3)
     c. Stain shows no foot marks, other than toe/finger drag marks. (BP,3)

  2. Some bleeding occurs.
     a. No spatter or droplets present. Probable source very minor drips or venous flow. (CS,3 BP,3)
     b. Possible source of blood, minor injuries to the feet from glass cuts and/or the minor head injury. If the head, the head was near the ground. (BP, 2)

  3. Victim pulled from this location by force from the rear.
     a. Edge of the large stain near the bathroom door is undisturbed. (BP,3)
     b. Stain boundary shows evidence of spines, indicating force of some nature was applied to the center. (BP,3)
     c. Drag marks present in stain are consistent with dragging of feet or hands. Marks show motion in the direction of the bed. (BP,3)

C: Primary assault occurs on bed.
  1. Victim was on bed with head in the vicinity of the headboard.
     a. Saturation stains in victim's blood type. (SR,2)
     b. All major bleeding injuries on victim's face. (MR,2)
     c. Impact spatter show a point of convergence in this area. (BP,2)

  2. Impacts occur here. Minimum of three blows.
     a. Impact spatter on two associated walls. (BP,4)
     b. Spatter establishes a minimum of three blows, but overall distribution is indicative of more. (BP,4)
     c. Wounds on victims face indicate at least three blows. (MR,2)

  3. Probable weapon is either the leg support or center supports of broken chair.
     a. Three sets of pattern transfers show characteristic measurements, which are consistent with the leg support. (BP,5)
     b. These stains indicate such an object was bloodied, rebloodied, and each time placed in contact with the bedding, near the victim's head. (BP,5)
     c. Wounds present on the victim's face indicate a weapon with a linear edge, consistent with the support. (MR,3)

D: Subject departs via window.
  1. Window open with items on the ledge disturbed here. (CS,6)
  2. Pattern transfer present on outer window ledge in blood.
     a. Pattern has dual linear boundaries, which are consistent with one measurement of the cross and leg supports. (BP,5)
     b. Pattern transfers indicate the object that made them came in contact twice at this location. (BP,5)

Using the five source reports, the analyst defines to some degree four events and their supporting event segments and sequence. In this instance, the victim, brutally attacked and nearly killed, is unable to provide much detail regarding the actual assault. The reconstruction objectively fills in sections where the victim's memory lapses and certainly corroborates the remainder of her story.

Body of the Report: Narrative Format

Although the outline format is functional and quite effective, in some instances, the subtleties of the analyst's logic are not always clear. In effect, the outline format requires the readers to put the pieces that support each event segment together for themselves. This issue is eliminated using the narrative form for the body of the report. A narrative format is exactly that, a running narrative of what the analyst believes and why he believes it. Outline or narrative, cross references to source documents are still required. The following narrative example is a small part of the total reconstruction report concerning a double murder:

Source Documents:

BPA: Bloodstain Pattern Analysis Report
CS: Crime Scene Report
FE: Firearms Examiner's Report
ME: Medical Examiner's Report
FM: Family Members
RA: Reconstruction Analyst's Report
SR: Serology Report
PR: Police Arrest Report

Event Segment Issues

Event Segment # 1 - How did the subject gain entry to the residence? There are four possible options.

1. Entry with a key.
2. The door was left unlocked.
3. One of the victims let the subject in.
4. The subject forced entry.

Related information:

A key to the lock was found in the suspect's vehicle. (PR,3)
The victim was terrified of the subject. (FM,7)
The victim was known to always keep the doors locked. (FM,7)
The child victim was too young to open the door. (ME,2)
The attack started at the bathroom. (CS,4)
No evidence exists of a forced entry anywhere in the home. (CS,3)

Evidence/information relationships: The attack suggests surprise as the victim was preparing for the day. There are no defensive wounds and no evidence of struggle. If entry were forced, some evidence of that process would likely exist. The child victim was too young to reach or work the door lock and knob. The victim reported she was terrified of the suspect and, although not impossible, it is unlikely she would knowingly open the door and allow him in. A key was found in the suspect's vehicle.

Best Explanation of Occurrence: The lack of forced entry, the victim's prior behavior, and her known level of concern with regard to the subject make it unlikely events B, C, and D occurred. The presence of the key on the suspect and his knowledge of the residence layout make it likely he entered unnoticed using the key, catching the victim off guard as she was preparing for the day.

Event Segment # 2: Initial contact: Were the victims awake or sleeping at the time of the attack? Two options exist in this instance. The victims were either awake or asleep.
Related information:

The bed appeared slept in and was unmade. (CS 4)
The normal schedule for sleep had passed. (FM 7)
The curling iron was plugged in and hot. (CS 3)
The victim was menstruating and a fresh, unstained panty shield was in her underwear. (CS 5, ME 4)
There is specific evidence that both victims were present in the hallway at the beginning of the attack. (CS 2)
Victim # 1 had fresh makeup on her face.

Evidence/information relationships: There is little to suggest that the victims were sleeping at the time of the attack. The condition of both the victims and the home make it almost a foregone conclusion that they were awake at the time the attack began.
Best Explanation of Occurrence: The victims were awake when the attack began.

Event Segment # 3: Mode of attack: In what order were the three modes of attack used on Victim # 1? There are three methods of wounding evident:

1. Gunshots
2. Knife wounds
3. Blunt trauma to the face

As we have three events with some sequence, there are several possibilities for that sequence. Using standard probability equations, these three options present numerous possible orders, as evident in the sequence matrix (Figure 9.1).

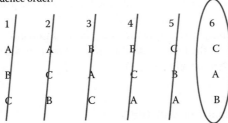

Sequencing Matrix Worksheet
Event Segment # 3: What is the order of the three modes of attack?

A. Gunshots
B. Knife wounds
C. Blunt trauma to the face
Sequence order:

Figure 9.1 When dealing with a number of possible sequences, it can be difficult to functionally demonstrate that each permutation has been considered. The sequence matrix allows the analyst to show that each possibility was considered in some fashion. In this instance, sequences 1 through 5 have been eliminated, leaving only sequence # 6 as possible.

Related information:

Relating to A:

> There is evidence of one gunshot to Victim # 1 after she was dragged to the bedroom. (BP 5, SR 6)
> There is no visible blood trail in the hallway leading there. (BP 5, CS 5)
> If shot, there is no need to strike the victim. (RA 6)

Relating to B:

> There is evidence of cuts to Victim # 1 in the bedroom. (BP 6, SR 7)
> The stabs and cuts are perimortem. (ME 4)

Relating to C:

> The blunt trauma was the least damaging injury, causing a minor lip bruise. (ME 3)
> This blow would not render the victim unconscious. (ME Interview 6-16)
> The victim's glasses were on the floor in the hallway. (CS 3)

Evidence/information relationships: The least injurious blows are usually the first struck in the altercation. There is no indication of Victim # 1's blood in the hallway outside the bathroom, but there is evidence of her blood from both cutting and gunshot events in the bedroom. As all knife wounds are perimortem, they most likely occur last. Based on information evident in Event Segment # 4, it is likely that Victim # 1 was unconscious when moved to the bedroom; thus there would be no resistance.

Best Explanation of Occurrence: The most likely order for this sequence of event segments is # 6, with a strike to the face coming first, followed by at least one gunshot, and then followed finally by the knife wounds.

Event Segment # 4: Mode of death: What is the order of the fatal wounds to Victim # 1? There are three different fatal wounds:

1. Gunshot to the left ear
2. Stab to the heart
3. Gunshot to C-2

Once again, three possible events produce six different possible orders as indicated by the following matrix examples (Figure 9.2 to Figure 9.4).

Related Information:

Relating to A:

> The shot to the left ear would have lowered the victim's blood pressure. (ME Int. 9-16)
> Such a wound would not cause paralysis. (ME Int. 9–16)
> There is time to use a pillow to muffle the noise for this gunshot. (RA 7)
> If first, the blood flow on the face should be different than as found. (BP 6)
> This is a distant shot, left to right. (ME 3)

Relating to B:

> There are no arterial spurts present. (BP 5)
> This is a perimortem wound. (ME 4)

Relating to C:

> This wound would lower the victim's blood pressure. (ME Int. 9-16)
> This wound would cause paralysis. (ME Int. 9–16)

Sequencing Matrix Worksheet
Event Segment # 4: There are 3 different fatal wounds.

A. Gunshot to the left ear
B. Stab to the heart
C. Gunshot to C2

Sequence Options:

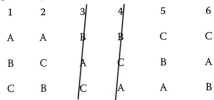

Figure 9.2 To fully understand the sequence matrix, consider how we arrived at the result demonstrated in Figure 9.1. Based on the ME's information, the stab to the heart cannot be the first wound. Thus, any sequence in which it is listed first is eliminated (sequences # 3 and # 4).

Sequencing Matrix Worksheet
Event Segment # 4: There are 3 different fatal wounds.

A. Gunshot to the left ear
B. Stab to the heart
C. Gunshot to C2

Sequence Options:

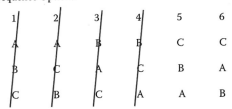

Figure 9.3 Using the ME's evaluation of the ear shots, any sequence in which the gunshot to the left ear is first is also eliminated (sequences # 1 and # 2).

Sequencing Matrix Worksheet
Event Segment # 4: There are 3 different fatal wounds.

A. Gunshot to the left ear
B. Stab to the heart
C. Gunshot to C2

Sequence Options:

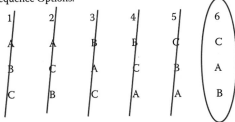

Figure 9.4 The stab to the heart (Wound B) is also the only perimortem wound based on the ME's information. Thus, any sequence in which it comes before the other two wounds is eliminated, leaving only sequence # 6.

There is time to use the pillow to make this shot. (RA 7)
This wound would cause little external bleeding. (ME Int. 9-16)
The wound is soft contact, left to right and back to front. (ME 4)

Evidence/information relationships: B is the only perimortem wound, it must occur last. This limits the orders to two (i.e., # 2 and # 6). Evidence indicates the victim was dragged by the left wrist and forearm without indication of resistance. There are bruises present to support this. These bruises could form after paralysis, but would not occur after a drop in blood pressure. The blood flow supports A having occurred after the drag from the hallway. Thus, C must occur before A.

Best Explanation of Occurrence: Sequence # 6 is the best explanation: gunshot C followed by gunshot A, followed by the stab to the heart.

Using the narrative-style report, note that for each segment the analyst defines the evidence considered, how that evidence relates to other evidence and information, and provides at least a glimpse into the reasoning process used to derive the conclusion.

The narrative report, although more time consuming to prepare than the outline format, doesn't require further action on the part of the analyst. All of the efforts detailed in the report are an integral part of basic event analysis. Whether using an outline or narrative format, the analyst must still accomplish each step. When using the narrative format, the analyst simply describes everything in a little more detail.

When considering critical issues of the analysis using either the narrative format or outline format, the analyst may wish to use a supporting worksheet (discussed and explained in Chapter 4) to help document his effort. In these instances, the worksheet should be retained as working notes.

Flow Chart

A reconstruction effort is almost always directed at defining what happened and in what order it happened. Thus, an integral part of any overall reconstruction attempt is sequencing the identified actions. How this is accomplished was described in Chapter 3. Part of the process of identifying sequence involves the development and validation of a graphic device known as a flow chart. Although a flow chart is not necessary in every instance, in most instances where there is any level of complexity for the incident in question, a flow chart should be prepared and included in the final report. As was previously discussed, the flow chart graphically allows others to see and better understand the sequential aspects of the reconstruction (Figure 9.5).

Keep in mind that the reconstruction product is not infallible. By incorporating the ideas discussed here, the reconstruction report offers the analyst a greater level of self scrutiny. Links between evidence become clearer and the analyst can often discover weaknesses in his own decision making. In particular, the analyst is far more likely to recognize situations in which he uses contradictory arguments. Such a product also makes it easier for the analyst to revisit his reasoning process in preparation for court. No small detail of the original analysis is forgotten, and nothing is left out. The reconstruction report also sets the stage for trial presentation. The report presents the investigative conclusions in a logical and structured form, which, if followed in terms of questions posed by the prosecutor, is more likely to be understood by the jury.

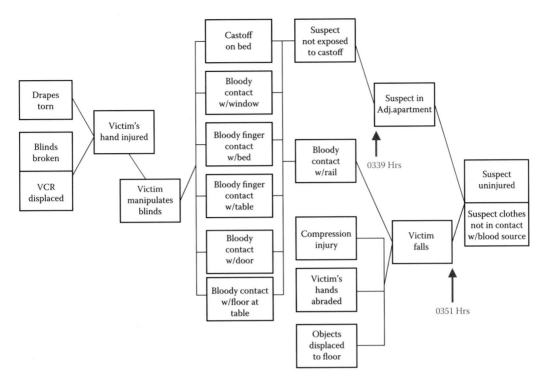

Figure 9.5 A flow chart is a graphic representation of the analyst's conclusions. It details the specific actions that occurred and the sequential order of those actions. In complex reconstructions, it is an essential element that should be included in the report, as it allows the reader to better understand the written conclusions.

Summary

Typically, the final form of any reconstruction effort is some type of a report. To be useful, the reconstruction report must be clear, concise, and to the point. The reconstruction report is a written account of the logic process the analyst utilized to reach the conclusions and should lead the reader through each point of the analysis.

Incorporating the concept of Event Analysis from Chapter 3, the reconstruction report should include each supportable event and event segment. The analyst should include any details regarding specific items of evidence or scene context that support the event segments. As the reconstruction report is a compilation of many different sources of information, the analyst should also cross reference this information. The cross reference serves an important function in keeping sight of all supporting evidence. It is often small, minute details scattered throughout the investigative reports that allow some specific conclusion to be reached. Without a cross reference, these details are often lost or forgotten in the total package. In the end, the conclusion described in the report should be functionally reviewable, testable, and repeatable.

Arguments and Ethics 10

There are two critical considerations for those involved in crime scene analysis: (1) understanding the arguments that frame our beliefs and (2) ensuring a viable ethos underlies the arguments we offer. The manner in which the analyst frames any argument is critical, demanding an understanding that the various elements of our beliefs are often based on a blend of inductive and deductive arguments. Scientific method seeks to combine both effectively to form the best explanation for a given phenomenon, but the strength of the overall belief is very much a characteristic of the individual arguments that make up its foundation. As we will discuss, deductive and inductive arguments are both important, but certainly not equal. Part of framing our beliefs correctly requires we recognize the many fallacies that any argument can fall prey to. Once we frame our beliefs, the analyst must also recognize his ethical responsibility when furthering that argument (e.g., when offering an opinion).

Deductive and Inductive Arguments

When framing an argument regarding some belief, the analyst always sets a foundation, a basis for the opinion offered. This basis is generally made up of a series of premises—statements regarding the context of the scene. Framing this concept in terms of Event Analysis, each event segment is a statement about some action—an investigative conclusion. For each segment, one or more data elements are offered in support of the action—premises that support that specific investigative conclusion. The event segment (the conclusion) is derived from the data (the premises).

Example:

Event Segment/Conclusion: The victim was mobile subsequent to his arterial wounding.
Data/Premises:
- A spurt pattern is present on the east wall extending from the foyer to the bathroom.
- The blood in the pattern is the victim's.
- There are no smear marks or evidence of dragging on the floor beneath the mark.
- Bloody palm prints are present along the length of the wall, consistent with a standing height.
- The palm prints were identified to the victim.

In asking others to believe a conclusion (e.g., that the victim was mobile), the analyst asks first that the premises be accepted as true. Note that the premises themselves can always be challenged. However, if the premises are true, must the conclusion in all instances logically follow with certainty? The answer is no, and it is this distinction that is the characteristic difference between deductive and inductive arguments. In a deductive argument, if the premises are true, then the conclusion must also be true. In an inductive argument, if the premises are true, then the conclusion should logically follow, but it doesn't have to.

Aristotle (384–322 BC) is generally acknowledged as the first advocate of deductive argument in the pursuit of science. Deductive arguments are often viewed as empirical knowledge (rules or laws) gained through direct observation (e.g., experiment) and, thus, they are the iconic view of scientific effort. Deduction is the process of "leading down" from general principles to specific cases.[1] A deductive argument begins with general premises (observations on the nature of something) that lead to a specific case (a specific conclusion based on those observations). The fundamental aspect of a deductive argument is that the conclusion is always encapsulated in the knowledge presented in the premises (Figure 10.1). In other words, the conclusion never exceeds the information offered in the premises.

Deductive Example:

Premise
     Joe is a man.
     All men are mammals.

Conclusion:
     Joe is a mammal.

As the knowledge of the deductive conclusion does not exceed the information within the premises, if the premises are true, then the conclusion *MUST* be true. If all men are mammals and John is a man, then John must by necessity be a mammal as well. Once again, the deductive argument is framed from general statements (John is a man, all men

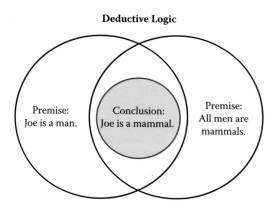

Figure 10.1 A deductive argument leads down from general premises to a specific conclusion. The information contained within the conclusion will always be inclusive or encapsulated by the premises. As a result, if the premises are true, the conclusion must follow without exception.

Deductive Logic

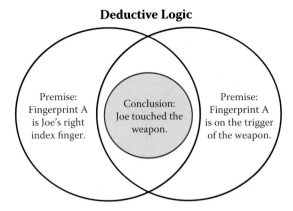

Figure 10.2 A CSR example of a deductive argument. If the fingerprint is natural (not planted by some extreme means) and belongs to Joe and it was found on the trigger of the weapon, then by necessity Joe must have come in contact with the weapon in some fashion.

are mammals), which leads to a more specific statement (John is a mammal). Consider a deductive argument in the context of crime scene analysis.

Premises
>Fingerprint A was naturally produced and is associated to Joe's right index finger.
>Fingerprint A is on the trigger of the weapon.

Conclusion:
>Joe touched the weapon.

If the premises are true, then by necessity the conclusion must follow that Joe was in contact with the weapon in some form (Figure 10.2). If any one of the premises is proven false, then the conclusion may suffer the same fate. But until that point, the conclusion remains a deductive argument and quite solid in its certainty.

Sir Francis Bacon (1561–1626) challenged Aristotle's beliefs about scientific discovery. Bacon thought of deductive reasoning as a dead end, and proposed that inductive method was as important, if not more so. Where deduction was based on rules and laws, inductive reasoning is based on rationalism. Induction is the process of "leading to," where observations and reasoning about specific cases lead to a general principle.[2] Thus, an inductive argument always proceeds from specifics and leads to a more general conclusion. As a result, the conclusion of an inductive argument exceeds the knowledge contained in the premises. For this reason, the conclusion of an inductive argument can be wrong, even if the premises are true (Figure 10.3). Nevertheless, an inductive argument is still valid and it allows for exploration. If properly framed, the conclusion of an inductive argument is said to follow the premises with a high degree of probability, but inductive arguments should always be examined in a critical manner to determine:

- How complete and representative is the information used in the premises?
- How reliable is the evidence?
- Have all alternative theories and negative instances been considered?[3]

Inductive Logic

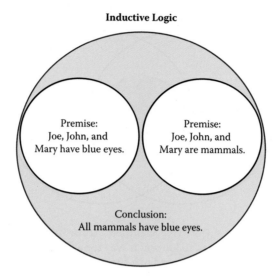

Figure 10.3 An inductive argument leads from specific observations to a general conclusion. As the information in the conclusion exceeds the knowledge provided by the premises, the conclusion may or may not follow. As a result, we have to consider how representative the data used are and whether alternative theories or negative cases have been considered. As this example illustrates, an inductive argument that is poorly framed (e.g., using a sample of three) can be wrong.

Consider Galileo's argument to the Holy Roman Church, which would ultimately be considered his crime of heresy. At the time of Galileo, Aristotelian thinking on the nature of the universe was very much accepted and held that the stars and heavens were made of a quintessential matter. This quintessential matter was unchanging and different from that of Earth and all matter known to man. This was an inductive argument itself, but a well-accepted belief even to theologians, as is comported with Christian theology. Galileo made observations relevant to the specific heavenly bodies he could see, which included the Moon, Sun, and Jupiter. From that he offered a general conclusion about all matter. His argument went something along this line:

Premises:
   The moon has a landscape, like the Earth.
   The sun alters its appearance day to day, month to month (e.g., sunspots).
   Jupiter has small orbiting moons similar to Earth.

Conclusion:
   Heavenly bodies are made of the same stuff as Earth and there is no quintessential matter. All matter must be generally the same.[4]

To date all subsequent observations have supported Galileo's inductive conclusion. Based on all available data, distant galaxies, stars and nebulae are made up of the same matter as our Earth. Thus, Galileo's conclusion logically follows, given the data available, we are all just stardust (as Carl Sagan would say). But that conclusion is still inductive. As we have not directly observed all matter, is it possible there is some form of "quintessential" matter (e.g., dark matter) somewhere, as yet undiscovered? As long as the inductive

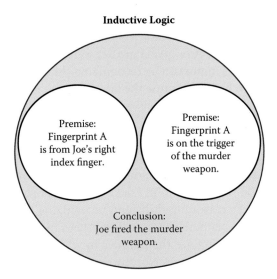

Figure 10.4 Our CSR example as an inductive argument. If the fingerprint is Joe's and it was found on the trigger of the murder weapon, then it is reasonable to believe that Joe fired the weapon. But we must consider any alternative theories (e.g., Did Joe enter the scene after the fact and touch the weapon?).

argument's premises are defined appropriately and are correct, the conclusion will follow with a high level of probability.

Consider an inductive argument in the context of crime scene analysis.

Premise:

Fingerprint A is associated to Joe's right index finger.
Fingerprint A is present on the murder weapon.

Conclusion:

Joe fired the murder weapon.

If the premises are true, then the conclusion that Joe is the shooter likely follows, but it is not a certainty given the inductive argument (Figure 10.4). Other possibilities exist. What if Joe arrived on scene after the shooting and picked the weapon up and in doing so deposited the incriminating fingerprint? Our decision to accept an inductive argument is based on our ability to reason. We must examine the argument and determine if we have sufficient data to reach the conclusion. A critical consideration for any inductive argument is to decide if all possibilities have been considered. Nevertheless inductive arguments are important as they allow for exploration. Crime scene analysis and all science rely on both inductive and deductive arguments.

The crime scene analysts in achieving the many small conclusions (e.g., the event segments themselves or sequence of event segments) will rely on a number of individual arguments. Some of the arguments may be deductive in nature, and others inductive. Each must be understood for what it is, as this blend in effect defines the level of certainty the analyst holds for his overall conclusion. It is not that the analyst must define each subargument as deductive/inductive, but he should recognize the certainty that each subargument holds. It is only by stringing together a series of subarguments that any overall conclusion is possible. The basis of our ultimate reconstruction conclusion rests on earlier conclusions made about items of evidence. Point A leads to Point B, which leads to Point C, ad infinitum. If we incorrectly infer Point A or give it greater weight than it deserves, we may taint the entire conclusion. Thus, as important as recognizing the nature of the argument itself, so too is recognizing how to properly frame the argument.

The Role of Logic in Crime Scene Analysis

Logic and reasoning consciously or unconsciously guides most human thought and behavior in some form or fashion. We are, as John Locke believed, born innately rational beings. But, by refining the analyst's reasoning skills and recognizing the dynamic nature of the events that analysts seek to explain, the analyst strengthens his ability to define a true "best explanation." Logic and reasoning are the manner in which we frame our arguments as they relate to the reconstruction task. As Nordby commented, "The purpose of the expert is to refine the context of the situation using the expert's understanding."[5] Logic plays a significant role in accomplishing that task.

Informal Fallacies Encountered in Analysis

Any analysis, at its heart, is an argument. Before we accept any argument, we should be clear on three things:

1. What does the argument choose to establish?
2. Is the evidence presented correctly, without unjustifiable weighting in either direction?
3. Is the reasoning of the argument valid?

In formal logic, there are three categories of fallacies that deal with these questions: fallacies of ambiguity, fallacies of relevance, and fallacies of presumption. Although the analyst may encounter any of the fallacies, presumptive fallacies are the most prevalent the analyst may engage in while defending an argument. If we include such fallacies in our arguments (either with intent or without realizing it), we fail some part of the objective standard for crime scene analysis. These fallacies in effect disguise incorrect arguments to look like correct arguments. Some of the more common presumptive fallacies the analyst may fall prey to include: the fallacy of bifurcation, sweeping generalizations, false cause, and irrelevant thesis.

The first presumptive fallacy of bifurcation presumes that something is either true or it is not. There is no in-between. Lawyers who ask us to "just answer yes or no" use this fallacy in their favor. They know the witness cannot answer all questions adequately with a simple yes or no. Thus, lawyers frame questions in ways to achieve the answers they want, without delving into background detail that might better reveal the truth of the matter. Analysts have a bad habit of accepting or including bifurcated positions about events and event segments in their reconstruction when such a position is unwarranted.

Sweeping generalizations are another fallacy of concern. In this instance, a rule, which is applicable to some situations, is applied to all situations. As an example of a combined argument (both a bifurcated argument and a sweeping generalization), imagine a question about the origin of a spatter following a gunshot. We know that shotguns can produce considerable back and forward spatter. Having found a small impact pattern that is consistent with a gunshot spatter, must we exclude it from having been produced by the shotgun simply because it is not "large"? Analysts have argued exactly that, claiming that shotgun wounds only produce large spatter patterns. A less presumptuous position demands we look at the empirical data. Gunshots, to include shotguns, do occur where there is little or no spatter. Between the parameters of "a lot" and "very little" reside many possibilities. The sweeping generalization attempts to apply a general rule (e.g., shotguns often produce large stains) to every situation. The bifurcated position bolsters the argument (e.g., shotguns only produce large stains) to make it look incontestable.

The ultimate issue, that is, was a small spatter pattern produced by a shotgun, remains unanswered based on this information alone. Is it possible to produce such a pattern by firing a shotgun? Yes. Obviously, it is not the most frequently occurring event, but the argument uses the bifurcation and sweeping generalization position to force a decision on the issue without exploring the possibility.

Another fallacy encountered in crime scene analysis is that of false cause. In these instances, the analyst draws a causal connection between two actions or an action and some item of evidence. Consider arriving at the site of a homicide and discovering bloodstains of various types. We observe the victim and note wounds that might account for these stains. If we simply assume all the stains to be the result of the victim's injuries, the fallacy of false cause has presented itself. We have not considered the possibility that other people (particularly the perpetrator) were injured and then created some or all of the stains in question.

A recent difficulty in bloodstain pattern analysis is a good example of the fallacy of false cause. A new type of bloodstain was presented in a high profile murder case; it was called a "painted fiber." This painted fiber was a cloth fiber, which had blood deposited all around the fiber itself, as if the blood was painted on. When introduced, those who coined the term stated categorically that "painted fibers" were a result of contact alone. In other words, the only way to create a "painted fiber" was to have direct contact with another bloody surface; they could not be produced by other mechanisms. As a new concept, the argument offered seemed reasonable on its face. Subsequent effort by other analysts determined that these "painted fibers" could also be produced when blood was projected onto wet cloth. The fallacy of false cause (associating a painted fiber to only contact) found its way into the analyst beliefs because they failed to consider other viable possibilities. There is no question that contact can produce a painted fiber, but other mechanisms produce it as well, thus, the true probative value of painted fibers is as yet undetermined.

An irrelevant thesis is another fallacy encountered. Simply stated, an irrelevant thesis attempts to prove something that is not at issue. It is then offered as proof that another issue is false. Imagine the question: Could a particular series of actions A and B create the result Z? The answer is likely to be put forth as a "yes" or "no." The irrelevant thesis answers this question by offering an alternate set of circumstances, C and D, which could also create the result Z. Irrelevant thesis is a constant strategy of defense in their effort to establish reasonable doubt. For instance, in a shooting incident a suspect and the victim were observed on a surveillance camera approaching a doorway to an apartment complex. The surveillance system jumped from one camera to the next; thus only a few frames for each camera were captured every few seconds. Although at some distance, in the frames from the shooting scene the two men were observed talking in front of the apartment, then the victim was observed falling with the suspect still standing over him, and finally the suspect was observed running away. The only thing not captured was the flash of the weapon. The terminal ballistics found at autopsy was consistent with the physical position observed on the tape between the two men. When asked to evaluate the scene, the requesting defense counselors were concerned with the possibility of claiming a third distant shooter. Based on the ballistic information available (the lab in question had failed to evaluate the victim's clothing for gunshot residues, so no distance determinations were available), the "possibility" of a third distant shooter could never be excluded. Yet given the data available, the claim of a third shooter was immaterial. Claiming a "phantom shooter" in no way altered the evidence against the suspect's involvement. Obviously, the analyst's opinion was not offered at trial.

The most deceptive thing about an irrelevant thesis is that it may offer valid information that might be of importance to the investigation. Yet the approach veils the answer in such a manner as to exclude or rebut the original issue without having dealt with it at all. The question of whether a third distant shooter "could" have been present, in no way rebuts the evidence against the suspect. Just because we cannot absolutely exclude a third party does not disprove the suspects involvement, which must still be considered in and of itself and either excluded or included based upon the evidence available.

An Ethical Approach to Crime Scene Analysis

Is it enough that we can build logical arguments and offer them to those who rely on our understanding? Is it "right" for experts to offer logical arguments (properly framed inductive or deductive arguments based on some foundation) to the court, even if they themselves do not believe it? For example, just because one cannot exclude the possibility of a third shooter as described in the example above, is it appropriate as an analyst to go in front of the court and simply pretend the data regarding the suspect's involvement don't exist and argue for the third shooter? Ethically that is wrong. If the analyst knows all of the data and there is clear evidence, how can he argue as if that data does not exist? The example comes from the defense, but analysts and investigators do the same thing from the prosecution side, either ignoring or hiding exculpatory information—once again a truly unethical behavior. We should be clear; arguing a position that is viable and relevant, just because it goes against the main body of evidence, is not inappropriate, so long as the primary data are not ignored. As an analyst, if I believe that there is a possibility that has been overlooked, I can always argue it so long as I acknowledge and give appropriate consideration and weight to any opposing data or theories.

In the morass of opposing ideas that courtrooms are, what guides the analyst in this effort? Can the expert witness play the game of lawyers, believing that "winning is everything"? If that is true, then isn't the law profession's "smorgasbord theory of science" acceptable as well, where rather than dealing with all facts and data, we simply choose that data that best suits or supports our preconceived ideas. If the expert witness takes the stand and offers the classic "Elvis is in the building" theory and has the gall to look the jury in the face and present it as if it were truly plausible, then in effect we have become nothing more than the unethical lawyers who we abhor. There must be some underlying principles of ethical action that guide the analyst when offering any argument. In fact, the analyst doesn't have to look far to find these guidelines. These principles of ethics are

found in the ethical standards of the many professional associations involved in forensics. Rather than reinvent the wheel with regard to ethical behavior, the authors offer a
synopsized look at these guidelines.* These ethical elements can be synopsized as:

- *Be objective*
  The mark of science is objective pursuit of truth. The analyst is concerned with
  discovering truth alone, regardless as to how that truth may or may not affect the
  outcome of some legal proceeding. The analyst approaches each problem using
  appropriate data; he assesses the evidence in an objective fashion and evaluates
  any reasonable hypothesis presented or any that he comes to recognize as reasonable. He never slants his conclusions for any reason. He must clearly recognize
  the certainty of any conclusion (e.g., recognizing a deductive versus inductive
  argument) and never give the conclusion greater weight than it deserves. What
  he knows or learns is not purposefully hidden from the opposing side. This latter aspect recognizes any ethical requirement to keep confidential information,
  but also demands that if expected to testify, the analyst makes himself available, if requested, for interview to opposing parties. The analyst cannot, however,
  become purposefully embroiled in the tactics of lawyers. For instance, he cannot
  agree to a prosecutor's request to delay writing a report until a few days before
  trial, or if required to provide a report when working for the defense, write an
  ambiguous document that fails to say anything. We may be, as the law profession
  believes, their handmaidens, but as handmaidens we can still retain some modi-
  cum of morality. Winning means nothing when it is based on half truths, lies,
  and deception. Finally, when dealing with lawyers, keep one simple rule in mind:
  lawyers can ask us anything, but they never tell us what we know! The same goes
  for judges. They may limit what we can say before the jury, but they do not get to
  redefine reality with their rulings.
- *Be honest*
  The honesty factor is an integral part of the objective standard just described;
  thus any conclusion is presented in as honest and objective a fashion as is possible. But the consideration of honesty extends to other aspects of behavior as
  well. These include properly representing one's discipline in the media, or any
  public forum, or how one represents himself before the court in terms of experience, background, and expertise in general. Thus, exaggerating or outright mis-
  representation of one's credentials, experience, memberships, or any other aspect
  of one's background is clearly outside of any ethical standard.
- *Be open*
  If the analyst is a true analyst, then he must be open to criticism of his technique
  and conclusions. When scrutinized, the analyst can't just assume the scrutiny
  is without justification. Recognition of procedural mistakes should be immediate, and the analyst must objectively decide if the mistake itself alters any aspect
  of the conclusions offered. If it does alter a conclusion, the analyst makes that
  clear as quickly as possible. Openness also entails describing methodology and

---

* Our deepest appreciation and thanks to Carolyn Gannet, San Diego County Sheriff's Crime Laboratory
for her effort to compile the ethical standards of the professional associations involved in forensics into
one document. Her document allowed us to quickly and easily synopsize those ideas.

procedure. Nothing an analyst does is a secret; the whole point of his effort is to offer information that may lead a jury or judge closer to the truth. The methods employed and utilized in doing that should be open to the opposing side (obviously utilizing appropriate discovery rules).

- *Be conservative*
  Objectivity and conservative behavior go hand in hand as well. The analyst, if he is conservative, recognizes the limitations of any analysis, and will not push his conclusions beyond where the data will allow. Some professional associations consider the conservative factor a part of the analyst's behavior before the court, stating that sensational methods of conveying a conclusion are inappropriate. That concern is a good rule of thumb and certainly one the analyst should consider in his courtroom demeanor, but in effect who decides what is sensational? To some analysts, the use of PowerPoint* is "sensational."

- *Communicate accurately, precisely, and without ambiguity*
  This is the true test of the analyst. Whether in a written report or verbally before the court, the analyst must communicate his conclusions in a clear, understandable fashion. The specifics of what he believes should be evident with no ambiguity.

- *Use proper tests, procedures, and methodologies, and remain current*
  Whatever the analyst does in support of his conclusions, he must use appropriate tests and procedures (which are open to scrutiny). If the case context requires deviation from some standard practice, this should be reported and any limitations imposed by the alteration of the method should be identified. This last requirement also imposes on the analyst a requirement to stay current in his field, altering individual methodology and technique when research in the field demands it.

There is one final ethical aspect of analysis, which to the authors' knowledge has not been identified by any professional association, but has been an issue on recent occasions. Analysis and science are not absolute. Analysts, no matter how qualified they are or how secure they are in their conclusions, were not present for the events being evaluated. Thus, no one has a crystal ball, and no one can state that he and he alone is right. The arrogance of such a statement would betray the analyst as not being objective. In the recent past, individuals of varying natures and backgrounds have begun to make claims that in effect state that because an opposing analyst did not agree with their conclusions, the opposing analyst must therefore be "unethical." If we can agree on anything, then a true scientist should believe that we can agree to disagree. Is it really unethical for a less-skilled analyst to follow basic methods and procedures, and come to believe something, even if another more skilled analyst believes the first is wrong? If the conclusions being offered in court are wrong, then a proper cross examination should bring this out. If the so-called "unethical" analyst is not following appropriate procedure, that too can be made evident during cross examination.

Another aspect of this concern is situations where the complainant goes ethics shopping (the complainant tries to sell the same complaint to a second or third professional organization, after other associations deny it as an ethical issue). This behavior, if not unethical itself, defies any claim of being professional. The whole purpose of an ethics committee in these professional associations is to *objectively* evaluate such claims, without agenda, and rule on them. Even if a complainant disagrees with a committee's findings, he should be professional enough to accept the ruling. As members, we should have faith that the system and the ethics committee did their investigation completely and fairly. If the complainant can't do that, then frankly speaking, he should resign from that association. By shopping for a second opinion, he is in effect stating he does not have faith in that association. The bottom line in all of this is that any claim of unethical behavior against an analyst should be based on clear unambiguous actions. Just because someone doesn't agree with you doesn't make him unethical. If you believe that it does, then perhaps it's time to put a mirror up to your own behavior rather than judging someone else.

Summary

The limitation in the reconstruction task is evident: the analyst seeks to look back in time and define an objective history of a particular incident. To do that, the analyst must frame his basic beliefs using a mixture of inductive and deductive arguments. In order to do that effectively, he has to make those arguments without interjecting logical fallacies. In most instances, the deceptive nature of logical fallacies occurs without intent on the part of the investigator or analyst. We are all capable of these failures and fall prey to unsound reasoning as a matter of our basic human nature. To avoid these subjective traps, the analyst must try to understand the basic application of logic and seek to define his arguments using acceptable reasoning. But framing logically sound arguments is not the end all of analysis. There must be an underlying ethos that guides the analyst's behavior. Objectivity, honesty, openness, and conservative action are all aspects of an ethical behavior for the crime scene analyst.

References

1. Honer, S.M., and T.C. Hunt. 1968. *Invitation to Philosophy*, Belmont, CA: Wadsworth Publishing Co., p. 16.
2. Ibid., p. 14.
3. Ibid., p. 16.
4. Van Doren, C. 1991. *A History of Knowledge*, New York: Ballantine Books, pp. 200–201.
5. Nordby, J.J. 1995. The Lady in the Lake. Presentation to a joint training conference of the Association of Crime Scene Reconstruction and the International Association of Bloodstain Pattern Analysts, Oklahoma City, OK.

Developing and Using Demonstrative Exhibits in Support of the Crime Scene Analysis

11

IRIS DALLEY

As discussed in Chapter 6, the fundamental purpose of the crime scene investigation is to collect information to determine what occurred and to preserve both the crime scene context and evidence in order to allow for subsequent analysis and to present the scene to the court. The scene may be preserved in images, sketches, models, notes, and physical evidence, each of which serves its own unique function in preserving the scene. Although the scene itself no longer exists, the goal is to preserve it in such a way that it can be understood and virtually reconstructed if needed. While the goal remains constant, methodologies have evolved over time. As with other aspects of life, automation has made manual tasks easier, faster, and more accurate. Methods for collecting data, analyzing the data, and representing the results of the analysis have evolved. Some of these methods originated from the crime scene investigative process, others within the forensic community, but many were adapted from industrial technology. The decision as to which technology to utilize in any analysis is based on various factors, including accessibility of the technology, the nature of the evidence being represented, the data collected from the crime scene, other aspects of the investigation, and the financial impact on the agency or analyst. Regardless of the technology used, the goal is to accurately depict the evidence and assist the court in understanding the scene and the evidence.

Collection of Data

Videography

Whenever possible, the decision to make or not make a video recording of the crime scene is made before investigators enter the crime scene. The adage "shoot-your-way-in/shoot-your-way-out" applies to both videography and photography. Videography is a good method of recording the overall scene, with the advantage of depicting spatial relationships within the scene. This can provide a virtual initial walk-through. Digital video is preferable to analog because digital image quality is better than analog and is easier to import into various software applications. Individual frames can be captured from digital video and stored as still images. Analog video can be converted to digital, but the process will adversely affect the image quality. Although newer technologies have simplified the process, still image capture from video should not be relied upon as an alternative to standard still image photography.

The quality of the captured still images will depend on the quality of the original digital video images and the sophistication of the software used to make the conversion. Captured video images, however, can supplement the crime scene photographs.

Photography

Photography is a major means of preserving the conditions of the crime scene and evidence during any examination. Film photography has served this purpose well over the past century, but advances in digital photography make it an excellent medium for crime scene and evidence documentation. An advantage of digital photography is the simplicity of use. One doesn't have to pack rolls of film and load and unload the camera throughout the scene investigation. Most, if not all, digital cameras have a "point & shoot" program that can adequately record some scenes. Many higher-end digital cameras perform the same manual functions as film cameras. An additional advantage of digital photography is instant availability of the images, which can be viewed immediately after they are recorded. Digital images can be recorded in a variety of formats that can be imported into various software applications, which will be discussed later in the chapter. In deciding which file format to use, consideration should be given to what uses will be made of the image, both in analysis and presentation. In addition to the image file, digital cameras also record a metafile with the image. The metafile includes information about when and how the image was recorded, including camera settings.

It is important to remain objective while photographing the scene, keeping an open mind as to what information may eventually be required from the scene and the recorded images of the scene. In effect, the photographs must record the entire scene context. In one instance known to the author, the analyst received a case for reconstruction in which a victim had a large-caliber gunshot wound to the face. Nearly a hundred photographs of the scene were produced; the vast majority depicted the victim and the wound. None of the photographs were at 90 degrees to the wound, none were close-up with scale, and very few depicted the surrounding area. This form of documentation leaves many questions unanswered. Did this shooting incident begin in another room, or in another area in the same room, and proceed to the victim's location? Was there evidence of other injuries, other victims, or other violent events? The information collected from the scene, including the information in the scene photographs, is used to determine what did or could have happened and what did not or could not have happened. This is one of the primary reasons the entire scene should be recorded. Determinations regarding what parts of the scene have probative value can change later in the investigation and formal reconstruction.

Items collected from the scene should be photographed completely with overall and with close-up photographs (Figure 11.1). At a minimum, the items should be photographed from the vertical and horizontal planes and from 90 degrees to the surface (Figure 11.2 and Figure 11.3). Items that need to be moved to capture important aspects beneath or hidden by them must be photographed in their original condition (Figure 11.4 and Figure 11.5). Particularly when bloodstains are observed on an item, each surface that is bloodstained should be photographed at a 90-degree angle to the bloodstained surface. These same photographs should then be repeated with the addition of a scale of reference placed at the plane of the stain (Figure 11.6 and Figure 11.7). These photographs can then be used for several purposes. One purpose is to show which stains were present before the items were moved, and distinguish those stains from postartifacts created by processing activity.

Figure 11.1 An overall photo depicting the bed and floor adjacent to the bed. Overall photos are intended to show the orientation of items in a general area.

In the process of creating these photographs, information about the relationship between the item and the scene is recorded. In this instance, properly recorded photographs can be used for analysis instead of the original stain. For example, photographs of bloodstains may be used to determine the angle of impact even if the original stain was consumed in laboratory testing (Figure 11.8).

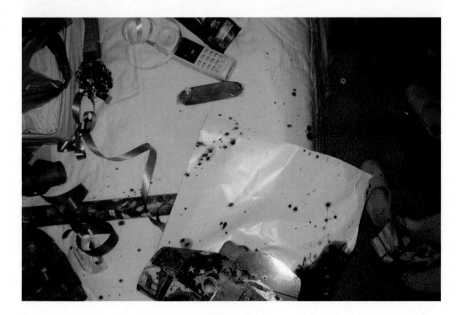

Figure 11.2 The film plane of the camera is oriented to the horizontal plane of the intended subject.

Figure 11.3 The film plane is oriented so it is 90° to the vertical surface being photographed.

Figure 11.4 A photo taken of the original conditions of the scene. The cap overlays blood-stains on the floor.

Figure 11.5 Photo taken after the cap was removed. Note the stain where blood had apparently saturated through the cap to the floor below and the presence of the casing. Both aspects require documentation.

Figure 11.6 Directional bloodstains on a truck bed. This photo was about 90 degrees to the stains on the truck bed.

Figure 11.7 A second photo of the bloodstain depicted in Figure 11.6 with a scale of reference added.

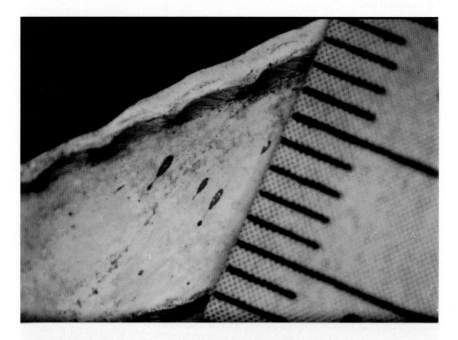

Figure 11.8 Each of the stains pictured are about 1mm long and are of sufficient quantity to develop a DNA profile, but the stains would likely be consumed in testing. The angle of impact can be determined from the photograph.

Measurements

Measurements are another means of documenting the crime scene and memorializing the position and relationships between items in the scene. Recording measurements in a measurement chart makes this data easy to display. The measurements support the crime scene sketches or scene mapping. In some ways the sketch duplicates information in the photographs, but provides a perspective not achievable in either videography or photography of the scene. The sketch may be a simple hand-drawn document with geometric shapes to represent items in the scene and notes-to-self, or consist of a sophisticated computer-assisted, two-dimensional, to-scale floor plan. In the latter, the accuracy of the sketch will depend on the measurements collected at the scene. The more measurement points recorded, the greater the degree of detail that can be put into the final sketch or model.

Manual measurement devices, such as a tape measure, are adequate for measuring points in a crime scene. Manual methods generally require at least two persons for measurement collection. The accuracy of the measurements will depend on the calibration of the devices used and the manner in which they are used. Most measurements need to be made in either the horizontal or vertical planes. The use of a level for horizontal measurements and a plumb for vertical measurements is recommended. However, this is cumbersome and will require more manpower.

Electronic measurement devices, or distance meters, are now available that can be operated by one or two individuals. When properly calibrated, these devices allow for more measurements to be taken with greater precision. Several models of hand-held electronic measurement devices are available. Many of these devices use a combination of laser and sonar technology to identify a target surface and measure the distance from the device to the target surface. The distance displays on an LCD screen. Product specifications need to be checked for the degree of accuracy of the particular device.

Automation of measurement collection facilitates measurement of more points within the scene while requiring less manpower and time. Whether using tape measures or electronic devices, it is important to ensure that the measurement being recorded is in the correct plane. The device must be level to obtain accurate horizontal measurements and must be plumb to obtain accurate vertical measurements. To record points that are not in the same horizontal or vertical plane, the horizontal and vertical components should be recorded. Either way, the linear and/or horizontal distances can be calculated using basic geometric functions.

Some devices record measurements in three dimensions. When those points are related to each other, the points can be accurately located in space. For example, the Nikon Total Station uses pulse laser technology to record points in a scene. It can be operated by one person and can quickly record a significant number of points compared to the manual techniques described above. The raw data collected by the Total Station can be imported into software applications that will convert the data points to either two-dimensional or three-dimensional sketches of the scene. Those applications will be discussed later.

In each of the above methods, the operator must decide which points to collect. The greater the number of points collected, the more accurate the sketch or model that can be developed from those points. Newer technologies combine digital imaging with pulse laser technology to capture the scene. These 3D laser scanners record millions of points in minutes and can be operated by one person at the scene. The area captured depends on the angle set by the operator, up to a full circle of 360 degrees. The result is a "point cloud" that can be electronically converted into a virtual replica of the scene for future analysis. High-resolution digital images can be developed from the raw data collected by the laser scanner. This technology has the added advantage of converting the raw data into various viewpoints of the scene.

There is a cost advantage to using the low-tech manual methods. The prices for tape measures range from a few dollars up to more than $100. Ultrasonic distance meters can be purchased for a few hundred dollars. Laser-based data collectors, such as Total Station, sell for thousands of dollars, while laser 3D scanners/cameras that produce virtual scene replicas sell for hundreds of thousands of dollars. The pulse laser technology requires software to retrieve and analyze the data collected.

Analysis of Data

Numerous computer software applications are available for use in the analysis of data collected at the scene. Attempts have been made to categorize the applications into generic groupings, but there is much crossover between the groupings. A software application can be both analytical and illustrative.

Image Editing

Properly documented scenes can be revisited by the jury or the analyst by viewing recorded video and images. Image editing software facilitates both review and analysis. Before reviewing digital images of the scene, an original copy should be saved and stored. All analysis should be done on copies of the original images. As with all evidence, a record needs to be kept of any enhancements or alterations to the evidence that occur in the analysis process for images that will be used as evidence. Adobe Photoshop CS2® is an image editing software program that records a history of the editing steps during the analysis. That history can be retrieved as needed.

For purposes of this discussion, image enhancements are those processes that improve the quality of the image. For example, many lighting problems in the image can be adjusted to improve the quality of the image (Figure 11.9). Adjusting the luminosity and color balance may help to refocus attention to various parts of the scene. Adjusting the histogram may increase the visibility of certain parts of the scene (Figure 11.10). Images that are presented for evidence must accurately depict the evidence. Enhancement of an image is sometimes necessary for the image to accurately depict the scene or evidence that it is purported to depict. Enhancement processes use elements in the image file. Enhancement does not add or subtract elements from the original image; it clarifies the existing information captured in the image.

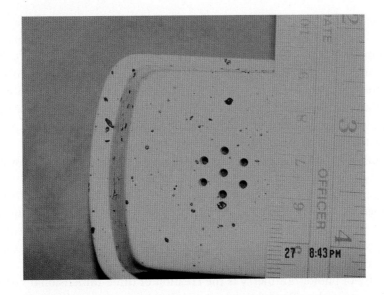

Figure 11.9 An overexposed image of blood spatter on a telephone handset.

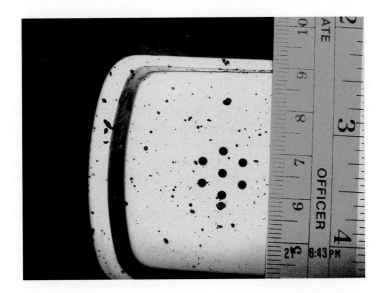

Figure 11.10 The same image as in Figure 11.9 after adjusting the histogram of the digital image.

Alteration in terms of this discussion means adding or subtracting elements to the image that were not in the original. Altered images may be admissible as evidence if they assist the court in understanding the evidence. Expert witnesses often use altered images to explain their interpretation of the evidence.

If necessary or helpful, images can be rotated. This is useful to display horizontal or vertical lines so that they appear as such in the image. Bloodflow patterns on objects that were moved after the flows occurred can be rotated to show the proper orientation of the flow to gravity.

Photogrammetry is the process of making precise measurements by means of photography. Images are then used to determine the dimensions of other unmeasured objects. The simplest method is to use a known scale that is in the image, such as a scale next to a bloodstain. This is best accomplished when the image is recorded perpendicular to the target surface. The scale can be used to determine the size of any object in the image that lies in the same plane as the scale. Objects of known dimensions, other than a scale, can serve the same purpose. For example, the diameter of a coin on a tabletop in a perpendicular image can be used to determine the size of other items on the tabletop.

Photogrammetry may be used to produce altered images. Images that were recorded at one angle can be altered to depict what the image would have been if recorded at a different angle, such as reorienting an image in order to correct perspective distortion. A foreshortened view can be altered to depict a perpendicular view. In a foreshortened view, a square block in an image appears as a trapezoid. The nearest side may appear square, but the block appears to narrow in the distance. In the perpendicular view, the block appears as an object with square surfaces.

Another use of photogrammetry is the creation of three-dimensional virtual models. Software programs such as PhotoModeler® and iWitness™ import the images and produce realistic models that can be used in animation. Software packages like these sell for about US$800 and up.

Regardless of the type of enhancement or alteration used, the end product must accurately depict the evidence and/or assist the expert in explaining the evidence.

Sketching and Mapping

A sketch or map of the crime scene can provide perspective not easily achievable by a single image of the scene. A sketch is a diagram presented as general representation of the scene. A sketch can also be accompanied by measurements of item positions and size or drawn to scale (both generally referred to as mapping). Sketches are visually appealing and easy to understand and depict the scene without including potentially objectionable visual material, such as the gore of traumatic injuries. If done to scale, geometric function calculations can be made to determine the approximate distances between various elements in the sketch.

In choosing a method for preparing sketches, consideration should be given to the target audience. Simple template sketches on prepared forms are sufficient for minor traffic accidents where the intended audience is the patrol supervisor who is familiar with the forms and templates, but may be confusing and uninformative to jurors. Likewise, blueprints of floor plans may accurately represent dimensions and locations of construction elements, but have little meaning to jurors outside the construction or architectural industries. Sketches produced as exhibits for jury trials need to accurately depict the scene and important elements (e.g., critical evidence) in a format that is easily recognized and understood by the average juror.

While it is necessary to preserve the data from the scene, including measurements, these need not be printed on the final sketch. The measurements can be preserved in a separate chart that can be produced as an exhibit if needed. Likewise, the sketch does not need to include every item that was present in the scene. Only items that have probative value and items that give a frame of reference need to be included in the final sketch. A bird's-eye view of a house may include walls and recognizable icons, such as a sink and stove in the kitchen and a toilet in the bathroom. This gives the viewer a frame of reference for the type of structure and its use.

As a general rule, most sketches are labeled "Not to Scale." Even though the sketch is based on measurements recorded at the scene, there are often elements within the sketch that were not measured. If any part of the sketch is not to scale, then the entire sketch is "not to scale."

Two-Dimensional

Hand-drawn sketches of the scene are acceptable. Drawing templates are available to produce standard shapes that are easily recognizable as common items. However, preparation can be time consuming and tedious to prepare accurately and precisely, and reproducibility can be problematic. At some point, even the hand-drawn sketch should be digitized for reprinting and storage.

A variety of simple, inexpensive graphic programs are available that provide a variation of the hand-drawn sketch. In computer-assisted drawing programs, such as Microsoft® Paint, a utility program provided with the Microsoft Windows® operating system, simple line drawings are made on the computer and stored as image files, such as bitmaps or jpegs. These programs offer an assortment of colors and shapes for use in depicting objects. Images can also be inserted into a Paint drawing by cut and paste functions. The sketch can even be done to scale by using either a grid background or inserting a ruler into the drawing. As cut and paste symbols are created, they may also be saved separately and reused in other sketches. The degree of precision in the resulting sketch will depend entirely on the user's skill.

Several computer-assisted drawing software programs are available that can perform these same functions faster, easier, and with a higher degree of precision. These programs have features for inserting the measurements from the scene into the sketch. Many of these programs also feature libraries of icons or models of common items. Additionally, home architectural programs can be used for this purpose and are very affordable. Many of these programs will convert the two-dimensional drawings into three-dimensional computer models. Other software programs, such as Cad Zone and 3D Eyewitness, have been specifically designed for depicting crime scenes and for the preparation of court exhibits (Figure 11.11 and Figure 11.12).

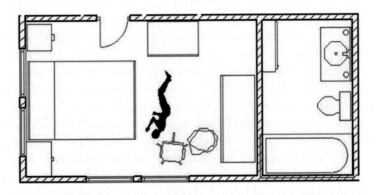

Figure 11.11 A two-dimensional sketch created in 3D Eyewitness.

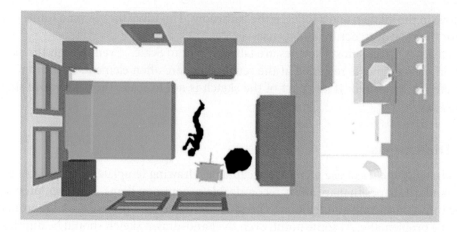

Figure 11.12 The same file in 3D Eyewitness can produce a more realistic three-dimensional view.

Some of these programs interface with laser devices and import the raw data collected by these devices. For example, data collected by the Total Station can be imported into Cad Zone. Directly importing the data is an important feature as it avoids the possibility of creating transcription errors.

Some programs have the added feature of creating a movie file from the two-dimensional sketch. This is done by successively recording snapshots of three-dimensional views of the scene. These movie files are useful as a virtual walk-through of the scene, created by successively repositioning the camera, or can be used to depict angles of view from a given point in the scene. Whether or not the view created by this type of movie file accurately depicts the corresponding view in the scene depends entirely on how accurately the scene was reproduced in the program. It should be noted that these virtual walk-through efforts are for demonstrative purposes only. They can show the scope of possibilities or demonstrate why certain views are excluded (Figure 11.13). If the sketch is prepared well, the virtual camera in the program can be placed in the same orientation as the camera at the crime scene to produce a drawing that approximates the image recorded at the crime scene.

Generally, the products of scene sketching software present line drawing images. Models in the 3D versions appear as geometric shapes. Some distortion appears in these types of movie files. More effective movie files are made from the products of the 3D laser scanners. Because the point cloud represents actual points in the scene, the result is an accurate virtual tour of the scene without the distortions seen in the computer-assisted drawing programs. The range of possible viewpoints depends on the settings of the original capture. If the original capture was a full 360 degrees, the resulting virtual walk-through will accurately depict all areas of the scene that were visible to the camera.

Physical scale models of a scene can be prepared from the scene data as well. Scale models can be very impressive and are easily understood by the jury, but they require great effort and are cumbersome to maintain and transport. Three-dimensional virtual models offer the advantage of examining an object or a scene from different viewpoints without the distortions seen in the sketched models. These virtual models are used to check the analysts understanding of the scene and also act as effective demonstrative exhibits in court. Realistic-appearing virtual human models can be prepared using animation software, such as Poser®.

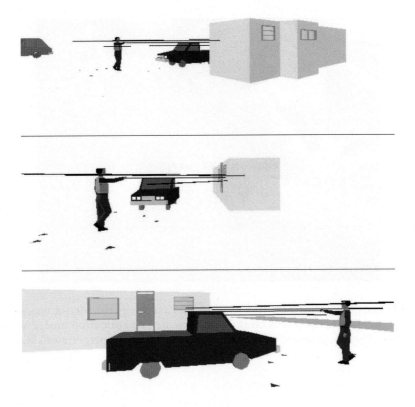

Figure 11.13 Images from a 3D Eyewitness movie file demonstrating the possibility that the bullet trajectories could have been fired from a point shoulder position by a person of the subject's height. In this example, the camera vertical angle, aperture angle, and height remained constant as the camera was moved a constant distance around the corner of the house.

Animation figures can be used in combination with crime scene images. A crime scene image is imported as background in the animation program, and then the animation model is positioned proportionally to illustrate specific scene information or interpretations (Figure 11.14).

Human figure models in animation programs are typically posed to duplicate the position of bodies in a scene, to demonstrate changes in position during an event, or to demonstrate motions. For juries, wound pathways as described in narrative formats and diagrams can be confusing. Wound paths are described by the medical examiner relative to the standard anatomical position (standing, arms down and facing out and forward). If a bullet passed through the body and the entry site was farther from the top of the head than the exit site, then the bullet path would be described as "upward." However, an upward bullet path described in the autopsy may actually be part of a downward trajectory in the scene (Figure 11.15). These relationships are better demonstrated to the court by positioning a rod through an animation figure to depict the described bullet pathway, then changing the figure's position as needed. The bullet pathway remains constant relative to the body, but the line of trajectory changes with the body position (Figure 11.16).

A virtual human model with a trajectory rod inserted (as described by the medical examiner's terminal ballistics) may be used to ascertain the body's position in the scene at the time that wounding occurred. If a bullet continued through a solid structure, such

Figure 11.14 The perpetrator admitted shooting the victim as the victim was sitting in the passenger seat, producing the stains on the driver's seat. The animation model was combined with the crime scene image to show the physical evidence and the perpetrator's statement were consistent.

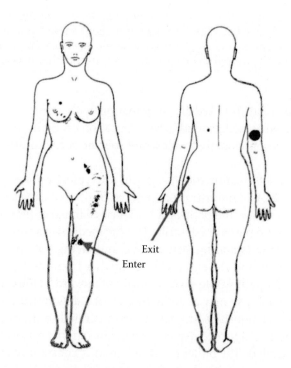

Figure 11.15 Based on information from the autopsy, a bullet traveled "sharply upward" through the lower left thigh and the upper left buttock, then exited through the left buttock. This description is based on a standard anatomical position and does not reflect what the bullet may have been doing in relation to the scene.

Figure 11.16 Once a trajectory rod is inserted into the animation model, the model can be positioned in any fashion (consistent with the known scene data) to better demonstrate the relative orientations. With the rod placed through the model along the wound path and with the left leg flexed, what was described by the medical examiner as a "sharply upward" wound in terms of the scene is actually consistent with a slightly rising and relatively flat trajectory. This path matched a trajectory in the scene across the location of the victim's body, and this posture was consistent with both that trajectory and the directionality of bloodstains near the body.

as a wall, a model of the wall with a trajectory rod is also prepared (based on the external ballistics defined by the crime scene investigator). Assuming both the gunshot wound in the body and the wall defect were produced by the same projectile, the figure model is positioned such that two trajectories are superimposed. This allows the jury to see an indication of the position of the body in the scene at the moment of wounding. This also allows testing body locations and postures at the time of wounding. Locations and postures that cannot be achieved while maintaining the superposition of the two rods are excluded as possible within the context of the scene. Additional information, such as muzzle distance determination, can further limit those possibilities. If no reasonable locations and postures can be accomplished with the rods superimposed, then the wound and wall defects were not likely to have been produced by the same projectile. This same technique can be applied to test multiple trajectories in a scene to bullet path(s) in a body.

As a general rule, wound pathology (terminal ballistics) alone will not define an order in which multiple wounds occurred. By analyzing the wound paths and comparing those paths to trajectories and/or bloodstain patterns in the scene, some sequential order may be possible and demonstrated using these techniques.

For the purpose of courtroom testimony, character animations should be limited to the data obtained from the scene. Bloodstain pattern analysis from the scene and wound analysis from the body together may be used to determine the location of a wound to the stained surface in the scene at the time that wound occurred, but cannot completely describe the body posture. For example, a bloodstain pattern on a wall that includes predominantly 0.5 mm diameter bloodstains, tissue spatter, and hair fragments located about 5 feet 6 inches above the floor and a 6-foot-tall body from that scene with a perforating gunshot wound to the head indicates that the body was standing near that wall at the time that gunshot wound occurred. Sitting, kneeling, and lying postures can be excluded as possible within the context of the scene. How was the body standing? Were the arms up or down? Were the feet together or apart? Absent other evidence from the scene, the exact posture cannot be known. An animation model may still be used for the purpose of demonstrating the relative position of the body to the stained surface at the moment the wounding occurred, so long as the limitations of position are taken into consideration and explained properly.

An animation of a sequence of motions that is obtained by the analysis of bloodstains in a scene may be appropriate with the caveat that the animation only approximates the action that occurred during the event. In the previous example, the evidence indicated the body was upright at the time that the wounding occurred. If the body was found lying prone on the floor in that same area, then one may reasonably conclude that the body fell to the prone position immediately after the wound occurred. An animation can demonstrate the analyst's view of that movement, as long as the analyst understands that many of the finer points of movement will never be known. Even giving particular attention to kinesiology relative to the instantaneous case, too many variables exist to know the exact and absolute movements. Did the head turn 5 degrees to the left or 10 degrees to the right? Were the biceps flexed or extended? Motion in an animation may assist the court in understanding the expert's interpretation of the evidence, but should always be used cautiously and include a clear explanation of the limits of that interpretation.

What crime scene analysis effectively defines are specific actions (e.g., event segments) at particular points in space and time. It may be possible to animate and represent a specific event segment, such as position of the body at the moment of wounding, appropriately. These presentations can either be in the form of still images or video files where the camera moves around a motionless character. Animations of this type represent the scene captured in that moment, but rotating in space, as if on a rotating stage. This technique can be very effective. In one case, multiple shots were fired into a vehicle and a virtual model of the vehicle was produced with trajectory rods placed to depict the paths of bullets through the vehicle. A video file was produced such that the vehicle appeared to rotate in space, thus displaying the trajectories from all directions. The video could be paused at any position to allow for further examination of any particular viewpoint.

An animation produced from data in video recordings can legitimately include full animation for one or more characters depicted in the video. One animation can incorporate the motion seen in multiple views of the same action or the same space and time to present a single coherent animation video of an event. For example, surveillance cameras at different locations may capture portions of a continuance motion or sequence of motions. A camera to the right of a person captures the motion and view to the right side, while a camera to the left captures the view to the left. A person's movement can be tracked by one camera as the person enters the area and by another camera as the person leaves that same area. The various views can be incorporated into a single animation. That animation could then be viewed from an infinite number of perspectives, including the perspectives of the original surveillance videos. This animation video clarifies the information present in the various views.

Witness statements are another source of information that may be animated. The animations may depict the witness's perspective and claims of how the events unfolded. The model of the scene is based on data collected from the scene; thus it accurately depicts the scene. Elements from the witness's statement are then added to the scene and animated according to the witness's statement, without altering the integrity of the scene. This can be useful in assisting the court in determining whether or not the statement is consistent with the known facts. For example, the position of a shooting victim in a scene may be determined from the physical evidence and an animation constructed from that information. Statements from the shooter may describe the shooter's position at the time the shooting occurred. The analyst should clearly state which portions of the animation are based solely on the physical evidence and which portions are based on statements.

When using human figure models, they should be specific enough that the court can easily recognize which individual the model is intended to represent, but generic enough so as not to be prejudicial or inflammatory. For example, appropriate gender models would be sufficient for distinguishing the intended representation where only two individuals of opposite sex are depicted. Clothing the models is optional, depending on the totality of the evidence being depicted. Genitalia should not be depicted except for probative purposes. Where two or more models represent persons of the same sex, the models can be shown in different colors, as long as the selected colors are not prejudicial. This method works well where all the persons represented by the models were similarly clothed. The models may be clothed similar to the clothing described in the evidence, but does not need to be identical to clothing in evidence. For example, a predominantly blue multicolored plaid shirt may be represented as a solid shirt. The intent is to make the character model easy to identify. Facial expressions (i.e., expressions intended to convey emotion) should not be included in these demonstrative exhibits.

An animation is prejudicial if the model or figure representing the perpetrator is depicted in such a way that it matches an image of the defendant, particularly if the identity of the perpetrator is at issue. Such an animation, in effect, suggests that the defendant and the perpetrator are one and the same individual. Evidence of the perpetrator's height, body shape, gender, etc. can be used in creating the animation model, but the model should not appear to be a particular individual.

A simulation is a type of computer-aided analysis in which the raw data is entered into and then analyzed by the computer. The computer is programmed according to scientific principles, incorporating scientific formulas and equations. The program can then develop a simulation animation. Simulation programs have been used for some time for traffic accident reconstruction. To date no simulation animation software is available for bloodstain analysis or most crime scene reconstructions.

BackTrack™ is a software program for the directional analysis of bloodstains. Images of bloodstains recorded at the crime scene and data to locate these stains in the scene are imported into the BackTrack program. The program then calculates the angle of impact and area of convergence of related stains and produces top view and side view graphs of the analysis. While accurate and informative, the graphs are somewhat lacking in appeal to the mathematically challenged. HemoSpat is a newer program that also imports bloodstain images and location data for directional analysis. The resulting data can be exported to a CAD program to produce a more realistic three-dimensional model.

Presentation

The information garnered during the investigation must be organized into formats that will bring the crime scene and/or evidence into the court. Computer presentation software, such as PowerPoint can be used both to organize information and to provide a means to publish the information to the court. PowerPoint is so enormously popular that the name has become virtually synonymous with any computer-generated slide show. There are other similar software programs on the market, such as Presentations, which is part of the WordPerfect® suite. Newer versions allow for migration of material from one program to the other, with varying degrees of success.

Slides in these software programs are prepared for linear presentation, but can be organized into looped segments. In a linear presentation, the slides are presented sequentially. This method works well in teaching situations. The operator manually controls the progression from slide to slide. Looped presentations include menu slides where each menu item is linked to another slide, to another presentation, or to another file. This method is particularly amenable to the courtroom. For example, a menu might contain a list of different types of exhibits (e.g., photos, videos, sketches, etc.), different areas of a scene (e.g., kitchen, bedroom, bathroom, etc.), or specific exhibits (e.g., Exhibit A, Exhibit B, etc.). Each menu item is hyperlinked to a specific slide or file. After presenting the linked portion, the presentation should always return back to the menu slide.

A similar technique is to hyperlink portions of an image in a slide. The crime scene sketch can be inserted into a slide, and then specific areas within the slide can be hyperlinked to other parts of the presentation. For example, an icon on the sketch that represents the weapon may be hyperlinked to an image of the weapon, while an icon that represents a bloodstain pattern may be hyperlinked to an image of that bloodstain pattern.

When using hyperlinks to lead to/from slides, it is a good idea to "hide" all slides except the menu slides. Bookmark slides are inserted that will force the presentation back to the menu after displaying the linked slides. Keep in mind that all files that are hyperlinked in the presentation should be stored in the same computer folder as the presentation.

Slide content and clarity is essential to the effectiveness of the presentation. The purpose of the slide is to focus attention on one idea or one item. Therefore, the content of each slide in the presentation should be limited to one subject simply presented. Generally, brief terms are preferable to sentences or paragraphs. Slides that are difficult to read or contain too much information will have a negative impact. Conclusions in text form should not be included in the presentation. If they are, an objection is likely to occur, and the content may be excluded until the offending material is redacted from the presentation. The content of the slides are used to illustrate the expert's opinion, not to write it out.

After an item is photographed in the scene, the item is examined more closely in a controlled setting, such as a laboratory where it is rephotographed. Both the scene and examination image can be shown together on the same slide. This is helpful for explaining and understanding evidence, such as bloodstain patterns on clothing and the relationship between the mechanism of staining and the location or position in the scene. Multiple views of a single item may be included in a single slide if it assists in conveying the concept presented.

In terms of demonstrative evidence, the use of artistic features, such as transitions and animations, should be limited to those needed to best describe the evidence or explain the expert's opinion. Custom animations in slides can be used for effect to highlight probative points, such as indicating a point in an image. In testifying about bloodstains, custom animation can be used to demonstrate the travel of a blood drop or a blood flow pattern.

One use of animation in a presentation is to demonstrate the mechanism of bloodstaining. To demonstrate a bloodstain mechanism, insert the pattern image into a slide and then use the *autoshape/scribble* function to trace the outline of the pattern. Select a color to fill the shape created by the tracing. In the *custom animation* menu, select an animation that will cause the created shape to appear over the image during the presentation in a manner consistent with the mechanism being described. For example, a wipe-down animation can be used to demonstrate a downward blood flow. This process can be repeated for stains within a pattern, such as cast-off. After creating the animated shapes over individual stains, sequence the animations such that the stains are "created" in the presentation consistent with the creation of the stains on the item of evidence (Figure 11.17 and Figure 11.18).

Slide transitions can also be used to simulate motion. This is done by creating two consecutive, nearly identical slides in which the position of one or more items is altered. Like

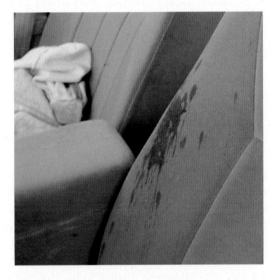

Figure 11.17 Bloodstains on a car seat as depicted in the crime scene photos.

Figure 11.18 Using presentation software, shapes were drawn over related patterns on seat. The shapes were then filled with color and a *wipe-down* custom animation applied to the shapes. In court, the combination simulates the blood flow down the seat that created the stains.

an early form of motion picture, the transition between the slides makes the items appear to move, although the two slides actually contain only still images.

Nearly any demonstrative exhibit can be displayed in a computer slide presentation. If audio files are needed, they can be linked to a slide. Video files are inserted into slides and played within the slide presentation or linked for display in a different application. Images of any nature (e.g., photographs or drawings) can be inserted into slides. Even written reports can be inserted into slides or linked for display in other applications.

Several multimedia case management programs are available that incorporate the above-described techniques, further automating the process. These programs simplify the presentation preparation by automatically creating links to any or all of the various types of information stored in a given case. These programs retain data in a proprietary format, but usually create a presentation in an industry-standard format that can be interactively viewed outside the program.

Courtroom Testimony

Regardless of the type of demonstrative exhibit used, the exhibit must accurately represent the scene and/or evidence and must aid the witness in explaining the scene and/or evidence.

The logistics of using demonstrative exhibits should be addressed prior to presentation in the courtroom proceeding. Newer courtrooms are often built with networked monitors installed for judge, jurors, and attorneys. Some courtrooms provide the technology of interactive monitors that allow demonstratives to be altered and recorded during testimony. However, with the portability of laptop computers and projectors, courtrooms without the latest electronic gadgets can still make use of computer-assisted demonstrative exhibits. Most personal computers will also allow the display to be directed to television monitors. When using a projector, the presentation can be projected onto any suitable surface, such as a projection screen or smooth white wall. Affordable wireless cursors and presentation controllers allow the witness to remain in the witness stand while controlling a presentation from a centrally located computer.

Courtroom Admissibility Issues

Demonstrative exhibits have historically been used to depict evidence and clarify detailed or complex scenarios. Exhibits have ranged from hand-drawn, pen and paper sketches and charts to photographs and video. Most people are visual; they process information more effectively visually. The mind interprets the written word or the spoken word into visual-like images. Presenting technical information, such as analysis reports, in a visual medium (maps, charts, and sketches) allows jurors to more easily comprehend and process the information. For purposes of courtroom admissibility, demonstrative exhibits must be authenticated, must be accurate, and must be probative.

As technology has progressed, so too have the types of demonstrative exhibits and their associated admissibility issues in the courtroom. After much debate over the past decades, courts routinely accept color photographs. The issues now as then are weighing the accuracy of the exhibits, the probative value of the information in the exhibits, and prejudicial nature of the information in the exhibits. Just because technology allows a particular exhibit to be prepared does not mean that the exhibit needs to be presented in the courtroom.

One of the most controversial types of technology to be introduced into the courtroom is computer-generated, full-scale animations. As with any demonstrative exhibit, a proper foundation should be laid before a computer-generated animation is introduced to the court. Authentication is accomplished by identifying who produced the animation and validating what information was used to produce the animation. The animation must be relevant to a fact at issue.[1] Animation of facts not at issue may be an excellent academic exercise, but, if they are not probative for purposes of a court hearing, they serve no function.

A critical question is: Does the demonstrative exhibit accurately depict the facts or events it is offered to illustrate? This is not only a question for admissibility in the courtroom, but also for the ethical conduct of the presenter. The witness presenting or sponsoring the demonstrative exhibit must be able to articulate the data that was used to produce the exhibit and how that data was collected and applied. If the evidence supports more than one scenario, a demonstrative exhibit depicting only one scenario may accurately depict that scenario, but not accurately depict the facts. The expert witness should depict any possible scenario and then discuss why one scenario may or may not be more likely than another scenario (Figure 11.19 and Figure 11.20).

Because "seeing is believing," demonstratives can be used to mislead and misinform. One only need look at the entertainment media to see the impossible demonstratively "proven." The argument can be made that improper use of demonstrative exhibits could cause the jury to confuse the animation (an illustration of the expert's opinion) as a reenactment of the actual events. Because of the potentially prejudicial nature of animations, some courts have prepared cautionary instructions to be read to the jury prior to the introduction of such exhibits. Although the specific wording varies, the common components of the instructions are an advisement that the animation is an illustration to be considered

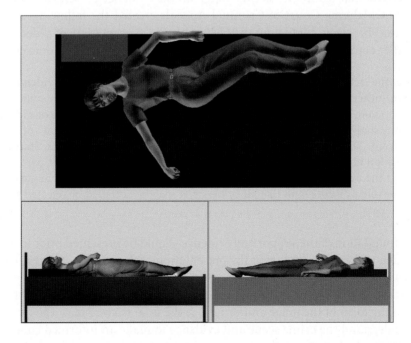

Figure 11.19 The position of a shooting victim as she was found in the final position is depicted in these animation images.

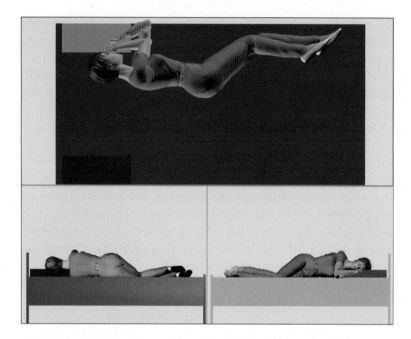

Figure 11.20 Based on the scene analysis, the final position depicted in Figure 11.19 is not the wounding position. The position of victim at the time the shooting occurred is depicted here to help the jury understand the alteration of position after wounding.

as demonstrative of the witness's testimony, and that the jury decides how much weight to give this particular testimony as they weigh all the evidence presented in the case. For example, the Oklahoma Court of Criminal Appeals created the following uniform jury instruction to "be given contemporaneously with the presentation of video, computer-based, or other comparable "reenactment evidence" to be used in Oklahoma courts:[2]

> **The State/The defendant** is about to present evidence in the form of a **video/computer animation/[other],** which is intended to help illustrate certain testimony or evidence being presented to you. The exhibit being presented is *not* an actual recording or video of the event that is shown. Rather, the exhibit is offered simply as a "reenactment" of what may have occurred. The exhibit is intended to help you better understand the **State's/defendant's** position about how an event occurred (or did not occur) and that party's understanding of the evidence supporting this interpretation. The exhibit is intended to assist you in your role as jurors, and like all evidence, it may be accepted or rejected by you, in whole or in part.

A clear foundation of the supporting evidence should be presented prior to the demonstrative exhibit and explained during the presentation of the exhibit, if permitted to do so by the court.

It is important to remember throughout the investigation and analysis of the case that the court, in the form of the judge and/or jury, is the final trier-of-fact. The court needs to "see" and understand the crime scene and evidence to make an informed conclusion. The best methods available to bring the crime scene into the courtroom should be utilized as objectively as possible.

References

1. *Clark v. Cantrell*, 332 S.C. 433, 504 S.E.2d 605 (Ct. App. 1998).
2. *Dunkle v. State* 2006 OK CR 29 139 P.3d 228 Case No: F-2004-621.

Chapter Author

Iris Dalley has 20 years of experience in forensics and crime scene investigation. She began her career with the Oklahoma State Bureau of Investigation (OSBI) in 1989 as a criminalist working in forensic serology and crime scene processing/reconstruction. She advanced through the Criminalistics Division of the OSBI to become the supervisor of the Eastern Regional Biology Laboratory before transferring to the Investigative Division to become one of the first designated crime scene agents. She now is a partner in the forensic education and consulting company Bevel, Gardner and Associates.

Dalley has a Bachelor of Science/Biology and a Master of Secondary Sciences degree. She attended over 2,000 hours of law enforcement/forensic training, including academies with the Oklahoma Council on Law Enforcement Education and Training, the OSBI, and the Southern Police Institute/Homicide Investigations. She received training in bloodstain pattern analysis from the OSBI, the Oklahoma City Police Department, the Kansas Bureau of Investigation, and Henderson (Texas) Forensics.

Dalley holds an Advanced Law Enforcement Certificate for the State of Oklahoma and an Instructor Certificate. She has taught courses in Evidence Collection and Preservation, Preliminary Investigations, Crime Scene Documentation, Crime Scene Investigations, Crime Scene Reconstruction, Reconstruction Animations, Preparing Demonstrative Exhibits, Sexual Assault Investigation, and Introduction to Bloodstain Pattern Analysis. She holds International Association of Identification (IAI) certification as a senior crime scene analyst.

Dalley is a Distinguished Member and Secretary of the Association for Crime Scene Reconstruction, is a regional vice president of the International Association of Bloodstain Pattern Analysts, member of the IAI Subcommittee on Bloodstain Pattern Analysis, and vice president of the Oklahoma Division of the IAI. She has done presentations for each of those organizations in their annual training seminars, and has instructed municipal, state, tribal, and federal law enforcement officers in crime scene investigations. She has done presentations in the United States, the Netherlands, and Switzerland.

Dalley has been court-qualified in the U.S. District Courts in Oklahoma and Texas, in Oklahoma District Courts, and in District Court in Idaho as an expert in Forensic Serology, Crime Scene Investigation and Reconstruction, Trajectory Analysis, and Blood Stain Pattern Analysis.

Dalley is also a member of the FBI Scientific Working Group on Bloodstain Pattern Analysis (SWGSTAIN).

Index